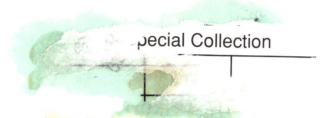

Special Collection

Nigel Calder

'Earth at Night'. A global image from space shows rich urban regions shining brightly, and pools of darkness in poor or sparsely inhabited regions. The Gulf glows with gas flares, and land-clearing fires are visible in West Africa. The extra island of Japan is its squid fleet. The image is composed from many midnight passes of a US military weather satellite. The aurora (blue) is an embellishment.

DMS SATELLITE DATA COMPILED BY W.T. SULLIVAN

Spaceship Earth

Viking

in association with
Channel Four Television Co Ltd

VIKING

Published by the Penguin Group
Penguin Books Ltd, 27 Wrights Lane, London W8 5TZ, England
Viking Penguin, a division of Penguin Books USA, Inc.
375 Hudson Street, New York, New York 10014, USA
Penguin Books Australia Ltd, Ringwood, Victoria, Australia
Penguin Books Canada Ltd, 2801 John Street, Markham, Ontario, Canada L3R 1B4
Penguin Books (NZ) Ltd, 182–190 Wairau Road, Auckland 10, New Zealand

Penguin Books Ltd, Registered Offices: Harmondsworth, Middlesex, England

First published in Great Britain by Viking 1991
1 3 5 7 9 10 8 6 4 2

100891175

Printed in Great Britain by Butler & Tanner Ltd, Frome and London

A CIP catalogue record for this book is available form the British Library

ISBN 0-670-83628-1

Contents

———

The television series *Spaceship Earth*, consisting of ten half-hour programmes, was first transmitted in 1991. A grant from Shell International Petroleum Company Limited made the production possible. It was produced by Network Television/Antelope Films for Channel Four (UK), Paravision (France), Teleac (The Netherlands) and South Carolina Educational TV (USA). A grant from the US National Science Foundation enabled SC-ETV to participate.

Some of the credits for the series are as follows:

Executive producer: Nicholas Barton   *Programme consultant:* Peter Montagnon
Producer-directors: John Selwyn Gilbert, Mike Kleinsteuber and John Dollar.
Graphics consultant: Colin Millward   *Associate producer:* Joanie Blaikie
Production team: Fiona Henderson, Gillian Strachan and Nicola Riley
Graphics and archive research: Rosalind Bentley   *Writer:* Nigel Calder

Commissioning editors for Channel Four: Naomi Sargant and Bob Towler
Project director for SC-ETV: Ruth Sproat

Warm thanks are also due to the cameramen, sound recordists, editors and others who made indispensable contributions to the production.

AUTHOR'S NOTE

Many scientists, scholars, officials and company executives gave unstinted information and advice during an odyssey through Australia, Benin, Bolivia, China, Finland, France, Germany, India, Indonesia, Italy, Japan, Kenya, Sweden, Switzerland, UK, USA, USSR and Western Samoa. Many others were helpful by correspondence and telephone. Several United Nations agencies and the Joint Research Centre of the European Community gave valuable assistance. Special thanks are also due to the many remote-sensing institutes and specialists who contributed essential information or images.

At the risk of being unfair I shall mention a few individuals, out of hundreds consulted, who were especially influential: Mike Baker (Paris), Gérard Brachet (Toulouse), J. Bodechtel (Ispra), Chen Shupen (Beijing), Ronald Cooke (London), Roland Fuchs (Tokyo), Norton Ginsburg (Honolulu), Chris Justice (Greenbelt), Kirill Kondratyev (Leningrad), Richard Leakey (Nairobi), Jean-Paul Malingreau (Ispra), Julian Minghi (Columbia, SC), John Mitchell (Bracknell), Ichtiaque Rasool (Washington), Piers Sellers (Greenbelt), John Townshend (formerly at Reading), Gilbert White (Boulder) and Alan Wilson (Leeds).

The adjective 'manmade' is used throughout in preference to the Greek variant 'anthropogenic'. If this implies that the male sex must take credit or blame for clearing forests, unearthing minerals, damming rivers, letting off nuclear weapons, and generally meddling with the planet, so be it. Acronyms swarm like locusts in Earth-system science.. Any not expanded in the text are decoded in the index.

Nigel Calder

The images in this book have been gathered from primary scientific sources, and permission to reproduce them is gratefully acknowledged. See also the explanatory credit lines beside illustrations. Numbers refer to the pages upon which the illustrations appear. Acronyms will be found in their expanded form in the index.

2-3 © 1986 Hansen Planetarium, Salt Lake City, Utah, USA

10, 19, 97, 101, 107, 108, 116, 120, 130 below, 139, 140, 141, 152 NASA GSFC, USA: 10 Plotting by Gene Feldman of data from C. J. Tucker NASA GSFC (land vegetation by NDVI), G. Feldman GFSC (ocean life by phytoplankton pigment), O. Brown University of Miami (sea-surface temperatures), C. Koblinsky GSFC (ocean currents by sea-level variability, also wind speeds), and W. Rossow GISS (mean cloud amounts). 19 Mark Schoeberl. 97, 101, C. J. Tucker et al. 107, 108 FIFE experiment. 116, 120 C. J. Tucker et al. 130 below G. Feldman plot of data from O. Brown University of Miami. 139, 140, 141 G. Feldman plots for US Global Ocean Flux Study Office of data from GSFC, University of Miami and University of Rhode Island. 152 J-P. Malingreau (now at JRC)

15, 48, 122, 132 Drawings by Chapman Bounford: 15 after ECMWF; 48 after US State Department; 122 after KREMU; 132 after JAFIC.

17 Graham Kelly, European Centre for Medium-range Weather Forecasts

27 © 1986 Gesellschaft für Angewandte Fernerkundung (GAF) mbH, Munich, Germany

29, 61, 167 French SPOT satellite images © CNES SPOT Image distribution

31, 91, 157 EROS Data Center, US Department of the Interior Geological Survey

35 Meteosat images supplied by European Space Agency

38 Artemis, FAO Remote Sensing Centre

44 Charles Elachi, NASA JPL, USA

46 Comalco Mineral Products, Australia

49, 87 top, 123 NRSC, UK: 49 NOAA data, 87, 123 Landsat images

52 M. Stern, formerly University of Lund, Sweden

60, 156, 199 John Dollar Network TV/Antelope Films

58 Bureau of Environmental Protection, Tokyo Metropolitan Government, Japan

65, 189, 204 NASA GISS, USA: 65 E. Matthews. 189 top and below after I. Fung et al. 189 middle after P. Tans, I. Fung and T. Takahashi. 204 William B. Rossow NASA GISS for ISCCP (World Climate Research Programme of WMO and ICSU).

67 From *Atlas of Tianjin*, Environmental Science Committee of the Chinese Academy of Sciences and Environmental Protection Bureau of the City of Tianjin, China

68 GMAP Ltd, Leeds University, UK

73 Earthquake Preparedness Division, Shizuoka Prefectural Government, Japan

77 top William Haxby, Lamont-Doherty Geological Observatory of Columbia University, USA

77 below C. DeMets, R. Gordon, D. Argus, S. Stein, and Northwestern University, USA

82, 111 photo, 176 John Selwyn Gilbert, Network TV/Antelope Films

83 Landsat image from ITC, Netherlands

87 below Centro di Ricerca IBM, Pisa, Italy

111 computer graphics   S. DeGloria, Cornell Laboratory for Environmental Applications of Remote Sensing (CLEARS), Cornell University, USA

114, 145 top, 153, 166 NOAA NESDIS, USA: 114, 166 R. Carey. 145 below, 153 R. Legeckis

115 Landsat images from INPE, Brazil

130 top O. Brown, R. Evans and M. Carle, University of Miami, Rosenstiel School of Marine and Atmospheric Sciences

132 JAFIC, Japan

143, 145 top FRAM group and Institute of Oceanographic Sciences Deacon Laboratory, © Natural Environment Research Council, UK

145 middle   K. Wakker, R. Zandbergen, M. Naeije and B. Ambrosius, Faculty of Aerospace Engineering, Delft University of Technology, The Netherlands

165 Landsat image from National Aerospace Laboratory (NLR), The Netherlands

170 Landsat image from JRC/EC Institute for Remote Sensing Applications, Italy

177 Space Media Network, Sweden

180 NASA and University of Chicago, B. Barkstrom (NASA), V. Ramanathan (Chicago), E. Harrison (NASA) and W. Collins (Chicago); images from Chicago for Earth Radiation Budget Experiment Science Team at NASA Langley Research Center, USA

195 High-resolution climate models (1989) by UK Meteorological Office (Mitchell et al.), Canadian Climate Centre (Boer et al.) and NOAA Geophysical Fluid Dynamics Lab (Wetherald & Manabe). Graphics collated for Intergovernmental Panel on Climate Change by J. J. Ephraums, Hadley Centre for Climate Prediction and Research, UK Meteorological Office

Sources of quotations in the text, by page number:

12   B. Ward, *Spaceship Earth*, New York: Columbia U.P., 1966

37   Exodus 10: 13–15

43   F. Rabelais, *Gargantua* (1534), trs. S. Putnam (1929)

69   S. Anderberg in Document RR-89-4, Laxenburg: IIASA, 1989

136   A. C. Hardy, *The Open Sea*, London: Methuen, 1956

149   J. Cook, *Journals*, Cambridge: Hakluyt Society, 1955

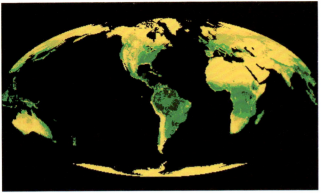

Land vegetation: NOAA satellites

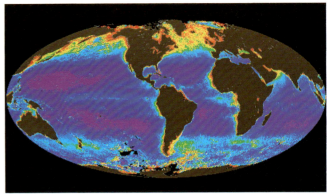

Oceanic life: Nimbus-7

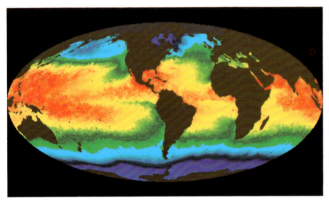

Sea-surface temperatures : NOAA satellites

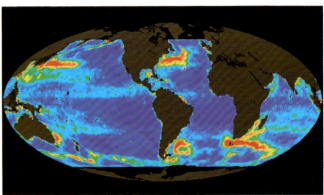

Major oceanic currents: Geosat

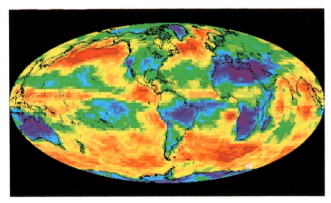

Cloudiness: GOES, NOAA, Meteosat, GMS

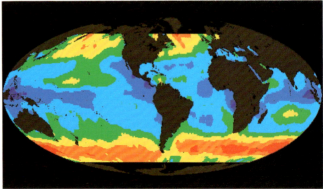

Oceanic wind-strength: Geosat

—

CHAPTER 1

The Look of the Planet

—

*E*VERY TIME YOU breathe or drink or eat, sow a seed, or ride in a car fashioned and powered with minerals from the ground, you take part in the Earth system. Atoms in your body have recently done duty in icebergs and giraffes. Endless interactions of rocks, air, water and living things, occurring at and near the surface of the Sun's third planet, comprise the Earth system.

Every half-hour a satellite poised high over the Equator takes an electronic snapshot of the part of the world where you live. At set times each day other satellites flit overhead unseen, using sensors of various kinds to see how the Earth system is getting on today. Once every 26 days, swooping southwards at 10.30 a.m., the French *SPOT* satellite takes a picture of your street.

Every day computers dream about the planet, conjuring up electronic wind and rain. As they wrap the whole world in a bubble of numbers, they picture a warmer Earth in the next century, and the human species frets. Are the growing numbers of people, each craving comforts or bare survival, leaning too heavily on the levers and push-buttons of their spaceship, and overloading the air-conditioning?

Facing:
Sub-systems of the Earth, seen from space. Gene Feldman, a NASA scientist, composed these images in map-like format using data from various instruments in orbit, as interpreted by specialist teams. In most images, red and yellow denote high activity.

11

This book is about current efforts to understand the Earth system and human interactions with it, at a level detached from fashionable environmental polemics. Even with the Olympian views that satellites and supercomputers give them, talented scientists come face to face with their own ignorance every day. Billions of dollars are starting to pour into research tagged 'global change', but so far the human species understands a black hole better than the Black Sea. Nothing in the Earth system is as simple as it looks, and the proper mood is wonder.

Fresh modes of thought are needed, too, that escape from the narrow specialisms of recent decades. Geography is by long tradition the great integrator that links the village and the world, and addresses the interplay between biophysical processes and the human factor. A new global geography is in the making, and the only question is how much of it the physicists will leave for geographers to do.

Remote sensing from space alters the ways of contemplating the Earth, as thoroughly as the telescope's invention revolutionized astronomy. Some civilian remote-sensing satellites begin to rival their military cousins in the close detail with which they survey the Earth's surface. Others with a broader geographical sweep and more frequent returns monitor the planet on continent-wide scales. Satellites over Africa discover the breeding grounds of locusts and give a preview of an astonishing new power to observe living systems from space.

All aboard the spaceship

A QUARTER OF a century ago, the economist Barbara Ward chose the title 'Spaceship Earth' for a lecture series. She wrote:

> Modern science and technology have created so close a network of communication, transport, economic interdependence – and potential nuclear destruction – that Planet Earth, on its journey through infinity, has acquired the intimacy, the fellowship, and the vulnerability of a spaceship.

Ward stressed the growing perceptions among social scientists of the limited size of the planet, but others had already described its compactness in quite different ways. Physicists reduced the Earth to a point of mass M to compute its motion around the Sun. Seismologists knew that earthquake waves could cross the Earth faster than a satellite flies. Air chemists could tell of pollution blowing off to the east and coming back from the west a few weeks later, or of an Asian volcano dimming the sunshine in the North America. Birds, fishes and whales commute as far and wide as any jet-setter, and the planet operated as an inside-out spaceship for a living crew long before human beings appeared. Whether its watchkeepers were microbes or dinosaurs, the Earth system of rocks, air, water and life worked like the life-support system of a manned spacecraft. It was always recycling and purifying the fluids, and maintaining an equable temperature that suited delicate biochemistry.

The gas and water tanks of Spaceship Earth are the air and the oceans. Habitual winds and currents take the place of piping. The top layer of the oceans, the mud of estuaries, and the crumbly soil on land are active surfaces, like absorbers and filters in a manmade spacecraft. Here key elements and compounds recycle, and the life of plants and animals finds direct support from water, carbon dioxide and oxygen.

The Sun is the spaceship's main power supply, for heating, lighting, and operating the photocells of plants. It is a thermonuclear-fusion reactor at a comfortable distance. The Earth's chief onboard power source is the natural radioactivity of the rocks of its interior. Although much feebler than solar energy, a trickle of heat moves the continents, and recycles and remodels the Earth's crust.

While clouds wring out the air's moisture, plants suck in its carbon dioxide, to make the plant tissue and oxygen on which animal life relies. Living things are not mere passengers, but active participants in the Earth system. Indeed, long-haul space voyagers may have to take many organisms from Earth, not only for food but for sustainable chemical purification of their air and water, as simulated in the assemblies of plants and animals sealed in the experimental habitat Biosphere 2 under test in the USA in 1990.

Human beings are just as much the products of the Earth system as the mountains, the marshes and the mynah birds. All are rearrangements of the same old cargo of atoms that gravity battened down on Spaceship Earth more than 4 billion years ago. Life's special talent lies in organizing atoms in useful ways repeatable from cell to cell and generation to generation. From the outset, life-and-death contests between species, and between living things and physical systems capable of appalling violence, ensured a continual destruction of species and the appearance of new ones. The mayhem of the present succession of ice ages threw up a strangely competent species.

With human life, the Earth system becomes self-conscious. For the

13

very first time it thinks about itself, and acquires skills and purposes that were never here before. It can now hold up a mirror to itself, as people venture into space and take pictures of the Earth from afar. Very beautiful they are, too, and in those shots of the whole round globe any human handiwork is so far hard to see.

Yet human beings are also the first watchkeepers with a sharp sense of guilt, and those same pictures from space arouse fears about the safety of the planet in human hands. The early dinosaurs that massacred their mammal-like predecessors had no such feelings. Thank goodness there were no conservationists around to prevent the annihilation of the dinosaurs that allowed the mammalian lineage its great comeback. Only the human species has the imagination to think of itself as a blight on the Earth.

Urgent questions abound about the effects of human action on the Earth system, at a time when the economy and the population are both growing. But a misanthropic strand in current thinking is perverse and dangerous. Self-styled 'deep ecologists', who are scientifically shallow, declare that humanity is doomed and they don't care. They are just as treacherous to their species as those who advocate its replacement by superintelligent robots or genetically engineered supermen. There is the same underlying belief that they have discovered some higher 'purpose' in Nature that would be best served by the human species' disappearance from the stage. The treason becomes lethal when people care more about an undiscovered species of beetle in the rain forest than the life of an Amazonian child.

Nature, misrepresented as a serene and benign mother, is in fact as clumsy as it is mindless. Yet the belief in a dichotomy between the human part of the Earth system and the rest only delays a surer grasp of their interactions. Many admired 'natural' landscapes, for example, were fashioned by human action. If the competent species ever ceased to marvel that blind Nature has conjured from the dust and vapours of the Earth the precious capacity of collective thought, it could easily misdirect its skills to self-destruction.

More positively, the human awareness of interactions with other species and the physical environment has been shrewd, if often sketchy, since our ancestors contended for survival with the ice sheets and the giant cave bear. That awareness now craves mathematical precision on a global scale. The pioneers of the new era of Earth-system science were meteorologists with computers and satellites.

14

How to be Right

*I*N LIVING memory, weather forecasters were stand-up comedians. When the man said, 'Enjoy the fine day, folks,' the audience chortled knowingly and reached for its raincoats. 'Watch out for the gales,' he would wisecrack, and in obedience to superstition small-boat sailors would paddle ashore. As they contemplated an unruffled sea, they swapped jokes about meteorologists, who ranked in public esteem higher than economists but below the better racing tipsters.

Computers and satellites have lopped off that branch of humour. No indulgent chuckles greet a mistaken forecast these days, but inquests into why the system blinked. As a rule, the forecast for tomorrow's weather is now boringly correct, and the predictions for three days hence are as good as the 24-hour forecasts of a generation back.

Global teamwork unmatched in any other enterprise set the stage for this transformation. The UN's World Meteorological Organization coordinates the World Weather Watch. All nations share their weather readings from ground stations, ships and aircraft through a telecommunications network. The world-embracing data and images from the weather satellites fill in the gaps where observing stations are scarce, besides giving vivid pictures of weather systems whirling across every continent and ocean.

The weather data go into the most powerful supercomputers on which the meteorologists can lay their hands. Forecasters no longer have to look at charts of the prevailing weather and try to guess what might happen next. A computer model calculates it. The model of the atmosphere is built of numbers and runs by mathematics. It is not so much difficult as elaborate, like the global weather itself.

Imagine a child's climbing frame as big as the Earth. The foot of each post defines a grid point on the surface, and further grid points on every post at various heights mark out box-like pieces of the air. Seven numbers define the state of the atmosphere at each grid point: the air's temperature, pressure, density and humidity, and the wind speeds north–south, east–west and up–down. Seven equations from the laws of physics describe how these numbers will change in space and time, as a moving parcel of air alters its speed or direction, warms up or cools down, expands or contracts, and absorbs or sheds water, according to the forces acting on it.

The computer model so constructed assimilates the best data on the

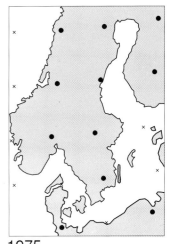
1975

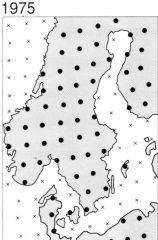
1985

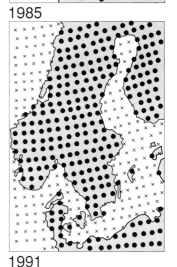
1991

European Centre for Medium-range Weather Forecasts tightens its grid.

current state of the weather, worldwide. Then it calculates changes at each grid point, taking account of differences at adjacent grid points, to arrive at new numbers for a few minutes later. When it has updated all of the numbers for all the grid points, the computer repeats the calculations for the next interval. And so on.

The numbers build raging tempests and calm anticyclones, send jet streams wriggling like hosepipes through the upper air, and drench computed hills with computed rain. This electronic drama in a metal box represents the weather as legitimately as the flickering intensities of light point-by-point on a TV screen reproduce a newsreel of a hurricane, or as the scanner of a satellite converts the tempest into signals for radioing to the ground. All are shadows of the real world.

The view from space would be useful for spotting the black eye of a hurricane, even if there were no computers, but only the machines can fully relish the feast of information coming from the satellites. The interplay between satellites and computer models is crucial to both. The human eye–brain system uses knowledge and anticipations of the world to enhance perceptions of it. Computer forecasts help to refine what a weather satellite sees, because the relations between height, pressure and moisture affect the way a weather system looks to the satellite's instruments.

The sums in a computer model must proceed much faster than the real weather unfolds, otherwise there is no forecast. Some 70 years ago, a far-sighted meteorologist visualized a forecast factory with 64,000 human beings using the primitive calculators of that era in a frenzy of collaborative arithmetic. Modern supercomputers are far more power-ful than that, but even for them the requirement of speed restricts the number of grid points they can handle.

In the most advanced models, the grid points are about 100 kilo-metres apart. Events within a grid box are too small to be seen except as a blur. These can include thunderstorms, for example. In large, multi-national experiments the world's meteorologists tackle tricky questions about how to represent, or 'parameterize', the sub-grid processes such as individual clouds or forests, in their computer models.

So far from being computational clerks, the people who run the forecasting systems are astute scientists who strive to refine their de-scriptions of the weather. The Earth is not a bare chessboard. Moun-tains, for example, help to steer weather systems, hamper the wind and trigger rain. Their representation in the models has been an area of

Facing:
Hurricane Hugo (1989) as seen by the US GOES satellite closely matched pressures and winds predicted 48 hours earlier by the European Centre for Medium-range Weather Forecasts. The cloud forecast, below, is compared with a poorer forecast (far right) using a coarser grid.

16

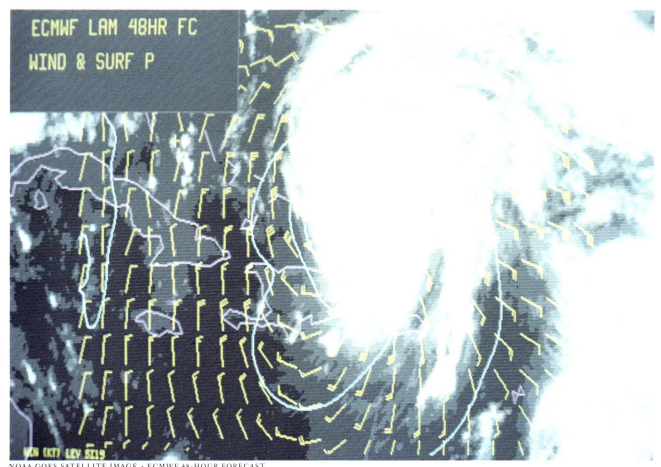

ECMWF LAM 48HR FC
WIND & SURF P

NOAA GOES SATELLITE IMAGE + ECMWF 48-HOUR FORECAST

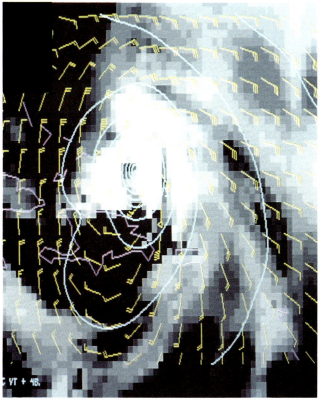

ECMWF

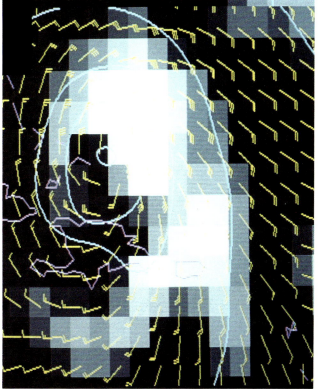

ECMWF

recent improvement. Oceans and vegetation affect the weather and are in turn affected by it. Such interplays tax the brightest minds in the field.

Decades of work slowly become translated into additional days of useful forecasting. But the 30-day forecasts promised when numerical forecasting began now seem like a mirage. The fashionable science of chaos had its origin in a meteorologist's notion that the flap of a butterfly's wing could influence the course of a depression on the far side of the world a week or two later. Present efforts concentrate on improving performance over periods of a week or so, and on extending the techniques to modelling the long-term averages and ranges of weather that comprise the climate.

The European Centre for Medium-range Weather Forecasts at Reading in England detected an error in the setting of a South African wind-vane, by inconsistencies between the forecast and reported wind-directions. Modern weather forecasting is a model of excellence for anyone who wishes to know the planet better. Central to it is the recognition that the atmosphere is a single, coherent system, and to understand the weather at any one place you have to take the whole world into account. A generation ago, the idea that Europe's weather, for instance, was directly influenced by sea-surface temperatures in the Pacific Ocean, 10,000 kilometres away, seemed the fanciful idea of a few bookish specialists. Now, when the eastern Pacific turns warm, the satellites see it lobbing depressions at Europe.

The Ozone Hole and after

*W*HEN WORD came that the British Antarctic Survey had detected a severe depletion in the ozone layer over the frozen southern continent, there was embarrassment at NASA's Goddard Space Flight Center near Washington DC. The Americans had a satellite flying called *Nimbus-7*, instrumented to look for just such a phenomenon. The satellite had duly observed it, but its minders on the ground had told the data-processing computer to ignore readings that seemed ridiculously low. Prompted by ground-based observations from a single point, at the British base at Halley Bay, Antarctica, the Goddard team dug out the tape of satellite data and immediately plotted the huge Ozone Hole as a new geographical feature.

That was in 1985. And when *Nimbus-7* showed the Ozone Hole over

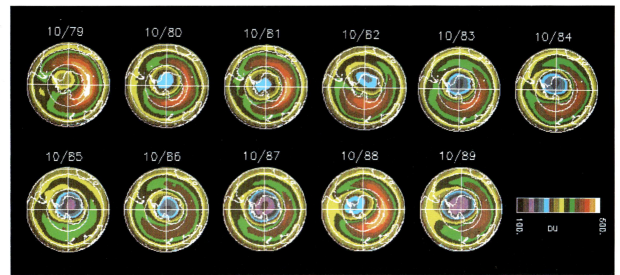

Antarctica to be not only large but tending to increase in extent and severity from year to year, it proved the power of satellites to observe surprising changes in the Earth system. More than any other discovery or prediction till then, the Ozone Hole focused the minds of the public and of scientists on the interactions between human beings and their environment. In fact it caused worldwide alarm.

The layer of ozone high in the atmosphere is created by ultraviolet rays from the Sun and screens the Earth's surface from the fiercest of those rays. Some scientists had been worrying about it 20 years earlier. Military minds toyed with using chemicals or nuclear weapons to punch a hole in the ozone layer and afflict enemy territory with crop-scorching rays. Fleets of high-flying supersonic airliners were thought capable of harming the ozone layer with nitrogen oxides.

Chemical studies pointed at manmade chlorofluorocarbons (CFCs) as another, more immediate threat to the ozone layer. These chemicals, escaping from refrigerators and sprays to the upper atmosphere, could there release chlorine to ravage the ozone in a series of reactions. A few geologists muttered about volcanoes releasing chlorine too, but following the Ozone Hole discovery it was on the CFCs that conclaves of governments focused their attention. By 1990 environmental diplomacy achieved an agreement to end all use of CFCs within 10 years.

Other satellites revealed holes in tropical forests, which were being cleared at rates faster than governments in some affected countries realized. If remote-sensing satellites had done nothing but look at the ozone of Antarctica and the forests of Borneo and Brazil, their place in

Antarctica's Ozone Hole from space. Centred on the South Pole, colour-coded images of atmospheric ozone from the US Nimbus-7 satellite depict low concentrations in purple. The images, from successive Octobers in the Antarctic spring, showed variation from year to year, but the hole tended to enlarge.

19

history would be secure, for having helped to push environmental concerns to the top of the international agenda in the mid-1980s.

At the same time, computer models of climate were predicting a global warming by manmade carbon dioxide and other gases in the atmosphere. And a team coordinated by the International Council of Scientific Unions (ICSU) looking afresh at effects of nuclear war reported that smoke from fires could dim the Sun's rays and cause crop failures in many parts of the world. The common factor in all these concerns – the Ozone Hole, deforestation, global warming and nuclear winter – was the notion that human action could have large and often unforeseen effects, not just local but global in scope.

The world-watchers have their share of fine comedians, of course. Back in the 19th Century they forecast that city streets would become knee-deep in horse manure as personal and public transport multiplied. A generation ago, peevish voices predicted mass famine in Asia by 1975 and exhaustion of the world's oil by the end of the century. In the 1970s, before the short-term global warming came to dominate the prognoses, some of us drew attention to the long-term risk of a new ice age (though a belly-laugh about that might be premature). Experts who in the 1980s vastly overstated the rates of growth of deserts and disappearance of forests have already had to eat their words.

When the world's scientists saw how poor their understanding of the Earth system was, in the face of demands from governments for firm advice about climate change and other problems, ICSU launched in 1986 the International Geosphere–Biosphere Programme (IGBP). A less forbidding name is the Global Change programme, and a related project is called Human Dimensions of Global Change. Over 10–20 years, the programme is expected to marshal resources worth many billions of dollars, although much of this will be by way of coordination of existing programmes, for remote-sensing satellites, oceanographic research ships, computer modelling of climate, and the like. By 1990 government funding for global-change research in the USA alone exceeded a billion dollars a year.

The declared objective of ICSU's Global Change programme is:

To describe and understand the interactive physical, chemical and biological processes that regulate the total Earth system, the unique environment that it provides for life, the changes that are occurring in this system, and the manner in which they are influenced by human actions.

In concert with this initiative, NASA advertised a Mission to Planet

Earth, to signify new resources set aside for remote-sensing satellites. When the space agencies of the world designated 1992 as International Space Year, they too laid special emphasis on the contribution that satellites could make to studies of the Earth system and global change. Plans for greatly increasing the number and variety of spaceborne instruments for observing the Earth are linked to the Space Station and its associated 'polar platforms', due to fly in the late 1990s.

Yet the workings of Spaceship Earth, the processes of global change and the interactions of the human species with them are all sufficiently mysterious for the aim 'to describe and understand' them to require major scientific discoveries. These could well alter the agenda of environmental concerns. As a challenge to the human mind the task ranks with grasping the origin of the Universe or the enigma of human consciousness, and requires those touches of genius where imagination counts for more than dollars. Unless reliable theories can aid thought, comprehension of the Earth may be befuddled by undigested data.

An attempt in the 1970s to fill the intellectual vacuum at the core of the subject gave a foretaste of what may be needed. The Gaia hypothesis of James Lovelock, an inventor of chemical instruments, sees the habitability of the planet depending on a conspiracy of organisms that regulates the chemical make-up of the air and the sea. If this were ever provable, it would be a giant discovery. The feature worth stressing here is that the Gaia hypothesis combines elements of many branches of science – 'from astronomy to zoology,' as Lovelock put it.

A challenge from physics

'WE'RE STUNNED,' Inez Fung said, 'we're all scratching our heads.' She was commenting to the author on the discovery of a Great Northern Absorber of manmade carbon dioxide. Sitting at computer terminals at the Goddard Institute for Space Studies in New York City, Fung and her colleagues had figured out that carbon dioxide in the air was behaving in a manner quite different from the way the pundits said it should. By 1990 they were testifying to the existence of a mysterious absorber on the land masses of the Northern Hemisphere, without being able to say where or what it was.

For geographers, there is no Northwest Passage or Great Southern Continent still waiting to be found by daring seafarers, no lost tribe to

21

be encountered in unpenetrated jungle, no Nile untracked to its source. Submarines haunt the North Pole and the South Pole is a permanent base. Even the deep ocean may have few surprises left, since the discoveries in the 1970s of ocean-bed ore-factories and giant worms.

The anatomy of the planet's surface being well known, most remaining discoveries will concern its physiology – how it works. Trade winds and ocean currents were historical examples of this kind. The jet streams encountered by high-flying military aircraft in the 1940s, and tropical cloud clusters first characterized from early weather-satellite images in the 1960s, were further items of this physiology, and so was the Ozone Hole of the 1980s.

The discovery by Fung and her colleagues concerns the Earth's bloodstream of life-giving gas. Where the arteries of the global atmosphere meet the Earth's surface, the carbon dioxide flows in unexpected directions. A widely held belief that the oceans are the principal absorber of the excess carbon dioxide put into the air by human activity appears to be untrue. Details of the research are postponed to a later chapter. Consider for the moment its provenance.

To be stunned by one's own work is the highest reward that science has to offer a happy few of its most faithful servants. The Great Northern Absorber may come to rank as an early triumph of the new global geography. But Fung is neither a geographer nor an atmospheric chemist. She is a fluid dynamicist by trade, a species of physicist. Central to her work are numerical models of the climate which she uses, for example, to compute the transfer of gases through the atmosphere from one part of the world to another.

The climate models are at the cutting edge of theoretical research on the Earth system. They are not really adequate for the political task of forecasting the climate of the 21st Century, yet they are, *pace* Gaia, the only reasonably comprehensive and precise description of the Earth system that exists. The state of knowledge in each contributory subject can be judged, in an important sense, by how usefully the climate models can assimilate it.

The modellers themselves see gaps in knowledge more clearly than anyone else, and they nag the specialists for information. They don't just go back to school. They argue with meteorologists about clouds, with oceanographers about deep currents, with botanists about plant growth, with hydrologists about river runoffs, or with economic geographers about fossil-fuel combustion. As Fung says: 'We have a new way of doing business where you have to talk several languages. The universities have not caught up.'

Because of ever-increasing specialization in education and research, an economist is *expected* to be ignorant about glaciers and a glaciologist about economics. So when experts discuss the state of the planet, it can be like hearing a chiropodist and a dentist arguing about a patient's heart condition. Worse than that, the experts eventually have to rely on outsiders to bring their own subjects up to date.

Many key scientific discoveries of the 20th Century, the age of the specialist, have come when talented individuals and groups, usually physicists, have invaded other people's sciences with novel instruments and fresh ideas. They put geologists right about the age of the Earth, continental drift and the rhythm of the ice ages. They told chemists how atoms react, and their new sensors revolutionized astronomy. They disclosed to biologists the molecular magic of the genes, and introduced some badly needed mathematics into ecology. If physicists now rush in where experts fear to tread, in the Earth system, one reason is that the remote-sensing satellite and the climate model are both applications of standard physics.

A cynic might suggest that the physicists now attending to questions at the planet's surface are refugees from the Earth's core. The dynamo there that makes a compass needle point north, but sometimes south, still defeats them 900 years after the Chinese invented the compass. Perhaps physicists hope that nothing at the surface can be quite as baffling. Be that as it may, they are for the moment the chief architects of the new global geography.

Reinventing geography

GEOGRAPHERS have always had good intentions about taking a grand view in putting together the pieces of the Earth system. Theirs is supposed to be the great integrating science that describes the two-way interactions between human life and its physical and biological surroundings, in a common framework of geographical spacetime. When other scientists speak of research on global change and human action they are reinventing geography 2400 years after Herodotus, 200 years after Alexander von Humboldt.

Herodotus, a Greek traveller and historian, treated the known world as a continuum. He was a crony of natural philosophers, and developed a mathematical model of silting in river deltas. Humboldt, a German mining engineer turned explorer, crusaded for the Amerindian slave-miners of Mexico, yet was fascinated by volcanoes, ocean currents and plant–animal interactions. These founding fathers of ancient and modern geography would quickly feel at home in a remote-sensing centre or computer-modelling lab.

Some individual geographers have played conspicuous roles in recent research on the Earth system, but their subject as a whole has languished. Perhaps geography lost its way as the great integrating science, when it divided the world too emphatically into regions and split itself into specialized sub-disciplines mimicking the work of geologists, economists or sociologists. When the state of the environment first became headline news in the 1960s, most geographers were looking the other way. 'We missed the bus,' many now admit. The best of them know that current concern for Spaceship Earth is another chance for their subject, provided they are ready both to recall geography's origins and to adapt to the era of satellites and computers.

What distinguishes geography most clearly from the natural sciences is its attention to human beings. Other disciplines such as agronomy, epidemiology and earthquake engineering link human, physical and biological factors in their special areas, but only geography offers to do so comprehensively. As people's lives, actions, and interactions with the environment are mainly focused in small areas, geography can never lose its interest in the village. But objects and activities in a village reflect worldwide arrangements and processes.

The region-by-region descriptions often favoured by geographers are at odds with a truly global approach from which no part of the Earth is ever excluded. Rather than leaving anywhere out, it is be better to reduce the whole Earth to that point of mass M. You can add numbers specifying its temperature, population, stock of dollars, and so on, and describe in dynamic models how these numbers change with time. That makes far more sense than a global model of a million grid points in which some points are inactive because Indonesia and Antarctica are not in the curriculum.

True global geographers would by force of habit identify *all* icecaps, farmlands, car factories (or whatever the items are) and not only those of privileged continents or regions. They could then, as they wished, home in on any region or any village and know its global setting from the outset – not just its latitude and longitude, but how it is enmeshed in global systems of geology, weather, ethnicity, economics and so on.

Most remote-sensing satellites deal evenhandedly with all regions. Their panorama is similar to what an astronomer on the Moon would see of the Earth as it spun every 24 hours, bringing the different parts into view – although the satellites cover the polar regions better. The larger oceans, continents, islands, ice sheets and cloud formations dominate the scenery. An infinity of detail waits to be filled in, but Indonesia, Antarctica and everywhere else are visible from the start. A remote-sensing specialist in Europe, say, can find out what is going on in New Zealand, by calling in the right space images. And besides their global reach in geographical space, the satellites give the first continuous overviews of the Earth in geographical time, as an ever-changing, dynamic system.

Where is all this leading? Imagine a 21st-Century model of the Earth system in a supercomputer a billion times more powerful than anything available now. It reaches from the action of individual genes in plants that govern their responses to the passing seasons, through to movements of continents that have set the climatic stage in the present geological age. Coupled into it are models such as river flow, human interactions with vegetation, and general human activity reflected in homes, workplaces, travel and economic data.

This ideal embodiment of the new global geography can tell at once how the price of rice in Bangkok, Asia, affects the demand for fertilizers in West Africa, what a sea-temperature change in the Atlantic implies for umbrella-makers' profits in Hungary, or simply how many tourists Alaska can expect next week. Satellite observations update the model from day to day, just as with the weather-forecasting models of the 20th Century.

Many components of such an ideal system already exist, at least in embryo. Computer models of various kinds, and computerized geographic information systems, can cope with pieces of Earth-surface spacetime of any chosen size, from a flowerbed to the entire world, and with topics from plant growth to pan-global manufacturing operations. And the scales of observation by the satellites already span the full range from the village, or the missile silo, to the world.

Big Brother in the sky

*C*LOUDS MOVE from hour to hour, and from month to month living things react to the changing seasons in waves of vegetation sweeping the continents and oceans. The remote-sensing satellites see all this, and their capacity to reveal changes over time, due to natural processes or human activity, is already impressive. No drought can strike, or river change its course, or volcano erupt, without the satellites observing it.

Any replacement of fields by houses or factories, or of forests by fields, is discoverable by comparing images from year to year. So is the creation of a new missile base; indeed techniques of remote sensing from space arose from military needs. The idea of a spy in the sky is much older than the Space Age, and balloons and aircraft have long played their part in military reconnaissance.

If you put a large astronomical telescope into a fairly low orbit and turned it to look at the Earth's surface, it could see individual bricks in a house. Some 'photoreconnaissance' or spy satellites have that capability. They can tell one type of missile, tank or aircraft from another. Built and operated at enormous cost, with armies of photo-interpreters to peer at the products, the spy satellites were the eyes of the USA and the Soviet Union during the Cold War and the Gulf crisis of 1990.

In 1956, the year before the first manmade satellite *Sputnik-1* flew and when many still regarded spaceflight as science fiction, the US Air Force ordered launchers and photoreconnaissance satellites. By 1960 the exposed film was being successfully mailed back from the satellites by parachute, to be caught in mid-air by a special aircraft. The Soviet Union followed suit with *Cosmos-4* in 1962. Spy satellites gave the nuclear superpowers a Big-Brotherly view of the world. They snooped not just on each other but on other countries at will. High-flying spy-planes played their part; the telescopes, cameras and instruments put into satellites can ride in aircraft too, for military or civilian purposes.

The first civilian spacecraft designed to look at the Earth was the American *Tiros* weather satellite in 1960. The 'T' in its name stood for 'television' and it transmitted the content of its images as TV-like radio signals to ground stations. All civilian remote-sensing satellites since then have relied on radio links. *Tiros* was the grandfather of the exceptionally valuable series of NOAA weather satellites, still going strong and finding new uses outside meteorology.

More detail of the Earth's surface became available to civilians from the *Landsat* satellites, general-purpose Earth-survey spacecraft of which the first flew in 1972. Six years later the *Seasat* satellite, using radar, failed after only 15 weeks in orbit. Rumour suggested that the admirals sabotaged *Seasat* because its images were far too good, but a design fault really takes the blame. The Soviet Union matched these American operations, although not until 1987 did it begin selling Earth-survey images to other countries.

Resolution is the key word defining the detail visible in images from space. Typical weather satellites can register an island more than one kilometre wide. The first generation of *Landsats* picked out fields more than 80 metres wide. *Landsat-4* (1982) introduced the Thematic Mapper with a resolution of 30 metres. This began to be militarily sensitive, with roads, airfields and large buildings becoming visible in the images.

The USA and Soviet Union were jealous of their privileges as orbital policemen. To a proposal from France in the 1970s, that an international photoreconnaissance satellite service should be created, they reacted like men watching a sex-show who find that their families want to see it too: 'It is not good for you to see all the naughty things that go on in the world.' With Gallic insouciance the French went ahead with the civilian remote-sensing satellite called *SPOT* capable of observing details down to 10 metres. With it came an open-skies policy that brooked no censorship except in the gravest crises.

Soon after *SPOT-1* was launched in 1986, the author showed a Soviet admiral an image of a naval base near Murmansk in the far north of the Soviet Union. A Soviet aircraft carrier was plainly visible and the admiral said of the image, 'We hate it.' Yet the Spot Image company would cheerfully sell to the Soviet Navy the scene showing Brest and the top-secret pens of France's own missile-carrying submarines.

Spot Image even advertises '*SPOT* as a penetration aid' to all the world's armed forces, using the satellites' capacity to generate 3-D images of selected target areas. But while anyone can buy any *SPOT* image, all acquisitions are catalogued, so if your enemy is studying his ground-hugging route to your palace, you should be able to figure that out. Open cataloguing is important also in the civilian field. Many countries are nervous about foreign companies using satellites to inspect their natural resources.

In contrast to the French, India too has its own remote-sensing satellite, *IRS-1*, yet is so worried about secrets passing to its old enemy

LANDSAT DATA 1985 • 1986, PROCESSED BY GAF, GERMANY

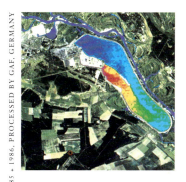

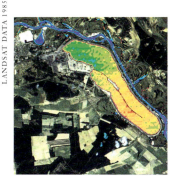

Crisis at Chernobyl observed using Landsat's heat-sensing abilities. Hot water, coded red in the upper image, enters the lake from the Soviet nuclear plant. After the disaster in 1986, more uniform temperatures indicated shutdown (lower image).

Pakistan that it restricts its use. An Indian scientist once let the author glimpse an I R S - I image of a farming district, as surreptitiously as if it were a dirty postcard. But proliferation has set in, with the Japanese (M O S and J E R S), the European Space Agency (E R S) and the Canadians (*Radarsat*). The genie of remote sensing will not go back into the bottle, however much the generals and admirals may wish that it would.

The press too is joining in. A small Swedish outfit called Space Media Network shamed the Soviet government into admitting to major nuclear contamination in the Urals, dating back to the 1950s, by publishing *Landsat* material showing the abandoned areas. An American project called *Mediasat* has envisaged a spy satellite for the press with a resolution of 5 metres. For users of civilian satellites who are preoccupied with honest civilian tasks, any military and political connotations remain an amusing sideshow.

Orbits, swaths and red grass

SOME WEATHER satellites seem to hover over particular regions, by using an Earth-synchronous orbit. While the planet spins, a satellite heading due east around the Equator keeps pace with the rotation if its orbit is about 36,000 kilometres above the Earth. From this orbit, often called 'geostationary', the satellite observes the same piece of the Earth all the time, and from so high an altitude that it has about a quarter of the entire planet in view. The edges are seen slantingly and less well than regions more directly below the satellite.

The US GOES first launched in 1974 was the earliest of the Earth-synchronous weather satellites. In principle, five such spacecraft stationed around the Equator give complete coverage of the Earth except for the polar regions. Nominally, two US GOES and one satellite apiece from Japan, India and Europe occupy these five stations, but the coverage has not been continuous.

A more typical remote-sensing satellite, like those in the American NOAA and *Landsat* series, visits every part of the Earth and always at roughly the same time of day, being synchronized to the Sun. Its orbit passes near the North and South Poles. From a height of 700–900 kilometres, it observes a succession of swaths, or strips, of the Earth's surface. During each 100-minute orbit the Earth rotates eastwards through about 25 degrees, and the satellite's path, steady as a gyro-

Facing:
A Japanese volcano seen by SPOT. The wind drives a smoke pall southwards from erupting Sakurajima. The tourist resort of Kagoshima appears grey on the bay's western shore. The predominant red areas are forests glowing brightly in invisible infra-red light, translated into red in the image.

scope, appears to shift westwards. So if it passes over Poland during one circling of the Earth, the next will take it over Britain, and five hours later it will visit the Great Lakes of North America. The next day's tracks are a little different.

The look of the Earth varies with the time of day, and differences between morning and afternoon images may owe as much to the lighting as to any real changes. That is why synchronism with the Sun matters. As the months pass and the Earth circles the Sun, the satellite must swivel its orbit like a slowly wobbling gyro. This happens spontaneously if the orbit misses the Poles by about 8 or 9 degrees.

A satellite can take a broad or narrow view of the Earth beneath it. The swath of the *NOAA* weather satellites is 3000 kilometres wide, and the resolution is about 1 kilometre. For *Landsat* the swath is 185 kilometres wide at the resolution of 30 metres. There is a trade-off between seeing a place infrequently but in great detail, or having a blurry view more often.

Successive swaths of the *NOAA* satellites overlap even at the Equator, where the separation between orbital paths is greatest, and observations continue during the half of each orbit that the satellite spends on the dark side of the Earth. As a result, each *NOAA* satellite sees everywhere at least twice in 24 hours. With its much narrower swath, and a need for daylight, *Landsat* takes 16 days to scan the whole Earth.

The choice of sensors for examining the Earth parallels the astronomers' options, when they scrutinize galaxies by telescopes tuned to X-rays, ultraviolet, infra-red or radio waves invisible to the human eye. In this vast rainbow of increasing wavelengths, visible light is only a narrow band between the ultraviolet and the infra-red. The Earth's atmosphere blocks the rays at many wavelengths, and remote-sensing satellites work mainly with visible light, infra-red and radio waves. They usually shun blue light, which scatters in the sky-blue air.

In the case of radar, the spacecraft itself illuminates the Earth's surface, but otherwise the sensors intercept radiant energy derived directly or indirectly from sunlight. By visible light, clouds dominate the scene, and when the ground is in sight the view is similar to that seen by eye from a high-flying aircraft. In images made with the various invisible rays, the planet can look very different.

At one infra-red wavelength, vegetation glows brightly. Another picks out swirls of water vapour. At a third infra-red wavelength, deserts stand out brightly because they are hot. Radio microwaves emitted by the Earth show patterns due to wet and dry soil. Radars probing the surface readily pick up hills, trees, sea waves and other features capable of bouncing the radar pulses back to the spacecraft, while the clouds disappear. Because radio and radar systems penetrate cloud, they are much less weather-dependent than other sensors.

Widely scattered ground receivers and data-distribution centres handle the torrent of information pouring in daily from the remote-sensing satellites. Technical processing enhances the raw signals and puts them in a correct geographical framework, having regard to the satellite's position and viewing angle. Different ways of dealing with the data then reflect different kinds of applications, that range from local mapmaking to taking the temperature of the whole world. Some users treat a space image as if it were simply a high-altitude air photo. In reality it is more of a confection of signals reporting activity area by area across the Earth's surface. Serious users often prefer to work from the data stored on magnetic tape.

Like a TV picture or a pointilliste painting, the space image dissolves on close inspection into a mass of blobs called pixels (picture elements). A typical image may consist of about 10 million pixels, each representing a square on the Earth equivalent in width to the resolving power of the spacecraft's sensor. A pixel shows no detail except a shade of grey, graded to the total energy received from that patch of the Earth in the band of wavelengths to which the sensor is tuned. Experts like to see the pixels, in a well-reproduced space image.

Simple processing can convert the grey scale to a colour scale, to emphasize differences in intensity from pixel to pixel and region to region. In another type of coloured image, primary colours represent signals for different wavebands. Superimposing them, pixel by pixel, paints the terrain in a wide range of colours, mixed according to the relative strengths of the signals. The colour conveys information about the character of the Earth's surface within each pixel.

The combined image must often be presented in false colours, when one sensor or more is operating beyond the wavelength range of the human eye. Only those who persist in thinking of the images as colour photos need be troubled by this. Maps have always used false colours, whether depicting roads in yellow or painting whole countries pink or purple. In a typical case, the remote-sensing bands are green, red, and near infra-red, where 'near' means not far removed in wavelength from visible light. A convention is to show the infra-red as red, red light as

An airborne sensor picks up strong infra-red signals from the trees. As the infra-red is invisible to human eyes, it has to be shown red in the image.

31

green, and green light as blue – shunting the bands one step along the spectrum.

Grass is red. That is one of the first things anyone finds out, when looking at false-colour images from satellites of the *Landsat* or SPOT type. This is simply because vegetation is bright in the near infra-red band shown red in the composites, but dull in visible light. As percentages of the available light, typical brightnesses in green/red/infra-red are 13/8/40. That is a remote-sensing signature for vegetation.

Expressed in the same way, for the same wavelength bands, the signature of bright snow is roughly 90/80/60, while liquid water free of sunglint is altogether darker, at 8/3/0. Rocks and soil become brighter towards the longer wavelengths, so that a signature of sand can be 20/30/45. These variations in the look of different surfaces are no different in principle from the blends of real colours that help human eyes to look at a scene. The numbers convey, better than any insistent words, that remote-sensing satellites do not simply 'take pictures' but measure the radiance of the Earth.

Three satellites from Europe

*A*S COMPARED with the USA and Soviet Union, Western Europeans have operated relatively few remote-sensing satellites but, starting late, they have chosen their systems and sensors with care. Three European spacecraft with very different personalities illustrate important techniques in remote sensing. They are SPOT, the leading miniaturist, ERS-1 the would-be king of the oceans, and *Meteosat*, which is Africa's guardian angel.

SPOT concentrates on a swath only 60 kilometres wide. In a telescope, a strip of 6000 small electronic detectors makes the most detailed observations, at the resolution of 10 metres. Sensing green and red light together, in a 'panchromatic' mode, each detector looks at an individual 10-metre pixel in a 60-kilometre line across the Earth's surface. The line moves down the swath like a pushbroom as the satellite flies forward in its orbit, completing the scan of a 60 by 60 kilometres scene every 9 seconds. Other pushbroom detectors observe with lesser resolution (20 metres) the three separate wavelength bands: green, red, and near infra-red. In its normal mode, looking straight down, SPOT takes 26 days to scan the Earth and return to any given place. But it carries two identical telescopes, and on command a mirror can switch one of them to look left or right of *SPOT*'s track. Oblique viewing can greatly shorten the interval between visits, while two views from different directions can make a 3-D picture.

SPOT was conceived and built in France, but Belgium and Sweden have stakes in the programme. By the time *SPOT-2* went into space in 1990, ensuring an uninterrupted service, Spot Image had a clear impression of the market for its images and magnetic tapes of data. The largest single use was for mapping, at 30 per cent of *SPOT*'s market. The detail in the panchromatic mode is good enough for making maps up to a scale of 1:25,000, where 10 metres corresponds with a moderately thick pen-stroke.

Vegetation studies, forestry and agriculture (20 per cent) is another important sector of *SPOT* applications, followed by geology and non-renewable resources (18 per cent) and public works and construction projects (8 per cent). Urban planning and coastal studies head a list of lesser and very varied uses for the satellite. The commercial prices of the material are rather high, and often beyond the reach of university researchers and teachers.

To watch the oceans by radar is the chief task of Europe's new *ERS-1*, launched in 1991. It also carries 'passive' microwave and infra-red sensors. But the 'clutter' of strong radar echoes from sea waves, always troublesome for designers of seagoing radars, offers a particularly powerful way of observing the sea from space.

Whenever *ERS-1* passes over Venice in Italy, a platform in the sea records the prevailing height of the water, while laser beams from five stations scattered around Europe pinpoint the position of the satellite. This is to check the radar altimeter in *ERS-1*, which measures the level of the sea below the satellite to an accuracy of 10 centimetres. Like a phrenologist handling a head, the radar altimeter feels lumps, humps and hollows in the shape of the solid Earth, and effects of currents and eddies in the sea. To observe sea-ice, the radar altimeter switches to ultra-short radar waves.

The sea waves stirred up by the wind can reveal the wind's direction and strength. Another radar in *ERS-1* aims three beams in different directions by the compass. Sea waves running towards one of the beams will return stronger echoes than for a beam looking along the crests. Comparing the echoes of the three beams gives the wind direction to within 20 degrees around the compass, and the wind speed to within 2 metres per second. A chain of buoys off the coast of Norway checks the winds and waves reported as E R S - 1 flies over.

The sharpest images from E R S - 1 show the sea, coasts and land with a resolution of 30 metres, across a 100-kilometre swath. Using a trick invented by radio astronomers and tested in space by *Seasat* and the Space Shuttle, a 'synthetic-aperture' radar (S A R) looks at the same objects repeatedly from shifting positions along its track, to accumulate signals that combine into a crisp images. But S A R is so extravagant with power and data that E R S - 1 can use it only for a few minutes at a time while in sight of a ground station, except for some very brief 'imagettes' of ocean swell.

Sea waves appear clearly, with highlights and shadows created in the slanting illumination by the S A R beam. Waves refracted around an island make patterns as if in a textbook diagram and S A R reveals sand-banks offshore, by the disturbed waves that cover them. The bow waves of ships show up plainly, while oil slicks appear as dark patches with weak echoes, because oil on troubled waters calms the waves.

The shadowing of relief in S A R images, seen with sea waves, becomes even more striking on land. Geological structures and fault-lines often stand out clearly, along with differences in texture between hard rock and loose deposits. Ice sheets and glaciers are important targets for the spaceborne radars. As for vegetation, radar's sensitivity to surface textures can distinguish between trees and ground cover and (experimentally at least) between different tree species.

At the other extreme from S A R and S P O T, *Meteosat* portrays a quarter of the world with the broad strokes of an Impressionist painter, every half-hour. It is Europe's Earth-synchronous weather satellite, or more precisely a series of spacecraft of that name on station since 1977, conceived in France and operated by the European Space Agency for a consortium of weather services.

Hovering at Latitude Zero, Longitude Zero, over the Atlantic Ocean just south of the protuberance of West Africa, *Meteosat* keeps continuous watch on a segment of the world dominated by Africa. It has slanting views of Europe, the Middle East, and parts of South America. *Meteosat* also acts as the meteorologists' own telecommunications satellite. Besides disseminating images, data, charts and forecasts, it relays information from about 250 'data-collection platforms' by land, sea and air – from flood-warning stations on British rivers, for example, and automatic weather stations in Africa.

Facing:
Simultaneous views of a quarter of the world, from Europe's Meteosat. The strangest image (top) shows water vapour swirling in the atmosphere, even over deserts, and air masses convolving in depressions. In a heat image (near, below) the hot Sahara appears black and the whitest, coldest clouds are those most likely to rain. By visible light (far right) stormy cloud systems over the Atlantic Ocean and off South Africa show up clearly, as do large rivers, lakes and other land features. These images are for noon on September 5 1990, but similar products are generated every half-hour.

34

The spacecraft is a spinning drum with a hole in the side, through which a telescope looks out. At any moment, each of four detectors sees a pixel a few kilometres wide. As *Meteosat* spins, the telescope scans an east–west strip of land and ocean. While turning away from the Earth, the telescope tilts a little, so that next time around it sweeps over a new strip, taking 25 minutes to complete one scan of the Earth.

A ground station in Germany picks up *Meteosat*'s signals, and computers generate three views of the Earth at different wavelengths. Sensors working by visible light see the clouds of depressions and other weather systems, white against the dark oceans and grey lands. Another, tuned to infra-red rays, at a wavelength strongly absorbed by water vapour, reveals great bands and swirls of moist air relatively high in the atmosphere. Lastly a 'thermal infra-red' channel in *Meteosat* registers wavelengths at which the Earth radiates its warmth most strongly into space, and takes the temperature of each pixel. Warm clouds, cold seas and snow-covered land all give readings close to 0 degrees C. High cloud tops, showing up as cold patches, denote clouds liable to shed their rain.

Meteosat numbers go into the computer models of the weather forecasters. They include percentages and temperatures of cloud in each segment, the humidity of the air, and the temperature of the sea surface. These are averages for segments about 200 kilometres wide. Automatic tracking of patches of cloud, seen in successive scans, reveals the speed and direction of winds at the height of the cloud tops.

Spacecraft versus locusts

ONCE AN HOUR, a computer at the UN Food and Agriculture Organization (FAO) in Rome searches the signals from the *Meteosat* spacecraft for African clouds likely to rain. Once every 10 days a courier arrives from Washington with tapes from a *NOAA* weather satellite's afternoon passes over Africa and adjacent regions. The computer looks for cloud-free areas and, by comparing the red and infra-red light reflected from the ground, appraises Africa's vegetation. Images and evaluations go out from Rome by telecommunications satellite, to receiving stations scattered across Africa. They give early warnings of famine, and help to avert plagues of locusts.

The name of FAO's system, Artemis, stands for 'Africa Real Time Environmental Monitoring using Imaging Satellites'. Operational since 1988, it generates images and maps to the relatively coarse resolution of 7.6 kilometres. Some show the number of days when rain has probably occurred in each sector, during each 10-day period. For the drought-prone belt just south of the Sahara Desert, the computer estimates the amount of rain. Vegetation mapping, to the same scale, picks the highest cloud-free readings from the land surface in each 10-day period. The highest readings of the month give a more definitive map of the vegetation. It covers all of Africa and nearby lands, including Arabia, the Levant and southern Europe.

While drought-watchers look out for an absence of vegetation in semi-arid lands near the desert margin, vegetation appearing abnormally in mid-desert is the danger signal for the locust-hunters. The ravenous insects have not changed their ways since the time of Moses.

And when it was morning, the east wind brought the locusts . . . They covered the face of the whole earth, so that the land was darkened; and they did eat every herb of the land, and all the fruit of the trees which the hail had left: and there remained not any green thing in the trees, or in the herbs of the field, through all the land of Egypt.

In 1986–88 it was much the same story, with a major locust plague afflicting farms in Africa, from Morocco in the northwest to the Sudan in the east. The desert locust *Schistocerca gregaria* is the most terrible and widespread of swarming insects. Harmless-looking hoppers living quietly in the desert are aroused by rain. The locusts feed on the opportunistic desert plants that salute the rain with a rare flowering. If an enclave of vegetation persists for a few months, the locust population explodes over three or four generations. Switching from a solitary to a gregarious life, the insects multiply into flying swarms up to ten billion strong capable of consuming a million tons of leaves in a few weeks.

Simultaneous upsurges from a number of desert districts, breaking out into farmlands, can annihilate crops, grass and trees in a plague of biblical proportions. The 'invasion area' at risk extends up to 1000 kilometres from the desert's edge. But by the time a locust swarm is large enough to darken the land, the time for effective action against it is already past. Control depends on finding the locusts in the first or second breeding generation, and spraying them with insecticides. The trouble is that the 'recession area' inhabited by the desert locust is very sparsely populated by humans, and hard to traverse. It stretches across the Sahara and Arabian Deserts and on into the dry regions of Iran, Pakistan and northwestern India. At 16 million square kilometres,

A locust breeding ground seen from space. The first image of Morocco shows normal January vegetation, by data from a NOAA satellite interpreted by FAO. In the second image, for January 1988, the desert was in bloom and the abnormal vegetation gave rise to an outbreak of desert locusts.

NOAA SATELLITE DATA PROCESSED BY UN FAO

almost twice the size of the USA, it is a huge area to watch even with aircraft, never mind attempting it with jeeps.

The satellites work magic for the locust-hunters. The Artemis maps and images of Africa and Arabia arriving every 10 days at FAO's Emergency Centre for Locust Operations in Rome give an unprecedented overview of rainfall in the desert, and of vegetation springing up in the moistened soil which could nourish a locust outbreak. The satellites cannot tell whether the locusts are actually swarming in such places, but persistent vegetation shows where to look on the ground. Equally, an absence of vegetation excludes most of the recession area from expensive searches, although there remains a risk of missing narrow strips of lush vegetation along desert watercourses that collect the rainfall.

Artemis will supply more detailed maps of vegetation, at a resolution of 1.1 kilometres. A start has been made with West Africa. As a *NOAA* satellite passes over the Canary Islands, off the African coast, a ground station of the European Space Agency intercepts its signals directly, and mails them to Rome. Vegetated wadis show up much more clearly. Checks on the ground confirm that the satellite maps miss very little locust-food at this resolution and are good enough for detailed planning of the locust-control operations.

The monitoring of vegetation from space, and the breakthrough in worldwide observations at NASA's Goddard Space Flight Center that made the FAO operation possible, loom large later in the book. For the moment, the battle against locusts represents the state of the art, as the remote-sensing satellites begin to play their part in real-time action in which living systems, the physical environment and human beings are interlocked.

CHAPTER 2

The Human Factor

To UNDERSTAND how the crew
of Spaceship Earth interacts with the the Earth system requires descriptions of the human factor that mesh with those of other sub-
systems. Computer models and remote-sensing satellites can help.
Reckoning the human population and its growth provides key numbers. Patterns of trade, industry and urban change define important
though often temporary features of life on the spaceship. Archaeology,
history and daily newspapers announce that the human sub-system is
highly variable on all timescales.

The task also calls for unprecedented ethnic detachment, to consider
the global human species without national, regional or cultural bias. An
obvious example, at the 500th anniversary of Columbus's arrival in the
Americas, is that the people he misidentified as 'Indians' had discovered
the New World long before, and built their own civilizations when
Genoa was a village.

Human beings are all actors in an unending tragicomedy, in which
their impact on one another and on Nature depends not only on birth
rates but on technology, politics, beliefs and fashions. Also on money.
Any realistic picture of the human sub-system must nowadays accom-
modate an electronic vortex of global business.

There are voids at the heart of human studies that this chapter cannot fill. Many researchers consider ways of forcing prices, and assessments of economic performance like the gross national product, to reflect any burdens on the environment or the potential exhaustion of certain resources. They propose, for example, enormous land prices to be charged for wetlands. But the real-life economic system can only prohibit such a sale altogether, tax it within reason, or let it proceed at a normal market price. The theoretical high prices have no testable meaning, because no one in his right mind would pay them.

More profoundly, there is no generally accepted formulation of human ecology that tells how ordinary people and local cultures interact with the environment. It is easy to find examples of behaviour, like defined hunting seasons, that are indeed shaped by available resources, but equally easy to find cases that embody no economic or ecological principle but only, say, the desire to make a football pitch.

While waiting for the Einstein of human ecology, one can sample salient global topics, and look at local examples of the global market intruding on people's lives, as in tropical Australia and the High Andes. People will never behave as predictably as ants. Yet geographical models and computerized mapmaking systems make distinctive contributions to describing the human sub-system, and scenarios can compare possibilities for the future.

Wealth at midnight

*T*HE NIGHT-TIME GLOW of cities visible from space shows where the world's well-to-do are concentrated. Few satellites attempt to observe the dark side of the Earth by visible light, but the Defense Meteorological Satellites of the US Air Force do so. One DMS satellite scans the planet at noon and midnight every day. Woodruff Sullivan, an astronomer at the University of Washington, has combined many midnight scenes in *The Earth at Night* (see title pages 2 and 3).

If an alien astronomer observed the planet's dark side, its 24-hour spin would bring the lit continents into view one after another, looking as they do in Sullivan's compilation. He could, for instance, trace the courses of China's Yellow River and Egypt's Nile by the lights of cities and towns along their banks. Coastal ports and cities hint at the outlines of the continents, in their richer and busier sectors.

Street lights are the main source of illumination and France, frugal in this respect, appears as a pool of relative darkness between the bright lights of Belgium, Germany, Spain and Britain. Paris makes only a modest dot of light compared, say, with Helsinki in Finland. The main Japanese islands of Honshu and Hokkaido are more readily recognizable from space at night than any other geographical feature on the Earth. The biggest surprise is the Japanese squid fleet, which lures its catch with lights so bright that it looks like an extra island of Japan.

Otherwise, the oceans are the largest pools of darkness in the image. Australia, with its population concentrated on its southeastern coasts, looks like a crescent moon. Other sparsely populated regions like the Sahara Desert in Africa and eastern Siberia in Asia are predictably obscure. Yet glaring lights from the northern Sahara and western Siberia, and also from the Arabian/Persian Gulf, the sea off Norway, and the Indonesian island of Sulawesi, have nothing to do with cities. They are gas flares, burning off uncaptured gas from oil wells.

South of the Sahara, smudges of light in the African Sahel show rangeland burning in progress, and manmade forest fires in East Africa and Indo-China are also visible in the image. Although the scenes used for some parts of the world were from the wrong seasons for burning vegetation, Sullivan estimates a million fires in his image. But when gas flares and bush fires are disregarded, the main meaning of *The Earth at Night* is wealth made visible.

If that alien astronomer tried to map the world's population from the lights he would err greatly. He would do better to assume that each glint represents, not a million people, but a billion dollars. The wealth glitters like diamonds, even when it is merely cultivating a taste for squid, or letting megawatts of street lighting leak into the Universe.

Japan, the USA and Europe have the most lights, with a goodly scattering of bright pinpricks corresponding to small cities and towns as well as large urban centres. The climatic effect of the Gulf Stream, which keeps Europe warmer than its latitude would otherwise imply, is evident in a northward shift in the shining, in that sector of the planet. The association of street lighting with electric power production and the use of road vehicles makes the *The Earth at Night* also a rough guide to the main sources of carbon-dioxide gas emitted into the air by burning coal and oil.

China and India, with a combined population of 2000 million, are outshone by Japan with 123 million. South America has a population

41

somewhat greater than the USA's but looks very dark by comparison. Most of the human species occupies pools of darkness scarcely distinguishable from deserts and oceans. Thus *The Earth at Night* illustrates the UN's distinction between 'More Developed Regions', comprising the USA, Canada, Europe, the Soviet Union, Japan, Australia and New Zealand, and 'Less Developed Regions' meaning (almost) everywhere else. In 1990, 1200 million people lived in the rich parts, 72 per cent of them in cities. More than three times as many, 4100 million, lived in the poor parts, and only 33 per cent in cities. Richest of all are Europe's Swiss, where the average man, woman or child benefits each year from goods and services worth more than $21,000 (gross national product per head, 1987 figures). The poorest country may be Africa's Ethiopia, where the comparable figure is $150 per person per year. When the disparity in wealth is more than a hundredfold, a Swiss barber is a millionaire beside even a successful Ethiopian peasant.

Terms that had quite different meanings before – 'Third World', 'South', 'developing' – have become euphemisms for a regionalization of poverty. 'Newly industrialized countries' such as South Korea and Argentina have climbed past $2000 per head, and the 'developing' countries also include some relatively wealthy oil-producing states such as Libya ($5500 per head). All these average figures can be very misleading, of course. There are pockets of poverty in the rich world, and superpoverty in slums and famine-belts of the poorest regions.

Winners and losers

*A*LMOST EVERYWHERE, the wealth-poverty axis seems to parallel the grey-scale of skin pigmentation. It's a white man's world. But if the alien astronomer imagined this to be an inevitable state of affairs, he would be overlooking the history of the human sub-system. The medieval French satirist, François Rabelais, encapsulated it thus:

A number are today emperors, kings, dukes, princes and popes of the Earth who are descended from certain porters and pardon-peddlers, just as, on the other hand, a number are almshouse beggars, needy and miserable, who are of the blood and lineage of great kings and emperors, as a result of the marvellous passing of realms and empires.

Had a remote-sensing satellite observed the Earth at night in the 9th Century AD, with an ultra-sensitive detector to register the feeble lights

Facing:
A pattern of rural settlements in China, imaged by radar from the Space Shuttle Columbia. Analysts at the Jet Propulsion Laboratory used the strength of the radar echoes from the densely populated Hopeh Province near Beijing to distinguish villages (red), fields (dark green), roads and canals (light green) and lakes (grey).

of a pre-electric era, it would have seen Europe literally in its Dark Ages. North America and Japan, too, would have been black holes. The largest cities were Baghdad in the Middle East and Ch'ang-an in China, both with around 2 million people. These were the capitals of the superpowers: the Muslim Caliphate of *The Arabian Nights*, and the Chinese T'ang Empire. In other eras, different cities and superpowers would stand out.

A sense of history is indispensable for global geography, starting with the evidence that everyone is African by ancestry. Around 100,000 years ago two subspecies of *Homo sapiens* coexisted: stocky Neanderthalers in Eurasia and neater folk in Africa. Something happened, probably full-blown language, that gave the Africans a decisive advantage. About 50,000 years ago, they began to spread all over the world in small bands of hunter-gatherers. The Neanderthalers did not survive.

The talkative hunters soon discovered every continent except Antarctica. Each group knew only its own territory and had to adapt to its climate and natural resources. By long separation, languages became mutually unintelligible, and trivial genetic shifts made various 'races' of mankind visibly different. Racial theories that ascribed these differences to separate origins were blown away by modern genetics, linguistics and archaeology. These combine to chart the great dispersal that peopled the continents.

After the ice age ended, 10,000 years ago, groups in Palestine, Indo-China, Indonesia, West Africa, Peru and Mexico began independently growing crops and herding domesticated animals. New dispersals began, as the denser populations sustainable by farming and herding sprawled into the hunters' territory. Subsequent migrations in Eurasia and Africa followed such innovations as the plough, the tamed horse, and the smelting of iron. From late prehistoric times to the present, conquest has been a dominant theme, as empires waxed and waned. With this was interwoven the religious strand, with beliefs of Asiatic origin making territorial gains mainly, though not always, through imperial power. Empires whose lineaments persist most plainly in the modern world are those of the Indians, the Chinese, the Arabs and the Europeans.

With sailing ships and guns the Europeans created the first world-encircling empires. The reunion of the human species after 50,000 years brought disease and slavery to many. And the rise of industry and modern science in Europe and North America during the imperial era ended the dominance of agriculture. By 1800, a post-agricultural life was first evident in Britain, with 60 per cent of the population earning a living by other means. By 1960, the USA had ushered in a post-industrial life, with 60 per cent of the labour force engaged in work other than farming or industry.

The advantages gained by the Europeans and North Americans from industry and science persisted when the empires broke up, but their economic ascendancy marked no innate Euro-American superiority. Indeed, the Japanese in a 100-year spurt overtook everyone as the most successful manufacturing nation. The oil of the Middle East has brought riches and power to people whose fathers minded the camels. On the down escalator, the decline of imperial, industrious Britain to a grumpy importer on the fringe of Europe took less than a human lifetime, and the Soviet superpower is now falling like a house of cards. The well-to-do might be prudent to show generosity towards their poor relations in the world because roles can switch very quickly.

Australian Aborigines stand beside the Amerindians as long-term losers who lost control of entire continents during the reunification of the human species. The story of their dispossession is now less relevant than their efforts to preserve traditional values while coming to terms with modern political and economic forces.

Ex-hunters meet the miners

ABORIGINES HAD occupied Australia for roughly 50,000 years before European settlers arrived about 200 years ago. They had never abandoned the life of hunter-gatherers, and their modifications to the environment, by the use of fire or by accidental overkill, arose in that context. In their Earth system, human beings and spirits interact for ever with hills, rivers, plants and animals, in accordance with supernatural dreams. Groups hold land in trust for their descendants, by the authority of the dreams.

The world's largest bauxite mine, at Weipa on the northeastern shore of Queensland, provides a concrete and not unhopeful example of the interplay between the land, the Aborigines and the newcomers. In opencast sites, huge shovels scoop out more than 10 million tons of ore each year, yet the satellite images show the opencast mine as only a small scar. The mining company, Comalco, fulfils a promise to restore

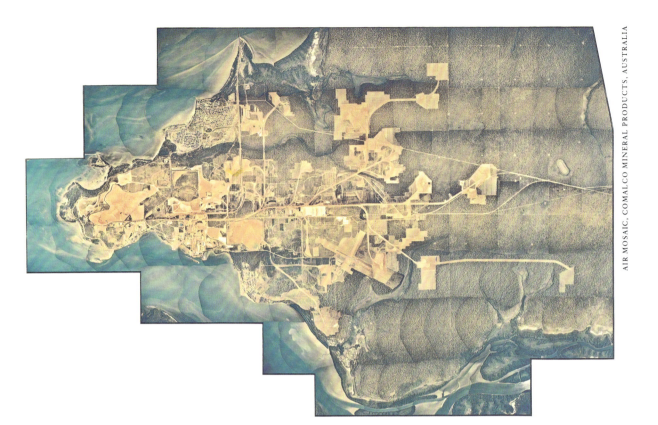

AIR MOSAIC, COMALCO MINERAL PRODUCTS, AUSTRALIA

Bauxite workings, in a mosaic of air photos of the Weipa peninsula. When they have removed the ore, rich in aluminium, the miners replace the soil and replant it.

the vegetation, section by section, as the layer of bauxite is removed. The setting is an open forest of fire-resistant species created by repeated burning, where kangaroos hop among stringybark trees, and crocodiles, turtles and abundant shellfish populate the rivers.

In this remote tropical region, 2600 kilometres from Sydney, the Aborigines persisted with their hunting, fishing and gathering until about 100 years ago. Apart from brushes with fishermen and would-be pastoralists, the first upheaval came with the arrival of missionaries during the 1890s. Weipa Mission gathered the Aborigines into a settled community. It failed to create any substantial economic activity to make up for abandoned skills and disrupted tribal life.

Peculiar geology and the global reach of the mining industry combined in the next upheaval. Many visitors had noted the red cliffs of Weipa, but they went disregarded until 1955, when geologists looking for oil discovered bauxite, the ore of aluminium, made by the dissolution of sandstone in the tropical weather. When mining began in the 1960s, some of the Aborigines joined the workforce, but unaccustomed cash and drunkenness created more disruption in the community.

The mining company made common cause with the Aborigines to

46

help them create the purposeful life that the missionaries and state handouts had denied them for a lifetime. The company would help with amenities and training, but the Aborigines had to handle the politics. The upshot was an inventive bending of the Australian welfare system to ancient traditions. The Aborigines at Weipa pool the state benefits of all individuals and use them to pay their own people to do useful work for the community.

Aborigine girls now handle the community's accounts by computer. A recent project has created a cultural centre open to other Aborigines in northern Queensland. And with rediscovered selfconfidence the Weipa Aborigines have joined battle with the state. They demand that when the stringybark forest has been stripped of its bauxite and re-planted, and reverts to government control, it shall swiftly return to its original owners.

The various groups of Aborigines defined the territories for which they took responsibility by features of the landscape memorized in songs. Farmers and chieftains, bishops and salesmen, have always had reason to define the limits of their terrain. In political geography, the borders of nation-states are nowadays the most significant feature – often fertilized with the human blood spilt to confirm them.

Carving up the world

SOMETIMES NATIONAL borders stand out remarkably clearly in space imagery, even when no natural dividing line such as a river or a mountain range is involved. Civilian remote-sensing satellites cannot see border posts or fences with much clarity, but border regions tend to be less populated than the heartlands of nations. There is a fashion for turning border zones into nature reserves, which can be seen in space images. Along the tense border between the Soviet Union and Iran, a strip of open ground remains out of bounds. Satellites register it as a band of vegetation spared the overgrazing apparent on either side.

Or the neighbouring countries may use the same land close to the border in different ways, discernible from space. Before reunification, large fields in East Germany contrasted with smaller fields in West Germany, and space images of the Soviet–Chinese border show the same transition. At some places along the US–Canadian border, American fields give way abruptly to Canadian grazing land.

On the other hand, a national border is hard to spot if it divides people whose cultures are identical. Africa is crisscrossed with crazy borders left by former colonial rulers who carved up the continent between them in the 19th Century. They simply drew lines on maps, lumping old enemies together and repeatedly cutting across traditional territories of ethnic groups. The post-colonial results have sometimes been bloody, as in the Biafran War in Nigeria, and sometimes comical, when the frontiers are scorned.

The border between Nigeria and Benin cuts through Yorubaland. In Benin, the official language is French and the currency is hard, backed by the French franc. Across the border, English goes with a weak Nigerian currency. For the Yoruba, speaking their own language and fixing their own exchange rates, smuggling is a way of life. In colonial days, they traded French brandy for British guns; now, Asian rice imports go one way, Nigerian gasoline the other. At busy crossings between Benin and Nigeria, everyone in sight may be a smuggler.

Only national laws stop dead at the frontier post. Weather systems disregard the borders, while for commerce, tourism, and legal or illegal migrations a border is at most a filter, with varying degrees of effectiveness. Modern technology penetrates borders – witness the role of television in the wave of democratization that swept across Eastern Europe in 1989.

More borders ostensibly come together at the South Pole than anywhere else. Antarctica is the spaceship's main refrigerator and the last unexploited continent. Nations laying claim to pieces of it define wedge-shaped territories by lines of longitude that converge with geometric inevitability at the Pole. Since 1956, the USA has cocked a snook at these claims with a thriving South Pole base that encroaches on them all.

The most beautiful of all space images may be the mosaic of Antarctica compiled by the UK's National Remote Sensing Centre from US *NOAA* satellite data. It shows an iced cake in the shape of a Q – the tail being the Antarctic Peninsula pointing towards South America. The Transantarctic Mountains divide the huge ice sheet on the high plateau of East Antarctica from the lesser ice sheet of West Antarctica, which straddles a bunch of islands.

Anyone who imagines that an island continent nearly twice the size of Australia will be readily abandoned to the penguins should remember chilly Alaska. The Russians sold Alaska to the USA as territory of

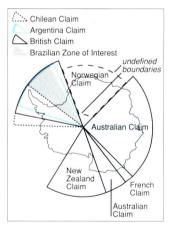

Claims to Antarctica.

Facing:
The frozen continent from space. British specialists carefully pieced together observations of Antarctica by US weather satellites, to produce an almost seamless mosaic.

US NOAA SATELLITE DATA PROCESSED BY UK NRSC

little value, only to see it transformed by discoveries of gold and oil. In Antarctica, offshore oil, sealskins, transpolar air routes and military bases are all potential payoffs, even before one looks to the minerals. These include gold in the Antarctic Peninsula and platinum in the Transantarctic Mountains.

For some 30 years, Antarctica has been in political deep-freeze, under a treaty that left the continent to the scientists. Serious research has included deep drilling into the ice for climate studies, the discovery of the Ozone Hole, and the quest for unique animal fossils from the time when Antarctica was ice-free. But much of the science is a charade, as some two dozen nations seek mainly to gain toeholds. They include countries like South Korea with no impressive tradition of Antarctic exploration or research.

The USA and Soviet Union have each considered laying claim to the whole continent. To demonstrate that they could exercise control, both countries deploy logistical systems by land, sea and air to many scientific bases. Scientists and military men of the various countries endure the long night of the Antarctic winter to prove they really live there, as a mute diplomatic struggle proceeds. The risk of bloodshed on the ice is not slight. Just 1200 kilometres from Antarctica and as recently as 1982, Britain and Argentina fought for the bleak Falkland/Malvinas islands. Both claim the same wedge of Antarctica itself.

Border-makers have gone to sea in an attempt to bring order to the seas and oceans, now that long-range fishing vessels operate in every part of the world, and the recovery of minerals from the seabed is becoming big business. An important application has been to define national zones for the offshore oil industry, as in Europe's North Sea. In former times, nations laid claim to a few nautical miles of territorial sea around their shores. Nowadays the norm is a 200-nautical-mile Exclusive Economic Zone (EEZ).

The national claim may be extended if the continental shelf stretches further offshore, or pushed back to a median line where two EEZs overlap. The status of the deep oceans beyond the EEZs remains uncertain, because several major maritime countries have rejected a regime for United Nations management of the seabed resources accepted by most nations.

The nation-state, which the newly independent countries emulate, evolved when Europeans streamlined their home kingdoms, city-states and confederacies for the purpose of empire-building. It is typically

50

centralized, militaristic and bureaucratic. Yet even in its European birthplace, the idea of the nation-state has a decidedly temporary air.

While vocal groups among ethnic minorities (Scots, Corsicans and so on) want to subdivide them, twelve nation-states of Europe are yielding much of their political and economic authority and control of their borders to a novel coalescence of nations, the European Community. Major industries are under the control of multinational corporations that may have their headquarters in Europe or anywhere else. Europe's aeronautics, space and electronics programmes are already collaborative efforts.

This changeability, not just of the size and status of countries but of the nature of their organization, has its place in any dynamic view of human global geography. Even before the crescendo of concern about the environment, the world's political and economic systems were severely strained by nuclear weapons, religious militancy, erratic commodity prices, mammoth trade imbalances and mounting debts. It would be rash to assume that present modes of government are worth dying for.

A number for the crew

*C*OUNTING HEADS has been considered the basis of sound government since biblical times, but it tests the organizational ability of even modern scientific nations. People may be on the move, or living out of doors. They may give birth or die at the moment of the census. They may tell lies, or deliberately evade the count, for fear of taxation or military conscription. Governments may falsify results for political reasons. Any figure for the total of people on the planet – said to be 5.3 billion in 1990 – is a brave try.

Census-takers have computers nowadays. Indeed, the US Bureau of the Census has a place in the history of computing, as the first to use a tabulating machine with punched cards, in 1890. By the census of 1990, the Bureau was operating a computerized 'geographic information system' called TIGER, which had the entire USA in mappable form down to individual census blocks and streets. The name stands for 'Topologically Integrated Geographic Encoding and Referencing'. It was used for planning the census-taking at every level, and it also provides the Bureau and outside users with a fine aid to interpreting the census results geographically. New settlements may come into existence unmapped, and in rich countries the retailing and restaurant chains sometimes identify in space images new residential areas for possible 'outlets'. In poor countries, remote-sensing satellites can help census-takers to see where to count. And in sparsely vegetated country in Africa, a geographer from Sweden's Lund University, Michael Stern, tested the direct use of satellite imagery for gauging the population.

West of the Nile river in The Sudan, Baggara Arabs live on sand in villages of closely clustered huts. In a *Landsat* black-and-white (vidicon) image, each village appears as a black dot of dirtied ground surrounded by a white halo of trampled land. From random visits to villages, Stern established a population density of thirty-six people per hectare. The sizes of the villages in the space image then gave a figure for the population of the test area with an accuracy of 70 per cent: not brilliant, but better than nothing at a time of rapid population growth.

Census from heaven. In a Landsat image, Sudanese villages appear as dots, the sizes of which provide a rough guide to their populations. The interpretation was by Michael Stern, working in Sweden.

 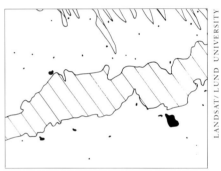

LANDSAT/ LUND UNIVERSITY

The world's total population, rising fast, is an important number for starting an assessment of the human impact on the Earth system. Some commentators make babies sound like a cancer on the planet. In fact, any impact depends as much on technology as on numbers, as evidenced in the uneven lighting of *The Earth at Night*. Populations in the rich countries have almost levelled off, but their economic growth continues apace. The world's human population has doubled in the past 40 years. The number of cars has multiplied seven times, and the rich countries have 88 per cent of them.

Population experts estimate that human numbers will double again, before levelling off during the next 100 years, at 10 or 11 billion. In her report on *The State of World Population 1990*, Nafis Sadik of the UN Population Fund warned that it could go higher. The question is whether a demographic transition will follow a reassuring track. Populations soared in the now-rich countries during the 19th Century, and almost stopped growing in the 20th Century. A similar slowdown may end the present demographic transition in the Third World. Growth rates have already eased in many countries but not in others.

The population explosion is uninvited testimony to the biological success of the human species. It would have ended in mass death already, if human beings were not so competent. In particular, food production has risen even faster than the population during the past 40 years. It put severe pressures on the soil and wild species, but hard work by farmers and scientists falsified the predictions of worldwide famine.

As compared with life expectancy in the 1960s, people in the Third World are living on average more than 20 years longer – further biological proof of improved wellbeing. Where individual countries have failed to grow enough food, malnutrition continues to affect perhaps 10 per cent of the global population. Against that must be set spare farming capacity in North America and Europe, where the embarrassments are mountains of surplus food, and overweight people.

The reasons for surges in population are debatable, but at present the fastest population growth occurs in countries with the highest rates of death among infants. This paradox suggests a primary human explanation of what is happening. Social and medical advances have cut death rates sufficiently to unleash a population explosion, but not yet enough to convince parents that babies don't die.

Religious leaders often oppose curbs on reproduction, and attitudes of governments vary widely. While some have tried forcible sterilizations or abortions, others want larger populations for economic or military reasons and give medals to fecund women. From recent UN data, governments of eleven countries with populations growing faster than 2 per cent a year consider the growth 'too low'. Eleven more with growth rates of 3 per cent or more judge the growth 'satisfactory'.

The money vortex

*P*ORTS AND sealanes visible from space mark the arteries of world trade, and roads and railways are its capillaries. In the Stone Age, stones of the highest quality for toolmaking or ornaments were traded over distances of thousands of kilometres. The unequal distribution of energy sources, minerals, natural products, and manufacturing centres still sustains an ever-growing need for trade. Yet geographers wanting

53

to explain the location of economic activities have always had a problem. The activities often defy geography.

The climate of northwestern Europe is unsuited to cotton production, yet 200 years ago the Industrial Revolution started with the British importing cotton from India and using machinery driven by waterwheels to make cloth for export – for example back to India. Japan has even fewer natural resources than Britain. Conversely, accounts that stress the mineral wealth of the USA and the USSR in explaining their economic geography and industrial development are misleading, if they fail to mention that Australia has mineral riches without the industries to match.

A few minerals such as diamonds occur in very few places, a few crops such as cinnamon are fastidious about where they grow, and a few commodities such as fresh milk do not travel well. But those are exceptions. On the whole the global market has access to many possible sources of commodities, from sugar to titanium. Transport by sea is so cheap that rice can travel half-way around the world, from Southeast Asia to West Africa, and still undercut the local rice farmers.

As for manufactured products, you can build a car or a computer almost anywhere in the world. Fifty years ago, steel production was the chief mark of industrial muscle. Today it is the mass manufacture of microchips for electronics. A recent boom in chip-making on the Japanese island of Kyushu illustrates the opportunism of manufacturers. They were lured there by airports built to serve the tourist industry in a pretty part of Japan.

Geographical patterns of economic activity are influenced largely by prices. These evolve to balance the supply against the demand. Companies or countries that can produce below the going price enjoy a piece of the action, while those who cannot retire from the market. This idealized picture is complicated by national subsidies and tariffs, and by trade wars and trade deals. Low wages traditionally gave the poor countries a cost advantage, but mechanization and automation can wipe that out. Synthetic materials can offer fierce competition to natural products, as with rubber, textiles and sweeteners. Technical innovations regularly make whole industries obsolete, in rich and poor countries alike, and grim cycles of boom and bust give typical enterprises a life expectancy comparable to that of human beings.

Skilful traders and moneylenders can play the market to stay in profit whether commodities or industries are doing well or badly. Nowadays that usually requires proximity to a major market, or a satellite antenna on the yacht. Information was always crucial, long before telecommunications and computers. The most valuable loot of the English pirate Francis Drake was Portuguese charts showing the trade routes to the Orient. Access to information as well as capital helps to maintain the rich countries' advantage over the poor.

'Addicted to the knife-edge' and 'hooked on speed' describe the present capitalist world economy, according to the geographer Nigel Thrift of Bristol University. With dealers and companies taking full advantage of modern telecommunications and information technology, huge amounts of money, reckoned in billions of billions of dollars, are in play internationally, and are themselves items of trade. Changes in prices, interest rates and currency exchange rates, which used to happen at intervals of years or months, now occur in hours or minutes. Unprofitable plants and operations are identified and shut down far more swiftly than even 20 years ago. In Thrift's opinion, the internationalization of capital is the most important economic event in the world at present, and he chides his fellow-geographers who persist in taking an insular view of economic trends in their own countries.

During the 1980s, multinational corporations, old and new, were busy internationalizing capital by setting up factories abroad, staging mergers, and forming alliances with foreign competitors. Perhaps one-third of all international trade now occurs between different parts of the same conglomerates. Ties between multinational corporations and banks have become stronger, as have those of the corporations and banks with national governments. The capital circulates especially between East Asia, Western Europe and North America, with Tokyo, London and New York acting as global centres. 'The developing countries have found the door to prosperity slammed shut,' Thrift comments. He notes that even as the financial pace quickened during the 1980s, standards of health, education and nutrition declined sharply in the Third World.

The computers chatter and a wave of business moves around the stock markets and money markets of the world, as the planet turns on its axis. Industries and offices migrate more slowly, yet more readily than many workers do. People unwilling or unable to leave their home districts are the most vulnerable to change, when decisions in distant boardrooms command a factory into existence in the jungle, or reduce an industrial centre to a rust bowl.

Although less visible than industrial smoke, the effusions of business computers blow across the world in the trade winds of commerce. They scatter money like rain, causing economic flash-floods here and there while leaving many other localities unrefreshed. When Earth-system scientists and global geographers try to see how human activity meshes with Nature's global machinery, their understanding will remain parochial if they look only at the man with the mechanical shovel or the chain saw. Who pays him?

Whether the new internationalization of capital will be good or bad in its overall effects remains to be seen, but at a conceptual level its debut is timely for the dawn of Earth-system science. Hitherto, worldwide economic decision-making was too diffuse to visualize clearly. Now human economic activity within the Earth system is largely governed, at least for the time being, by the vortex of money and information in electronic form, whirling around the Northern Hemisphere. Activity shifts in synchronism with the Sun, as dealers in Tokyo, London and New York wake up or go to bed – though perhaps the bright lights of *The Earth at Night* should be seen as sleepless capital and moonlighting labour.

City slickers

P ATCHES IN space images that look like miniature deserts, in their lack of vegetation, draw the eye to the filigree of streets and buildings characteristic of cities. The jewellery of *The Earth at Night* fades to a dull grey in the morning pass of the high-resolution satellite. To the infra-red sensors of weather satellites, measuring temperatures, cities are islands of heat, a little warmer than their surroundings, with a tendency to promote cloud formation and rainstorms downwind of them. Used water discharged by cities into rivers and seas also tends to be warm, turbid and to varying degrees polluted. Sensors at ground level register noxious gases, smoke and photochemical smog.

In global models of weather and climate, cities almost disappear, being smaller than the grid boxes used in the computations. But they exert many indirect influences on the Earth system, not least because of their roles in decision-making, price-fixing and fashion-setting. For thousands of years, cities have been equated with all that is smartest and most 'civilized' in human existence. Urbanization, a great geographical theme of the 20th Century, has already made city slickers of four human beings in ten.

The growth of large cities has not been as inexorable as some experts were predicting a quarter of a century ago. According to their projections the 50-million-people city should already exist. Noisy, dirty, congested and impersonal megacities eventually lose their pulling power, while countervailing forces including new technologies encourage growth in towns far removed from the big centres. In Europe and North America many city dwellers have opted for greener suburbs and satellite towns. In southeast England well-to-do people love their countryside so much, they sprawl all over it, often expelling its rustic inhabitants by driving up land prices. Their geographical range and political power recently confounded attempts to find an overland route for a high-speed rail link from the Channel Tunnel to London.

Tokyo remains a prime example of urban growth in a rich country, as the 20th Century draws to a close. The satellite images show the Japanese capital pressing like a grey tide against the surrounding hills, and into suburbs and satellite cities around Tokyo Bay. Land reclamation extends it into the bay. The population of this conurbation passed the 30-million mark in the 1980s, but by then a drift to the suburbs was stabilizing the Tokyo Metropolis itself at about 12 million.

By the doughnut effect, as geographers call it, the resident population of Tokyo's historic heart, now the business centre, has shrunk to less than 300,000, while more than 2 million commute into it every working day. Astronomical land prices in central Tokyo have led architects to contemplate extreme remedies: living underground, or on offshore platforms like those of the oil industry.

Over the centuries, there have been many local and temporary answers to the question, 'What is this city for?' Tokyo originated 400 years ago as a fortress. Today it is unremarkable as a port or a manufacturing centre, but it possesses is the lion's share of Japan's computers, banks, corporate headquarters, universities, newspapers and television companies. Tokyo is the very model of a post-industrial megacity, as a centre for transactions in money and information.

Tokyo Teleport Town on the waterfront is meant to consolidate that role in the 21st Century. So-called 'intelligent' buildings, designed around optical-fibre and satellite telecommunications, will provide companies with instant and copious access to Japan-wide and world-wide information. A hope is that Teleport Town will welcome foreign businessmen as cheerfully as the Rialto of old Venice did when the Italian city was Europe's first centre for global capitalism.

For its ordinary citizens, Tokyo is not a very pleasant place. Commuting takes up much of their time, and overcrowding, noise and pollution pursue them to their suburbs and satellite towns. And a succession of satellite images since the first *Landsat* flew in 1972 records a continuing disappearance of the metropolis's vestiges of open space. The loss of greenery is not the only cause for concern. Without open spaces, many people have nowhere to run to for safety in the event of a major earthquake and fire – an ever-present risk in Tokyo. Only after years of campaigning by an architect, Suminao Murakami, has the Tokyo Metropolitan Government accepted that open spaces may be as important for human survival as for the trees and birds.

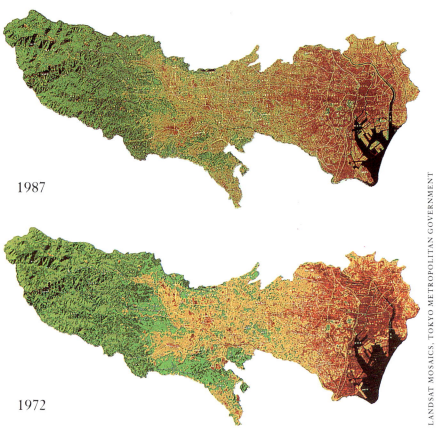

1987

1972

The de-greening of Tokyo. Landsat mosaics of the area covered by the Metropolitan Government confirmed the loss of open spaces in urbanized zones. Satellites are a powerful means of monitoring changes in land use.

LANDSAT MOSAICS, TOKYO METROPOLITAN GOVERNMENT

Here interactions in the Earth sytem link money and geotectonics. A major earthquake in the top information city could, according to some, cause a worldwide slump. That would ease some obvious economic pressures on the Earth's resources and atmosphere, but could create a myriad of local crises threatening the environment, as desperate people tried to scrape a living. At a simpler human level, the seismic risk will extend even to a corporate president at his computer terminal in Tokyo Teleport Town.

For a contrast with Tokyo consider La Paz, in South America's poorest country, Bolivia. It advertises itself as the world's loftiest capital city. Here, landslides are the chief natural hazard, and the SPOT satellite is helping the city authorities to map the danger zones. Nearly half a millennium ago, Spanish conquerors found shelter here from the icy winds off the High Andes, in the canyon of the Choqueyapu river. The city has spilled into other valleys, and also up the sides of the canyon.

Rivers cut easily through the boulder clay laid down by ice-age glaciers in the Altiplano, the plateau between the twin snowcapped ranges of the High Andes. In most parts of the world, the rich and powerful tend to diagram their high social status by occupying the fortified hill or the skyscraper penthouse. In La Paz, 3500 metres above sea-level, the climate turns this urban convention upside down.

The zones of La Paz seem laid out with an ethnic altimeter. There is more oxygen and warmer air down the valley from the old administrative centre, and here the well-to-do live among trees and flowers in the closest approximation to European normality that the city has to offer. They are not exempt from the risk of muddy floods. Middle-class people of European descent also have homes on the floor of the canyon, but higher upstream. Poorer folk, many of them mestizos of part European, part Amerindian ancestry, occupy the slopes of the canyon, where they invite death by landslide.

The Amerindians themselves – mostly Aymara people – are mainly housed 500 metres above La Paz, on the Altiplano plateau itself, in the new satellite city of El Alto. Sited alongside the airport of La Paz, where incoming tourists gasp for air, El Alto might have been an analogue of the shanty towns of other Third-World cities, if shanties were not useless in the windy and frosty climate. Simple concrete houses line a neat grid of streets. El Alto's municipal government tries to bring order and touches of civilization to the bleak city of the poor.

Many of El Alto's citizens commute by bus or on foot to jobs in the capital – or to street-vending pitches where bowler-hatted Aymara women will sell you anything from a box of matches to a magic potion. Although there is no official apartheid in Bolivia, the contrasts in vegetation density, varying from the lush gardens deep in the valley to the sparser growth on the canyon walls and the near-barren Altiplano, could almost substitute for a genetic map.

Thousands of years of habitation in the High Andes have left the Amerindians with a respiratory system better able to cope with the thin air than the Europeans'. That and the coca plant helped them to survive the centuries of slavery and near-slavery that followed the Spanish Conquest. The Aymaras descending like a river each morning into La Paz consider themselves better off than their rural cousins, or their mining cousins who lost their jobs. But then the impacts of the global market on Bolivia have been unusually grim.

Supply and demand in the Andes

THE FABULOUS wealth of the Amerindians in Inca times whetted the avarice of Spanish conquistadores and drew them to the High Andes. Some 200 million years of geological turmoil left a province of silver and tin ores perched at around 4000 metres above sea-level. A single mountain, Cerro Rico, yielded enough silver to cause runaway inflation in Spain.

The hard work of hard-rock mining always relied on the Amerindians' adaptation to the thin air. But whether they laboured for the Spanish conquerors, or for the private and public enterprises of independent Bolivia, the miners needed their coca-breaks. Coca grows in Bolivia, and chewing the leaves make the High Andes bearable by alleviating cold, hunger and exhaustion.

In recent decades, tin was Bolivia's prime export. When during World War II the Japanese occupied Malaysia, then the biggest tin-producing region, Bolivia rose to prominence as a supplier. An early application of the *Landsat* imagery was to make a mosaic showing the lineaments of the country's mineral-rich terrain, for the Geological Service of Bolivia. The mining towns of the tin belt prospered until geological roulette suddenly impoverished them.

In the Amazon forest at Pitinga, in neighbouring Brazil, Nature has done the miners' work for them. Grains of tin ore carried by a river formed large alluvial deposits, which a mechanical shovel can scoop up by the ton, like the bauxite of Weipa. The Brazilians developed Pitinga into the largest and cheapest tin mine in the world. In 1985, in obedience to the law of supply and demand, the price of tin in the

*Facing:
The airport of La Paz is conspicuous on Bolivia's bleak Altiplano, in a SPOT image. Many Amerindians live in El Alto, a new city on the plateau beside the airport. Better-off Bolivians of European descent inhabit the canyons (centre right of facing illustration) which shelter the city of La Paz (above).*

global market collapsed. Every tin mine in Bolivia became uneconomic overnight. Most miners lost their jobs, and those who kept them had their wages slashed. Thriving communities became ghost towns in which a few families continued to scavenge the workings and tailings for pennyworths of ore. Efforts to keep working the mineral riches of the Andes have led companies back to silver and gold, using modern (though controversial) methods of cyanide extraction.

Some of the more enterprising of the sacked miners crossed the eastern Andes to the valley of the Chaparé river, where the product was 'green gold'. The miners adapted to the farming life, to help grow more coca bushes. The global market was crying out for coca leaves. The law of supply and demand that had crucified the Bolivians in the matter of tin, now favoured them in respect of coca.

Of course, the crazy gringos of North America and Europe did not chew their coca leaves or make an infusion, like sensible Andean folk, but preferred to sniff a concentrated extract first isolated as an anaesthetic. Ordinary Bolivians who toil in the coca plantations of Chaparé remain far poorer than any competent cocaine peddler in New York or Amsterdam. They are nevertheless glad of the work, arranged by the local cocaine barons who become rich on the inflated proceeds of an illicit trade. But when the Bolivians started to relieve their desperate plight by growing more coca, the USA suspended the law of supply and demand.

Like other rich cocaine-importing nations, the Americans failed to enforce their prohibitions of this and other drugs on their city streets. Spectacular interceptions on the smuggling routes only proved how much was in the pipeline. So the rich countries thought it easier to declare war on the growers and traders of the Third World. The Bolivian government and its neighbours in the High Andes, Colombia and Peru, were pressured to make illegal at least some of the coca-growing in countries that had run for thousands of years on legal coca.

As this also affected the foreign-exchange earnings of the Andean countries, the US government urged a policy of crop substitution. Why not coffee? But for that permitted addiction, supply-and-demand still operated, and overproduction of coffee worldwide depressed the prices paid to growers. When Bolivians pinned their hopes on soya, the US soybean farmers complained about the competition.

Even on civilian satellite images the plantations of Chaparé and other coca districts stand out clearly, as the softest of soft targets. The USA used photoreconnaissance satellites and military spyplanes, and all the techniques of espionage devised for hunting down Soviet missiles, to trace the coca stocks, processing plants and smuggling facilities in the High Andes. The military scientists who destroyed tropical forests in Indo-China with dioxin during the Vietnam War offered to drench the coca plantations of the Andes with chemical or biological weapons. That help was declined, but the extradition of Andean traders to stand trial in the USA became a major objective.

The alien astronomer might wonder how a tobacco-grower in North Carolina would react if the outside world declared his crop illegal and seized him by helicopter to stand trial in a non-smoking country. The mentality behind the assault on the primary producers in the drugs war bodes ill for policies on global problems. It would seem no less logical to curb carbon-dioxide emissions by bombing oilfields.

The geographers' own models

A KEY TERM in modern geography is GIS, for geographic information system. It means a computerized aid to generating instant maps from data stored in digital form. The term originated in Canada in the 1960s, where the Department of Agriculture adopted digital techniques for mapping land-use. With an unlimited range of applications, GIS relates on the one hand to formal cartography, which nowadays relies ever more heavily on computers, and on the other hand it ties in closely with methods for processing and analysing satellite data. Software is commercially available.

The TIGER system of the US Census has already been mentioned. Another example of GIS in action is the GRID system of the UN Environment Programme. This Global Resources Information Database handles many different kinds of data, from soil types to political boundaries, for the whole world and in close-up for Africa. World Data Centres of the International Council of Scientific Unions amass information on many scientific topics (mainly geophysical) and provide a starting point for a digital-mapping system suitable for the Global Change programme (IGBP). Among many other GIS developments, the CORINE system of the European Community seeks to bring together self-consistent environmental data from the various countries of the Community, with special reference initially to nature reserves, acid rain and coastal problems of the Mediterranean. The name of CORINE is said to be an acronym for Co-ordinated Information on the European Environment.

Numerical models of global weather, river systems and the like frequently use geographical frameworks that provide a stage on which physical and biological events can unfold. They are often developed by non-geographers. But distinctive models of the geographers' own devising deal with the human use of geographical space; they tell how objects and activities occupy it (location) and how they function as dynamical systems (spatial interaction). Geographical theorists have long sought to transform their subject from a descriptive art to an analytical and predictive science. In the early days of computers, logistical problems of fighting a global nuclear war stimulated geographical systems analysis at the RAND Corporation in California. A civilian geographical model came from RAND in 1964. It explored the ways in which transport systems affect the use of land, and vice versa. Since then, academic geographers have acquired computers, and developed models, the scale of which is more likely to be that of a city, a county or a small nation, than of a continent or the whole world. The human and economic factors are usually dominant, and for that reason they are here called human-geographical models.

Before computers, geographical theories were necessarily rather simple. German geographers were their main inventors. Early in the 19th Century Johann von Thünen imagined an isolated city with roads radiating from it. He theorized that cheap land far from the city would carry cattle, and rings at intermediate distances would be farmed at increasing intensities, with dairying and vegetable-growing close in. More complex and more realistic patterns emerged when von Thünen introduced a river providing an axis of cheap transport.

Alfred Weber (1909) reasoned that an industrial firm would locate itself where its transport costs were least. In an ideal case of a firm with two sources of supply and one market, its factory would lie inside the triangle they made on the map. To make sense of the distribution of towns in southern Germany, Walter Christaller (1933) developed his 'central place' theory. Large cities served a wide area, while a village met only basic local needs. Towns therefore spaced themselves according to their reach, in a honeycomb pattern, with a characteristic distance separating settlements of a given size.

These and other classical theories in geography had to ignore many

Facing:
The world mapped by computer.
To assess the human impact on
natural ecosystems (above) by
farming (below) Elaine Matthews
of NASA collated data from
atlases and space images, in a
geographic data base. the major
ecosystems distinguished by colours
in the upper map are six
categories of forest and woodland
(green and yellow), three of
shrubland (mauve), four of
grassland (blue), tundra (red),
desert (brown) and ice (grey). In
the lower map, the intensity of
cultivation increases from 20 per
cent (blue) to 100 per cent (red).
Squares are 1 degree by 1 degree.

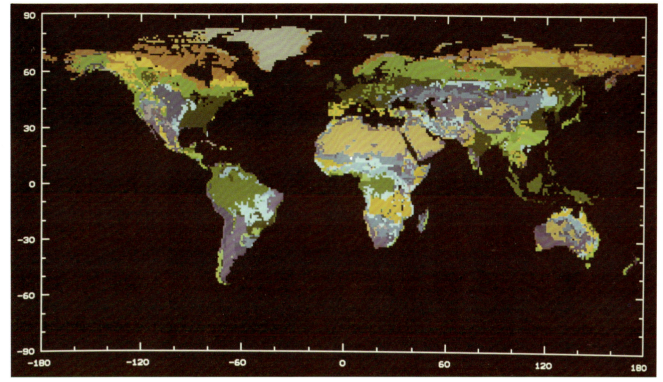

DATA FROM ATLASES CROSS-CHECKED BY LANDSAT, NASA GISS, USA

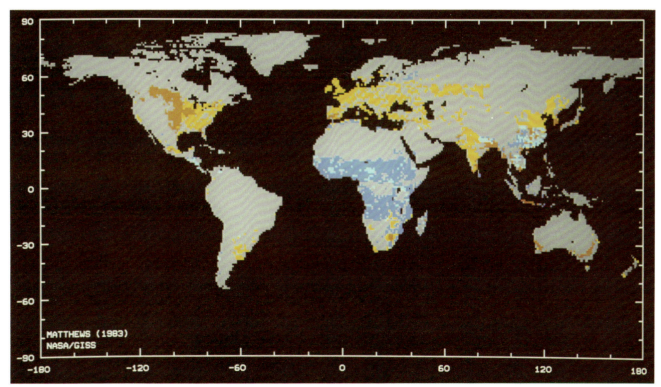

MATTHEWS (1983)
NASA/GISS

DATA FROM ATLASES CROSS-CHECKED BY LANDSAT, NASA GISS, USA

real-life complications of topography, geology, water supplies, transport routes, wages costs, technological change, and so on. They are not so much contradicted as swallowed up, in more powerful and complex models that can easily reproduce Thünen's rings, Weber's triangles or Christaller's hexagons, if required.

A typical human-geographical computer model divides geographical space into a grid of an appropriate scale, and computes flows from each square to every other square. The flows can be of people from home to work, for example, or crops to market, or new cars to customers' homes. The modern geographical theorist prefers to deduce locations from flows, rather than flows from locations. Equations often specify that, as distances or transport costs increase, the volume of a flow halves and halves again. Human-geographical behaviour frequently fits that simple law, which matches the everyday perception that near things are much more useful than far things.

Geographers at Leeds University in England have helped the Toyota company to explore marketing strategies for its Japanese cars, first in Britain and now in other European countries. Geographical Modelling and Planning, or GMAP, is a commercial spinoff from fundamental work on human-geographical models at Leeds, led by Alan Wilson. Aimed at enabling businesses and public services to discover how best to reach the public, GMAP uses spatial-interaction models that can run on personal computers.

The number of people using a shop, hospital or other service depends on where it is located in relation to where people live, and what competition exists in the area. The models express and compute these relationships as flows of people, goods and services. Complexities arise because people vary in their requirements according to sex, age, ethnic origins, income, and so on. Access from home to shop depends as much on transport and routes as on simple distances.

In the case of Toyota Great Britain, the first step was the creation of a nationwide geographical information system. It incorporates data on the demography, economic characteristics and pattern of car ownership for every postal district. Its computer memory also holds the locations of all car dealers, monthly sales of new cars by manufacturer and type to each postal district, and Toyota's own sales in more detail. The GIS allows the company to call up any of 60,000 maps. These can show, for example, the reach of a Toyota dealer's sales by its share of the market in neighbouring districts. This varies for different cars, with the

Facing:
Infant mortality in Tianjin, China, mapped in a geographic information system. The Chinese Academy of Sciences promotes the use of computers in geography, as a powerful tool for relating health, for example, to social, economic and physical factors.

66

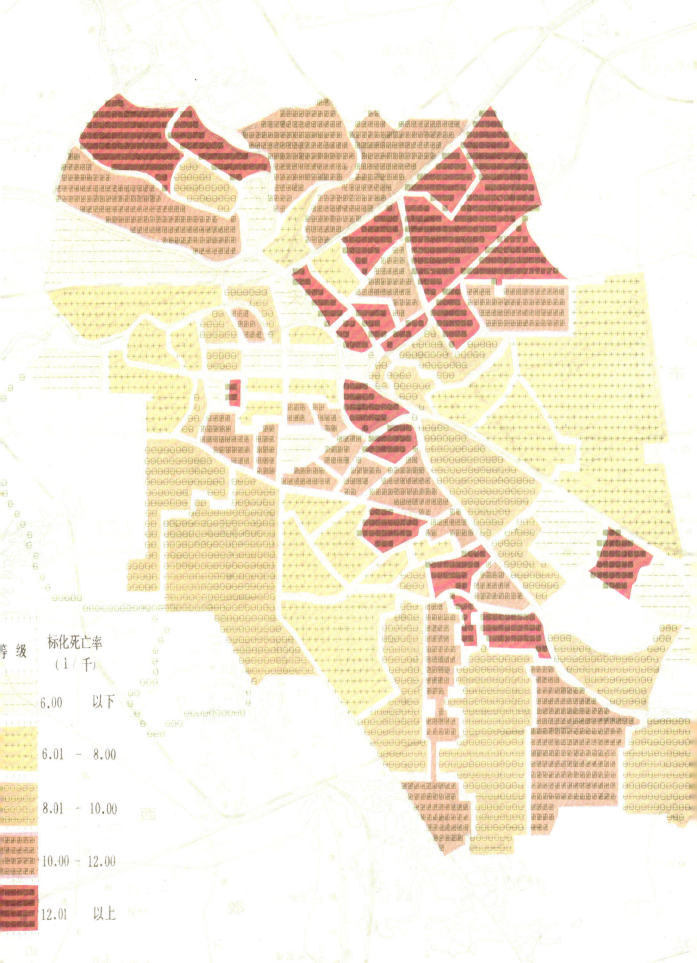

等级　标化死亡率
　　　（1／千）

6.00　　以下

6.01　－　8.00

8.01　－　10.00

10.00　－　12.00

12.01　　以上

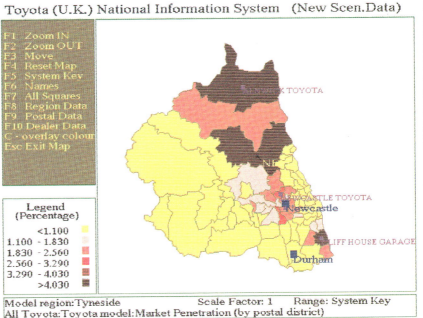

GMAP LTD MODEL FOR TOYOTA GB

Marketing strategies in a geographical model. In a screen display, theory predicts the market share for a car company, district by district near Newcastle, England, if a new saleroom were created north of the city.

more expensive ones selling to more distant customers. In the human-geographical models, the second part of the Toyota package, the Leeds geographers gave the company the means of answering questions of the form, 'What if . . . ?'

Toyota had to explore entirely new marketing strategies and re-appraise its network of dealers, because a decision then impending, to build Toyota cars in England, would circumvent import quotas that restricted the company to about 2 per cent of the market. The geographers adjusted the mathematical equations in the GMAP models until they correctly 'predicted' the present flows of new cars of all makes, from dealers to customers. Then Toyota's managers could forecast their own sales by various sales strategies, and with various geographical scatterings of the dealers. Like competing centres in Christaller's central-place theory, dealers handling the same make of car will ideally space themselves to minimize mutual interference.

GMAP's other clients include retailing chains and a water company. Geographers have always provided public and private users with maps, and with written descriptions of districts and regions. While geographical theory was still at a simple-minded, arm-waving stage, its predictive powers were severely limited. Armed with computer models, geographers now exert a more active influence on geographical changes.

COMPUTERIZED confections of another kind are less concerned with the geographical location of activities than with overall trends and interactions within the human part of the Earth system. They have more in common with computer models of national economic systems and international trade, and with the business analyses of large corporations. An early 'socioeconomic' model of the world was behind *The Limits to Growth* (1972) in which a group at the Massachusetts Institute of Technology predicted a crash in the human population in the 21st Century following a large-scale conversion of most of the Earth's natural resources into various forms of industrial pollution. Other assumptions gave far less pessimistic conclusions, and later models were subdivided into large regions, so introducing into the global analysis a little rudimentary geography. Some concentrated on particular sub-systems, notably population, agriculture and energy supplies.

The sixteen-nation International Institute for Applied Systems Analysis (IIASA) was founded at Laxenburg in Austria in 1972 to bring together analysts from East and West, despite the Cold War, to study problems of common concern with the help of computer models. In 1989, IIASA published a critical review of socioeconomic models, as part of an exploration of 'the possible environmental implications of alternative patterns of future socioeconomic activity', related to the Global Change programme (IGBP) of the International Council of Scientific Unions. Stefan Anderberg assembled a Conventional Wisdom scenario for the 100 years from 1975 to 2075, from some of these existing models.

This scenario assumes that world population will stabilize at 10 billion, and that the present rich world will remain dominant. For example, energy consumption per head does not increase at all in South Asia, 1975–2075, but trebles in North America. Overall energy consumption increases to six times the 1975 level, with coal replacing oil as the chief fuel of international trade. But Anderberg himself was sceptical about the models on which the Conventional Wisdom scenario was based. He commented:

They usually assume that the dynamics of the present system, as perceived from studies of the recent past, will remain basically the same. In most studies the global economic, political and social structures are implicitly similar to the present.

69

Introducing surprises into the contemplation of the future was an important feature of the IIASA study. At a brainstorming workshop in Sweden, multidisciplinary groups of experts concocted alternative scenarios for the period up to 2075, to show how global totals and regional distributions for population, agriculture and energy could change drastically as a result of unexpected events. In a Big Load scenario, the surprise is the global population growing out of control, and passing the 20 billion mark in 2075. Energy use multiplies by twelve. Political power passes to autonomous ethnic and religious groups, and to multinational corporations.

Greatpox is a hypothetical disease that kills a billion people in 1997–2000, in another of the IIASA surprise-rich scenarios, Rurban Arcadian Drift. People flee the cities and, in the rich industrial North, rural and small-town societies emerge, with a high degree of self-reliance. Global trade is disrupted. Lower prices for energy and other natural resources enable Asia, Africa and Latin America to achieve high rates of economic growth. Key numbers for 2075 after greatpox and the Rurban Arcadian Drift are a global population of only 6.4 billion, and energy use up 3.7 times.

Such surprise-rich scenarios are just science fiction in a computer, yet they conform with the surprise-rich history of the species better than Conventional Wisdom does. And a free-ranging consideration of 'What if . . . ?' is a stimulus to fresh thinking about global geography. Thus IIASA's Big Shift scenario has India emerging as top nation, in a world of 8 billion people. A sixteen-fold increase in energy use in South Asia by 2075 contrasts with a mere 30 per cent increase in Europe.

To people with only a smattering of geographical knowledge, the possibility of India usurping the power of the USA, Europe and Japan might seem laughable. But Anderberg notes that big changes often come from the periphery of the old order, and from countries with burgeoning populations. He mentions the long entrepreneurial history of India, and the vigour of its nuclear research. To these can be added its space programme, and India's success in multiplying wheat production fourfold in less than 20 years. Thus dull-seeming facts about faraway places acquire, for the scenario-makers of the new global geography, the fascination of clues in a new and purposeful form of thriller-writing.

CHAPTER 3

Refurbished Decks

*E*ARTHQUAKES AND volcanoes are outward signs of Nature's unending reconstruction of the planet's surface. Although the schedules of its projects for making new oceans and refreshing the land extend over millions of years, these sudden hammerings are the most alarming of natural hazards. They are repeated reminders that the solid Earth is just as much a part of the life-support system as the air and the water.

The distribution of mineral riches such as oil follows ancient patterns of the Earth system's operations in its geological mode. The solid Earth also keeps the surface layers resupplied with the nutrients that plants need. Nowhere is this more apparent than in the intensely volcanic island of Java, where people risk death to farm its fertile soil.

Volcanoes are the jokers in the pack of global cause and effect. A lull in major activity in recent decades has let even experts forget that volcanoes can pollute the environment more comprehensively than most human activities, and draw veils of dust across the sky that can chill the world. The monitoring of volcanoes with remote- sensing and relay satellites therefore has broader purposes than just warning the regions directly affected by an outburst.

The chapter ends in Kenya's rift valley, a different and enigmatic volcanic area where early humans evolved. While visiting geophysicists probe the crust to try to understand the rifting process, the Kenyans themselves are more concerned with practical matters like useful heat from the ground.

Waiting for a disaster

NATURAL STAIRCASES in Japanese sea-cliffs proclaim that big earthquakes repeat themselves. On a peninsula near Tokyo, the lowest step being carved by the waves came up to sea level in the great earthquake of 1923, and the mini-beach before it sprang into the air. Higher steps in the cliff match earlier earthquakes, going back many centuries. But in the country where seismic violence and technical skill confront each other most strenuously, Japanese experts worry less about an imminent repetition of the Tokyo earthquake than an overdue event down the coast.

The Japanese Prefecture of Shizuoka wraps itself around Suruga Bay, just south of the sacred volcano, Fuji. A fault in the crust runs out to sea in the bed of the bay, and every 120 years or so it unleashes a major earthquake. The last one was nearly 140 years ago. Since then, subterranean forces have dragged the western shore down by half a metre and narrowed the bay by a metre. At any time now, the western shore will jerk up like the escapement of a ticking clock, and send seismic shocks racing through the region.

About 11,000 people may die, by official calculations, as the buildings and traffic of Shizuoka are reduced to burning wreckage, and great sea-waves, the tsunamis, assail the shore. This is the grim toll expected despite unprecedented efforts to prepare for the earthquake as if for a war, with sea defences hardened, buildings and bridges reinforced, hillsides strengthened against landslides, first-aid stations designated, and a population drilled in what to do when the earthquake strikes.

Dozens of scientific instruments have the region's crust in intensive care. Seismographs, tiltmeters, tide gauges and so on are dotted around the prefecture and on the seabed. The hope is that unusual activity preceding the event will give a warning, though earthquake prediction is a doubtful art. Preparations include computerized geographic information systems, used to prepare maps of areas judged to be most at risk

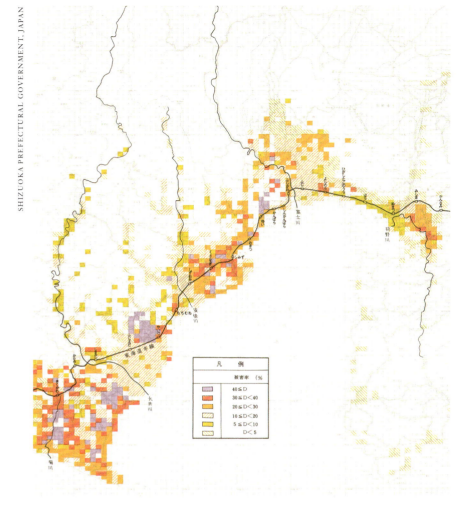

Earthquake hazards near Suruga Bay in Japan, charted by computer. This map, showing the risk of collapse of wooden houses, is one of a series prepared in anticipation of a major earthquake on a fault in the seabed.

from structural damage, landslides, fires and tsunamis. A video-disk system has 7000 air photos of the entire prefecture available for instant consultation in an operations room provided with all the telecommunications that Japan can muster. Yet high technology aggravates the risks outside. Last time, there were no cars to run amok, no bullet trains to derail, no electricity lines and gas mains ready to split and feed the flames, no nuclear power station on the Shizuokan shore relying on automatic systems to shut it down.

Most earthquakes concentrate in an irregular network of narrow seismic zones, that became largely visible from space when the US *Seasat* flew. It caressed the sea surface with the pulses of a radar altimeter, to feel its humps and hollows. Local variations in the level of the sea reflect the presence of huge underwater chains of mountains, the mid-ocean ridges, and of chasms in the seabed, called trenches. The

73

ridges and the trenches are seismic zones in the oceans. They mark boundaries where large, mobile plates of the Earth's crust diverge at ridges, or converge at trenches.

Japan's earthquakes are associated with trenches in the nearby ocean floor. Others occur in regions where an ocean separating two continents has disappeared, as in the collision between Iran and the main body of Eurasia, which caused recent severe earthquakes in Armenia (1988) and Iran (1990). California's earthquakes are in a setting where two plates slide past one another. As the earthquakes are local adjustments to inexorable movements of plates thousands of kilometres wide, they are not preventable. Lubricating a fault at a plate boundary could make its earthquakes gentler but no one dares try, for fear of triggering the very disaster they want to avert.

The plate theory explains why intense geological activity is confined mainly to that irregular network of narrow seismic zones. Besides the earthquakes, most of the world's volcanic eruptions and mountain-building occur at or near the present plate boundaries, where Nature is busiest with its never-ending maintenance work on the Earth's crust. Earthquakes can still happen in other places, where ancient faults near former plate boundaries are still settling down.

The most important activity beyond the plate boundaries occurs at hotspots, where narrow, rising plumes of molten rock remain fixed in position in the body of the Earth. A hotspot punches out a row of volcanoes through any plate gliding over it. The islands of Hawaii are a classic example, where the biggest island stands over the hotspot, belching volcanoes, and a line of diminishing, eroded, ex-volcanic islands stretches far to the northwest.

Split-level decking

*T*HE *SEASAT* data on the oceans' surface topography gave a novel view of Spaceship Earth's machinery for refurbishing its decks. The largest pieces of decking are the ocean floors, and these are completely renewed every 200 million years. The mid-ocean ridges create new ocean floor, from heavy, black basalt rising hot from the Earth's interior. A mid-ocean ridge breaks through the surface of the North Atlantic, in the island of Iceland. Satellite images show lines of new basalt at the plate boundary, where the ridge grows from the middle outwards.

Heat that drives the crust-building is apparent in warm patches seen by infra-red sensors.

At the trenches, old ocean floor dives back into the Earth for recycling. The grinding action of its slanting descent causes strong and often deep earthquakes. The fierce heat and pressure melts the rocks and throws up a line of volcanoes on the far side of the trench. Mineral transformations create a slag of less dense material, including granite, that floats on the heavy rocks of the Earth's interior and thereafter has little inclination to sink.

The buoyant slag establishes split-level decking on the spaceship. While oceans come and go, the slag gathers into rafts, making land masses. These have been slowly growing in total area since the world began. The ocean crust remains in charge of events, and new oceans (the narrow Red Sea, for example) tear continents asunder and push the pieces apart. The death of oceans (as in the Mediterranean) brings different land masses into collision, squeezing remnants of the ocean bed into high mountains.

Continents and islands ride on the plates, like lunch on a cafeteria tray. A rough impression of the present directions of relative movement of the main land masses comes from an inspection of the *Seasat* image. Continents on either side of a mid-ocean ridge, Africa and the Americas for example, are drifting apart. On either side of a trench, as with Australia and Asia, the continents are heading for a collision.

Visualization of these movements is complicated by the Earth's roundness. Plate tectonics is first and last a mathematical theory about the behaviour of rigid plates on a spherical surface of finite size. It is inherently global in scope, because plates on one side of the planet have to adjust to changes on the far side. The plate boundaries follow the curvature of the Earth but in close-up they look like straight lines, and linearities in many landscapes and seabeds parallel the lines of plate boundaries past and present.

In *Landsat*, SPOT and radar images from space, linear features of a plate-ruled crust stand out. But continental rocks are less rigid than those of the ocean floor, and they crumple and fracture, complicating the scenery. Even the great San Andreas fault in California is kinky. Geologists use satellite images to interpret the crumpling and faulting that created present mountains. For example, images of Tibet testify to the shifting of large blocks of the Earth's crust as Asia yielded to the impact of India, in the collision that is still building the Himalayas.

Seasat and a later American radar satellite, *Geosat*, gave hints of the sluggish rocky motor deep in the Earth that drives the crustal changes. Stirred by a trickle of heat from radioactivity, deep-lying rocks rise, cool and sink. They slightly deform the roundness of the ball-like planet, in broad-scale humps and hollows seen by the radar satellites. The rocks of the interior seem to be rising under Western Europe and the adjacent Atlantic Ocean, under the ocean bed southeast of South Africa, and under New Guinea in the western Pacific. They are sinking under India, off the two seaboards of North America, and between New Zealand and Antarctica. How these deep convections couple to the plate motions remains uncertain.

The speeds of the horizontal motions of plates would disgrace a snail. They are typically a few centimetres a year, and you would have to wait for centuries before displacements became visible in remote-sensing images. But the Global Positioning System (GPS) is a high-grade US system of navigation satellites that can measure the relative positions of ground stations a thousand kilometres apart with an accuracy of about a centimetre. It makes the measurement of plate motions a matter of routine, directly applicable to earthquake studies. The drifting of the continents becomes as observable as the migrations of birds.

Yet consider this. Only 30 years ago most geologists refused to believe that the continents had ever moved, and scoffed when physicists deduced that the present ocean basins were much younger than the continents. Drilling to the ocean bedrock settled the issue in the late 1960s. The geologists raised a white flag and surrendered their textbooks for rewriting. What other profound misconceptions still lurk, one wonders, in current beliefs about the Earth system?

To explain the evidence for ancient glaciers in India, desert sand dunes in Europe, and coal in Antarctica, the old geology required preposterous changes in the global climate and weather patterns. In the new, mobile version, the pieces of the present continents simply wandered between the polar regions, the desert zones and the coal-rich tropics. The extents of those zones have, though, in a fluctuating global climate. The stage was set for the present generally glacial phase of the Earth's history when Antarctica became isolated at the South Pole and froze up. Then northern land masses thronging around the Arctic Ocean provided platforms on which, during an ice age, snow could pile up as ice sheets, like Greenland's now.

Facing:
The seabed charted from space. A US geophysicist, William Haxby, used radar-altimeter readings from Seasat to picture humps and hollows in the sea surface corresponding with ridges and trenches in the ocean floor (upper image). The latest computer model of the Earth's outer shell (lower illustration) shows plates diverging at the ridges and converging at the trenches. The plate boundaries are the main earthquake zones.

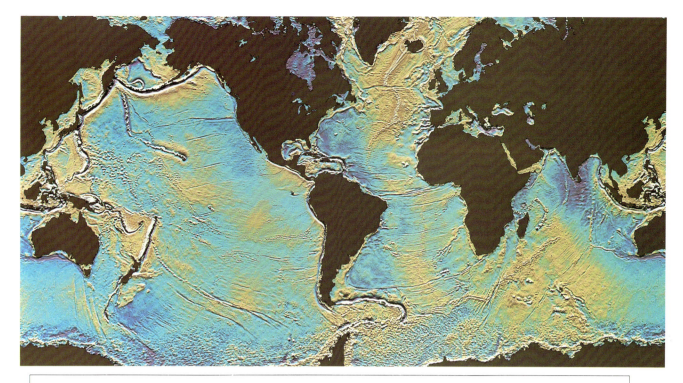

Present−day Relative Plate Velocities

Plate Boundary Type

⟷ Divergent

→✕← Convergent

100 millimeters/year

Mercator Projection

Vectors not distorted

Sources

DeMets et al. [1990]

Pelayo & Wiens [1989]

Phil. = Philippine

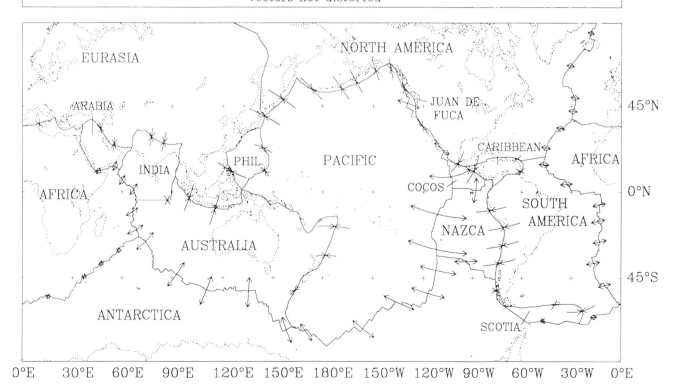

Where to look for oil

CONTINENTAL DRIFT and plate tectonics tell a single, coherent story of the whole world's geology. The lines of oceanic islands, or the lines of metal ores like Bolivia's tin, make sense, at last, as products of plate action. So do the great mountain ranges of the world, which result from plate convergences and collisions with islands, as in the Andes, culminating in continental collisions as in the Himalayas.

The demolition of mountains, almost as fast as they rise, releases huge volumes of sand and mud into the rivers. These sedimentary materials plaster the plains below or continue out to the beds of adjacent seas. The deposits congeal into sedimentary rocks. Low-lying parts of continents are often flooded by the sea, on a continental shelf far shallower than the ocean basins. Here marine organisms with carbonate shells thrive, and make limestone when they die. Most spectacular in the present world, and well observed by satellites, is Australia's Great Barrier Reef, built of coral skeletons. Subsequent plate actions can crush the sedimentary rocks and reefs into new formations, which is why fossil seashells turn up on mountain-tops.

To make fossil fuels – coal, oil and natural gas – the organic remains of living things have to become trapped in airless sediments before they can rot in the usual way. Coal comes mainly from land plants, which can make scrappy deposits almost anywhere. The richest seams form when swampy tropical forests become caught up in a continental collision.

This happened in Europe and North America around 300 million years ago, and provided the coal with which the inhabitants of those regions rose to industrial dominance in the 19th Century. Before the industrial era almost everyone found energy supplies where they lived – firewood, running water, wind power and so on. Coal was the first fossil fuel to be used on a large scale. Europe and North America have 31 per cent of the world's coal, and China and the Soviet Union have another 52 per cent. That leaves another 60 per cent of the world's population with 17 per cent of the coal.

Even spottier is the distribution of the oil of the rocks, petroleum. More than half the world's known reserves are concentrated in the region of the Arabian/Persian Gulf, where fewer than one in fifty of the human population lives. The Soviet Union, Mexico and various other countries are quite well-endowed with oil, but many have virtually none. These include Japan. Although the USA and Europe have oil of their own, they import it too. The world's thirst for oil aggravates the geopolitical issues in the war-torn Middle East.

Oil oozes naturally to the surface in many places, and the tarry asphalt left by its evaporation was valued as a waterproof material in prehistoric times. Many whales perished to supply 19th Century industries with lubricants, and fuel for lamps, until pioneers in North America and Europe drilled for liquid petroleum. It provided potent liquid fuels, and inventors made engines that ran on their vapours. In the 20th Century oil overtook coal as the world's most popular fuel. Together with its newly prized associate, natural gas, oil accounts for more than half the commercial energy supplies of the human species.

To start making petroleum, Nature needs a warm, shallow, stagnant sea where a superabundance of rotting corpses of marine plants and animals exhausts the oxygen at the seabed, allowing organic material to accumulate. Other sediments must then pile up on top of it so that it can be pressure-cooked deep underground by the Earth's internal heat, to form oil and gas. These will tend to escape unless faults in the rocks or sealing layers of salt can trap them.

The requirements for large amounts of oil to survive are exacting. They are met only in rift valleys and sedimentary basins, made by a stretching and sagging of the crust of a continent, which become flooded with sea water. Europe's North Sea is an example. It is a sedimentary basin created when the British Isles eased away from the European mainland, thinning the intervening crust. Oilfields lie mainly on a line down the middle of the North Sea. There, in dinosaur times, a large crack formed a deep rift valley where organic sediments could accumulate and cook. Flooded repeatedly by the sea, and intermittently drying to salt, it provided ideal conditions for amassing oil and gas.

The spaceship's largest tanks of liquid fuel lie far from where the oil is most wanted. This mismatch creates the world's greatest trading system. From the oil-making sedimentary basins, much of the oil goes to those old provinces of the coal-making forests, which are still industrially strong. Images from space show the night-time illumination of Arabian and other oilfields by those flares of uncaptured natural gas. The satellites can pick out pipelines, and the wakes of supertankers rounding Africa en route to Europe or thronging the narrow seaways of Southeast Asia on their way to Japan.

Other scenes from space show the huge refineries beside the sea that swallow the crude oil from the tankers and turn it into fuels, lubricants,

79

tars, and raw materials for the chemical industry. Oil spillages at sea are a chronic problem, and remote-sensing experts working for the European Community have developed ways of detecting slicks from the air, before the offending tankers have time to sail away.

A generation ago, the big worry was about the oil running out. With human beings extracting it a million times faster than Nature accumulated it, and individual fields running dry, oil was the very model of a nonrenewable resource. When commentators predicted its exhaustion by the end of the 20th Century, a sense of scarcity should logically have pushed prices up. Yet by 1980 the complaint was that oil was too dear.

Big price rises during the 1970s, when Arab and Iranian oil producers flexed their political and economic muscles to restrict production, caused demand to level off, as people economized without greatly altering their habits. The global economy faltered a little, and Third World countries without oil of their own suffered badly. Prices roller-coastered during the 1980s, but generally stayed higher than before, and took off again in the Gulf crisis of 1990. They vindicated the exploitation of fields in difficult regions like the North Sea and Alaska, and encouraged worldwide searches for new fields.

Sedimentary basins old and new are clearly the places to look for oil, and prospectors were quick to take advantage of fresh interpretations from plate tectonics. On land, the oil companies became big users of satellite images, to form first impressions of the geology of areas to be prospected. In parts of the world lacking good maps, the images can do instead. Some companies also use the space images to study and minimize environmental impacts of their operations. The sea and the seabed are rather poker-faced to remote-sensing satellites, but explosives and airguns can set up earthquake-like shocks to explore the sediments of the world's shallow seas by seismic soundings. Supercomputers enable oil geophysicists to translate the results into 3-D pictures of subterranean strata, and so pinpoint even small reservoirs.

Fresh oil discoveries and re-evaluations of known fields are increasing the reserves faster than oil is taken out of the ground. This cannot go on much longer, in conventional areas at least. But most of the present margins of continents started as rift valleys when their parent continents were ripped apart. Where the continental shelf has remained undisturbed by later geological action, extensive undiscovered oil deposits may exist beneath the seabed in relatively deep water.

By 1990, in another lurch in opinion, fears of too little or too costly oil had given way to anxieties about too much oil. Its burning makes a large contribution to the manmade carbon dioxide going into the atmosphere. General issues about carbon dioxide and climate change are deferred to a later chapter, but note here that fossil fuels differ in the amount of carbon dioxide released for each unit of energy provided. Coal gives the most carbon dioxide and natural gas (methane) the least, with oil in the middle of the range.

The newly-perceived advantage of natural gas as a low-carbon fuel can only encourage an already growing appetite for it. Large-capacity pipelines have delivered Soviet natural gas to Western Europe in ever-growing quantities since the oil crises of the 1970s. High temperatures and pressures deep underground generate gas in preference to oil, from organic materials. In the northern North Sea, for example, oil and natural gas coexist, while in the southern North Sea, natural gas predominates. Although the ways of distributing and using liquid and gassy fuels differ greatly, the oil and natural-gas industries are thoroughly entwined, with the same companies engaged in finding and recovering both.

Some poor countries depend heavily on earnings from oil, and this must figure in any consideration of the industry's future. Indonesia is a case in point, as the largest exporter of oil in eastern Asia. Its efforts to expand its oil production provide a vignette of the state of play, in global economics, technology and geology. Japan is a major customer. Twenty per cent of Indonesia's oil already comes from offshore fields, and important new fields are turning up in the Java Sea.

The oil-explorers visualize the island of Java as a piece of Asia's shore that became detached by continental plate-stretching of a kind well known to geophysicists, though not well understood. The separation thinned the continental crust between Java and the mainland, to create a sedimentary basin. It is flooded by the high sea level of the present interglacial period, but during an ice age you could walk dryshod through tropical forests on the bed of the Java Sea.

A complex history left the basin crisscrossed with faults, allowing blocks to drop and make miniaturized rift valleys, now filled and hidden beneath the seabed. In 1988, by pinpointing such a buried chasm by seismic soundings and exploratory drilling, the prospectors made Indonesia's biggest oil discovery in 10 years. Called the Widuri field, it is already the scene of intensive corporate effort of the kind for which the oil industry is well known, with half-a-dozen platforms and an export terminal appearing in the midst of the Java Sea, to tap Nature's gift of liquid energy. More important than these manmade islands, yet too obvious to be noticed, is the Indonesians' much longer use of another and more basic geological gift – the land itself.

Life among the volcanoes

*A*N AIR PASSENGER flying over the Indonesian island of Java sees impressive volcanoes poking through the clouds. Their regularity and conical forms gives them an engineered look, like the pyramids of Egypt. Descent through the clouds brings into view the terraced farms that climb precariously up the slopes of the volcanoes, and on the plains the long, thin, glinting paddies where the rice grows. Despite its mountainous terrain, Java supports a dense population.

Landsat images show a complex, pockmarked landscape in the interior of Central Java, with lake-filled craters left by volcanic explosions, large and small volcanic cones, and untidy lava flows. Hot springs blast out sulphurous steam and lure engineers who want to use them to generate electricity. In 1979, an eruption in a crater lake suffocated more than 140 people in an exhalation of carbon-dioxide gas.

Dieng village stands in a crater that used to be occupied by a lake. Nearly 1300 years ago, unknown travellers brought the Indian religion and Indian hydraulics to Central Java, and drained the lake. New crops, farm animals and diseases arrived fom other parts of the world; tobacco and mushrooms are the present novelties at Dieng. But the inhabitants are still the Austronesians whose ancestors were cultivating bananas, yams and coconuts here, 9000 years ago.

The rugged volcanic terrain has not kept out waves of intruders into Central Java, including Portuguese, Dutch and Japanese. Indonesian nationhood was, in effect, invented by the Dutch when they lumped a thousand inhabited islands and diverse cultures into an administrative entity, dominated by fertile Java. Stretching more than 5000 kilometres from Sumatra in the west to part of New Guinea in the east, Indonesia is so wide that only the Japanese Earth-synchronous weather satellite, far out in space, can take it in at a glance.

The Indian Ocean to the west is almost perpetually cloudy, while the desert of Australia to the south is almost cloud-free and therefore easy to spot. The long, thin island of Java is usually clear in July, but lost in

Facing:
Volcanic landscape of central Java, Indonesia, in a Landsat image. Black fingers of debris flow down the western flank of the ever-active Merapi (above). The red tinge denoting vegetation shows large areas fertilized by the volcanic minerals.

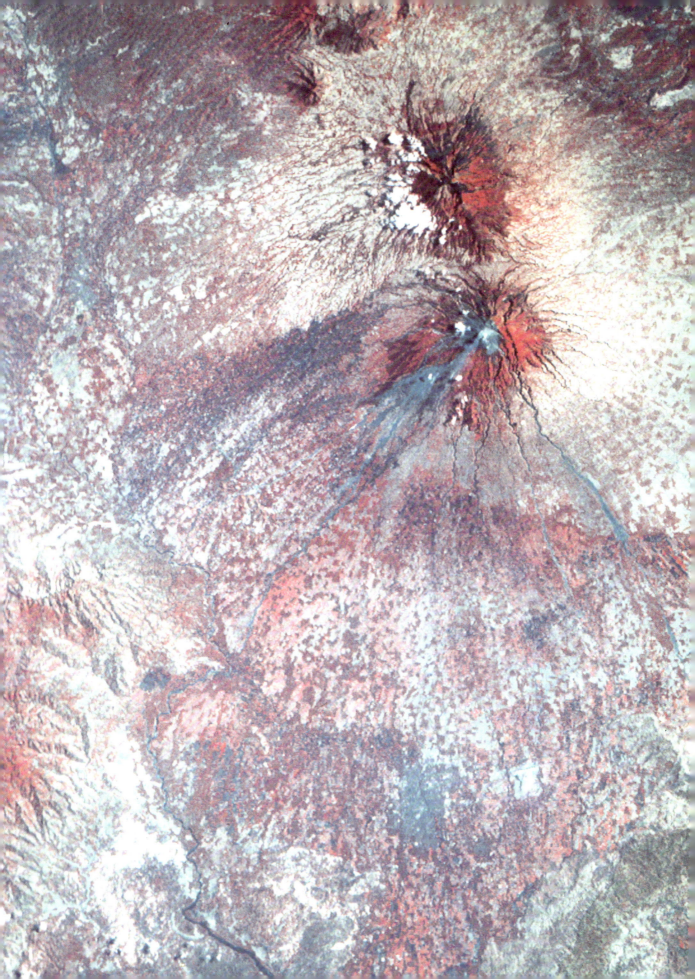

cloud in January, at the height of the rainy season. Every few years, satellites show fewer clouds and less vegetation than usual over Java, because of the great shift in the world's weather called El Niño. Abnormally high air pressure in Java is by long tradition a warning to the world's climatologists of a swing in the seesaw.

The essence of Java is best signalled by the radar altimeters in space that reveal the deep trench just south of the island. Here the ocean floor is diving to destruction under Java, as the last scrap of ocean between Indonesia and Australia gradually disappears. Their collision will come to a climax some 10 million years from now. Their former separation explains Java's place beside a fault line in biogeography, that separates the native mammals and trees of Asia from the peculiar marsupials and gum trees of Australia.

The ocean floor disappearing into the grinder under Java and other islands meanwhile makes Indonesia the most active zone in the world for volcanoes. Unexceptional for Java was the offshore islet of Krakatau which blew up in 1883, taking thousands of lives with its tidal waves and causing scarlet sunsets and blue moons all around the world for many months thereafter.

North of the Central Javan city of Yogyakarta, Merapi is a long-playing volcano 3000 metres tall. Always smoking, it is noted for its frequent eruptions, with dangerous but relatively small outbursts every 10 years or so and major events each century or two. The last big eruption was in 1930, and the last substantial one in 1984. Yet 10 million people live on Merapi's slopes and the plain below it.

Outpourings from Merapi include glowing avalanches of fine volcanic particles, and porridge-like 'lahar' flows of dark volcanic cinders mixed with water. Gravity propels the flows and landforms guide them down the steepest and clearest routes – typically along the small ravines made by streams. Heavy rain can reactivate the loose material in secondary flows of lahar.

Just below the naked ground near the summit of Merapi, a young forest replaces trees destroyed by a glowing avalanche in the 1984 eruption. Close by, farmers work the land as near to the summit as they can. A supposedly forbidden zone is thronged with people and vehicles gathering rubble and sand from the lahar-strewn landscape, for building purposes, and artists seek out the bigger blocks to make stone carvings for sale.

Satellite images and air photos show dark fingers of recent lahar flows

84

concentrated on Merapi's southwestern flank. Some other governments content themselves with drawing circles around an eruption centre to define zones of various degrees of hazard, but the Indonesian Directorate of Volcanology pays closer attention to the pattern of recent eruptions and the lie of the land. On Merapi the forbidden zone, which is supposed to be permanently abandoned, extends up to 16 kilometres from the current eruption centre (a lava dome) towards the west and south, but only 1 kilometre in the opposite direction, where the scarp of an old centre shields the northern and eastern slopes.

A 'first danger zone' about 2 kilometres wide covers areas outside the forbidden zone that were partially or completely destroyed in previous eruptions. No houses are supposed to be built in this area. In a 'second danger zone', extending down river valleys, people have to be prepared to evacuate their homes. While the lahar and officialdom press them downhill, the land-hungry farmers of Java drift uphill. The Volcanology Directorate has enlarged the forbidden zone beyond its own scientific criteria, in an effort to dissuade them, but the 'first danger zone' is thick with people and crops.

A watchtower keeps the volcano under surveillance, and so do seismic stations, while geochemical tests and surveys of ground movements heighten the vigilance. A weather radar and rainfall gauges monitor the rainfall which can loosen existing lahar. Wires stretched across the ravines are meant to break and send an automatic warning in the event of a lahar flow.

By excavations and the heaping of rubble into dykes the authorities try to regulate the landforms of the volcano's flank and guide future lahar along harmless paths. But it has to go somewhere, and protecting one place can put others at risk. Check dams athwart the ravines help to slow the rush of lahar into inhabited areas, but one eruption can sweep away or overtop the check dams, and clog a ravine with rubble.

Some geographers question the policy of trying to keep the lahar flowing down particular routes. Encourage it to spread more widely, these experts say. Then the rain will have a better chance to re-excavate the ravines to cope with the next eruption. Arguments of this kind illustrate the problems of playing God even on a small scale, when Nature is dealing out death.

The Javanese boast that you could plant a walking stick in their soil and it would grow. The warm, moist climate certainly helps, but the volcanic material of which the land is built must take much of the credit. Life cannot live by carbon dioxide and water alone. Another ingredient, nitrogen, is abundant in the air and microbes in the soil and roots fix it biochemically, making it available to plants. But mineral elements essential for life, phosphorus for example, have to come from the solid Earth.

In the global picture, limited supplies of nutrient minerals gradually disappear from the land surface, either by burial or by travelling downhill, eventually into the sea. They can only be replaced by the weathering of rocks, in which the weather itself and chemical and biological action release new supplies of the elements into the soil. The chemically rich volcanic rocks of Java, fresh from the bowels of the Earth, weather easily to make excellent soil. Hence the life-and-death bargain between the farmer and the volcano, in the land that Merapi built.

Down the slope towards the sea, the coarse lahar of the summit comminutes to an ever-finer black sand, and the absence of mountain chills favours rice. Here stands the city of Yogyakarta. Its first king, so the story goes, married the queen of the sea and they went to live inside Merapi. They still share their wedding feast with the people, in generous handouts of rich soil. This folklore anticipates the geophysical tale of the seabed diving under the land and making magma.

The precautions concerning future eruptions of Merapi can only cope with events falling in the range of 'normal' local experience. A catastrophic event that could turn Merapi into a crater lake, like Tambora on nearby Sumatra in 1815, defies anyone's horror-struck imagination. When scientists try to think of ways of taming volcanoes, only nuclear weapons seem equal to the task.

A typical image of a dormant volcano seen from space shows a necklace of latter-day Pompeiis surrounding the cone. On the slopes of Vesuvius in Italy, grape-growers collect fresh volcanic dust to put around their vines, as assiduously as colleagues in more tranquil places gather manure. Dense populations live in areas of volcanic danger, not only in Indonesia and Italy, but in Japan, the Philippines, Mexico, and the countries of the High Andes.

In order to cultivate some of the world's most fertile fields, individual farmers risk their children being burnt alive. Only they can elect to live on the volcano's slopes. If they all fled, the loss of a slice of the world's food output would be compounded by pressure on land elsewhere. Like miners, fishermen and lifeboatmen, farmers in volcanic areas are willing to live dangerously, but they cannot be ordered around as

Facing:
Vesuvius by satellite and computer. Nearly 2000 years after its ash buried Pompeii, Vesuvius is still surrounded by towns and villages. Italian researchers combine urban data from Landsat (top) with a model of expectable fallout of volcanic ash (near, below). They compute a map (far right) of roofs at risk of collapse under the weight of ash, from yellow denoting a low risk, to violet the highest.

86

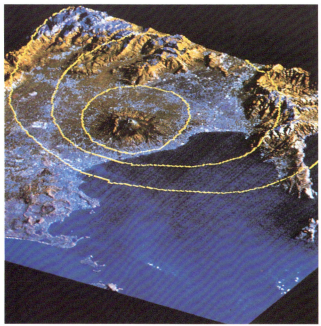

TEPHRA FALLOUT MODEL, IBM, ITALY

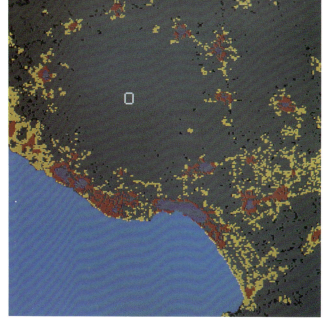

URBANIZATION FROM LANDSAT AND COMPUTED FALLOUT, IBM, ITALY

casually as national or would-be global planners might presume. Their self-reliance matches Nature's own anarchism.

The bladder-emptying terror aroused by molten rock fountaining from the ground, by the choking, poisonous steam, and by the hot pumice pattering on your head and shoulders, is a rapid cure for two of the 20th Century's favourite delusions. One is that Nature is a loving mother. The other is that human beings are in charge of Spaceship Earth.

Dusting the stratosphere

*I*T WAS A sign of the times that a squib like Mount St Helens seemed shocking. The events that removed the top of that mountain in the western USA in 1980 were feebler by far than many in the historical and geological records, but a dearth of major volcanic events during most of the 20th Century left the public and even experts unprepared for it. The worst consequences of earthquakes, tsunamis apart, are confined to the shocked area. Even mild volcanoes fling ash and gases into the atmosphere as a kind of natural pollution. The severest ones alter the global climate.

Extinct, dormant and active volcanoes line up like soldiers on islands or continental margins around the world. Those that rise from hotspots, either at the edge of a plate as in Iceland, or in the middle of a plate as in Hawaii, ooze more often than they explode. The most violent volcanoes occur with the destruction of the ocean floor, as in Indonesia. A Ring of Fire surrounds the Pacific because that ocean is compelled to shrink while the Atlantic grows.

Satellites are excellent eruption-spotters. As a *Landsat* passed over South America one day, its infra-red detectors registered heat coming from Lascar, a neglected volcano on the desert's edge in Chile. Scientists at Britain's Open University compared the intensities at different wavelengths and inferred the presence of red-hot rock seen through a thin, cracked crust. That was in 1985. In the following year, Lascar erupted and scattered ash across hundreds of kilometres of sparsely inhabited land.

A quite different method enabled Japanese scientists of the National Research Centre for Disaster Prevention in Tsukuba to observe warning signs before the eruption of a submarine volcano, Teishi, off the

Japanese coast in 1988. This was an early application of GPS, the Global Positioning System mentioned earlier. The scientists were able to detect ground movements on the coast near Teishi, in the days before the volcano blew, due to underground movements of molten rock.

Such anticipations from space have been rare so far, but weather satellites, observing the whole Earth daily, see important eruptions almost instantly, by their heat or by the clouds of material streaming from them. Compare this with the situation in 1912, when the 20th Century's biggest eruption darkened the sky in Washington DC. Four years elapsed before it was traced to Mount Katmai in Alaska, where the Valley of Ten Thousand Smokes is now a tourist attraction. That eruption was forty times greater than Mount St Helens.

When the El Chichón volcano in southern Mexico erupted in 1982, after lying dormant for some 600 years, satellites were able for the first time to trace a cloud of volcanic dust spreading right around the world, in the upper atmosphere. The force of gun-like explosions helped to create the dense, persistent, detectable cloud, and an extraordinary amount of sulphurous gas released in the event turned into droplets of sulphuric acid in the stratosphere.

The El Chichón material travelled due west over Hawaii, where a ground-based laser saw a stratospheric cloud 140 times denser than that from Mount St Helens two years earlier. The cloud continued westwards at 70 kilometres an hour, over Indo-China, India and the African Sahel, and returned to Mexico three weeks after the main eruption of El Chichón. Weather satellites, working as a team, saw the cloud by visible light, as it formed a smoke ring around the world, but soon lost it. An infra-red detector in the *Solar Mesosphere Explorer* and an ultraviolet detector in *Nimbus*-7 continued to sense the cloud for some months. These specialized instruments registered infra-red emissions from the cloud, and absorptions at wavelengths characteristic of sulphur dioxide.

Dust in the upper atmosphere can veil the Sun and cause a cooling at the Earth's surface. Unlike dust at lower altitudes it does not fall out rapidly, and there is no rain in the stratosphere to wash it out. Mineral dust can persist for months, while sulphuric acid droplets and fine soot particles can stay up for some years. Stratospheric veils have figured in various recent trains of thought about threats to the Earth system – from volcanoes, from collisions with small planets or comets, and from nuclear war.

89

Volcanic winter

*H*ISTORICAL EVIDENCE confirms that dust injected into the upper atmosphere by violent volcanic eruptions can temporarily cool the world. The British climatologist Hubert Lamb cites, for example, two eruptions in Indonesia in the 19th Century. Tambora (1815) was followed by an exceptionally cool, wet summer in Europe and North America. After Krakatau (1883) measurements of the intensity of direct sunlight at various places around the world showed it dropping 10–20 per cent below normal in the following two years. Colleagues of Lamb reported a cooling of the Northern Hemisphere by about 0.2 degrees C within three months of the El Chichón (1982) eruption.

At that time the scientific world was debating the theory that the extinction of the dinosaurs 65 million years ago was due to a cosmic collision. The events that terminated the Mesozoic Era extinguished all land animals of more than 25 kilograms, and left the oceans almost dead for a while. The discovery that the dinosaurs' demise coincided with a worldwide dusting by iridium, a material very rare at the Earth's surface, revived the hypothesis that an asteroid or comet hit the Earth, causing a stupendous explosion. Apart from direct effects of blast and fire, the dust hurled into the upper atmosphere could have spread as a dense pall around the world, blotting out the Sun and suspending plant growth for some years.

The third related story concerned nuclear winter. In 1982, the Dutch atmospheric chemist Paul Crutzen, with John Birks, an American ecologist, noted that smoke from forests set alight by nuclear weapons could bring 'twilight at noon'. A group at Cornell University in the USA then pointed out that blazing cities would be even smokier. The international Scientific Committee on Problems of the Environment (SCOPE) mobilized 300 scientists to picture the worldwide spread of smoke and its effects, with computer models, and to estimate the ecological and human impacts. They concluded that billions could die of starvation in noncombatant countries.

Yet the Earth system is capable of generating a volcanic winter far worse than the nuclear winter. A mountain exploded 78,000 years ago on the Indonesian island of Sumatra, with a violence equivalent to 4000 Mount St Helens. Lake Toba, 100 kilometres long and 30 kilometres wide, partly fills the crater that it left. In the course of a week or two it injected into the upper atmosphere billions of tons of dust, water

LANDSAT DATA, PROCESSED BY US GEOLOGICAL SURVEY

Alaskan volcano from space. Landsat's heat sensors helped to image the molten crater, hot material spilling downhill, and an ash cloud blowing downwind. This eruption of Augustine Island endangered intercontinental flights into Anchorage, Alaska.

vapour and chemicals such as sulphur. The Toba blast produced a short-lived ice age, clearly recorded in the ice of faraway Antarctica and in changes in fossil pollen in Europe.

The most remarkable volcanic event known to geologists built much of the territory of India, 65 million years ago. It marked the first break-through of a new hotspot. A flood of basaltic lava covered an area of a million square kilometres (larger than France or Texas) to an average thickness of more than a kilometre, to build India's Deccan Plateau. This coincided with the extinction of the dinosaurs, and Vincent Courtillot of the French Institute of Physics of the Earth, who recently confirmed the date and speed of the Deccan event, sees a likely connection. Robert White of Cambridge University offers a scenario in which any cosmic impact was just a sideshow, and the real killing was done by volcanism.

White visualizes the Deccan basalt pouring out in pulses every few thousand years. Forest fires would carry soot into the upper atmosphere, along with dust and gases blasted there by explosive volcanic activity. Loss of sunlight and severe changes in temperature, aggravated by natural acid rain, would disrupt the Mesozoic life at every pulse, and explosive events may have administered the coup de grâce. A three-way argument continues between physicists who favour either the comet or the volcanism, and fossil-hunters who detest any non-biological explanation for their favourite catastrophe.

New hotspots appear at intervals of roughly 30 million years, and the last flood basalt event created the Columbia River Plateau in North America around 16 million years ago. It may or may not have been responsible for the founding of Antarctica's ice sheet. While there is no cause for alarm about another Deccan-like event in any time-frame of current interest to human beings, and while Toba-like events are also rare, there is plenty of reason to take lesser volcanoes seriously.

For example, the Tambora eruption of 1815, mentioned earlier, was only equivalent to 100 Mount St Helens, but its release of chlorine may have done more harm to the Earth's ozone layer than all the manmade CFCs since their invention 60 years ago. Some sceptics wonder if the effects on ozone by past volcanoes mean that the deadly sunburn, widely advertised as a consequence of ozone depletion, has been exaggerated. But the behaviour of volcanic chlorine, mainly in the form of hydrogen chloride, is poorly understood.

Although climatologists can point to volcanoes as a means by which any warming of the global climate might be interrupted, they cannot predict the eruptions of, say, the coming 50 years. Computer models of climate change sometimes throw in a few imaginary volcanoes and register hesitations in the rising temperatures. A chorus of volcanic eruptions, or a truly gigantic one, would be needed to cancel the warming predicted in the models, or precipitate an ice age. And the dearth of eruptions leaves the volcanologists whistling for public attention.

They want a global monitoring system that puts automatic instruments on every important volcano not demonstrably extinct. They would use relay satellites to harvest the data, the Global Positioning System to watch for gross ground movements, and remote-sensing satellites to register outward activity. This may be the only way to cope with volcanoes in remote spots, or with long-dormant volcanoes in populated areas that would usually be a waste of a volcano-watcher's time. The observing system may reveal how to predict major eruptions. Meanwhile volcanologists can only note, with fascination and concern, ominous signs in various parts of the world.

Iwojima looks like a new Krakatau in the making. The American marines who stormed this Japanese volcanic island in 1945 would have found it less formidable in the Middle Ages. Iwojima has risen 120 metres in the past 700 years. Coral reefs perched high above the sea testify to this uplift, which is probably due to molten rock accumulating under the island. A comprehensive eruption would be equivalent to perhaps 10 Mount St Helens. The sea would aggravate its effects, with explosive steam generation and chemical reactions, and would carry tsunamis to ravage distant coasts, as happened in the Krakatau event.

A disagreeable feature that giant volcanic eruptions share with major earthquakes is this: the longer they are postponed, the worse they are likely to be. And even as a global overview of volcanic activity becomes possible for the first time, it brings a touch of farce to present grandiose ideas about management of the Earth system. What grandson of Canute will command the tides of molten rock to stop rising in the Earth's crust?

Riddles in the rift

*H*UMAN BEINGS evolved among volcanoes, in the rift valleys of Africa. Plaster-like volcanic ash in Tanzania, nearly 4 million years old, preserves the oldest known footprints of a hominid walking on two legs. Fossils found along the rifts reveal several species of apemen and early tool-making human beings. The rifts cut through the crust of East Africa like giant scars, where the continent swelled into a large dome, and the crust cracked. Sagging blocks dropped 2 or 3 kilometres to create the rifts, which volcanic debris and other sediments have largely filled. Africa has widened by about 10 kilometres here.

Images from space show parallel lines of long, wall-like scarps. The high ground on either side of the rifts attracts more rainfall and appears better vegetated. The valley floors are decorated by chains of lakes. Hot rocks rising from below the land surface have punctured the crust to create many volcanoes. Most are now extinct, but some expired explosively, leaving large craters. The volcanic cones of Kilimanjaro and Mount Kenya rise high enough into the cold upper air to carry glaciers even in tropical Africa.

As the best example of recent rifting on dry land, it seemed impressive to geologists, before the confirmation of continental drift. Now they know that during the past 200 million years far more decisive rifting has torn from Africa, in turn, the continents and microcontinents of North America, India plus Antarctica and Australia, Madagascar, South America, Italy, and Arabia. That leaves the East African rift system seeming less imposing than enigmatic.

Is it set to make an island of part of East Africa? Is it a failed attempt at doing that? Or is it a phenomenon different from the continent-splitting that created, most recently, the new ocean of the Red Sea between Africa and Arabia? The continent of Africa seems to be nearly stationary over the Earth's interior, and doming and rifting in Ethiopia seems to be the product of a long-playing hotspot. There may be a second hotspot under Kenya.

In 1990 the Kenya Rift International Seismic Project (KRISP) mobilized a hundred experts from seven European countries, from the USA and from Kenya itself. They set off explosions in lakes and boreholes, and registered the arrival of seismic waves at distant detectors after they had swum deep into Kenya's underworld. The signals revealed a wedge of dense, semi-molten rock from the Earth's interior rising under the rift, perhaps from a hotspot, and sending chimney-like plumes to volcanoes at the surface.

Intensive studies of natural earthquakes were part of KRISP, and gave information relevant to the safety of dams and other structures. Kenya is also looking for oil, not in the present rift valley, but in another, older rift valley that crosses underneath it. By probing the deep structures where the rifts cross, KRISP's results may help the oil-explorers. The old rift was flooded by the sea for a while, when a piece of East Africa broke off to make the island of Madagascar. Oil has already turned up in it, though inland from Kenya.

Kenyan engineers who exploit the seething underground heat of the rift valley obtain from KRISP a literally deeper understanding of the sources of this geothermal energy. Where a volcano last erupted 5000 years ago, south of Lake Naivasha, rainwater trickling into the rocks comes back to the surface scalding hot. Now boreholes at Kenya's first geothermal power station harvest natural steam to generate electricity. Ironically, perhaps, the Kenyan villagers in this part of the rift valley appreciate the clean water most. Any water can be hard to come by in Africa, and it often carries disease. The condensed steam from the geothermal plant is as pure and safe as anyone could wish for.

CHAPTER 4

The Look of a Leaf

S EEN FROM the sky by the human eye, rich grasslands and forests appear almost black. That is just as it should be. The vegetation is tuned to the same wavelengths as the eye and it grabs all the daylight it can, to grow by. But water and some rocks are a dark grey too, and a satellite observing a landscape only by visible light would confuse them with vegetation. As already noted, though, plants glow bright in the near infra-red, closest in wavelengths to visible red light.

Take the signals from a satellite for red light and the near infra-red, pixel by pixel. Find the difference between them by subtracting the red signal from the infra-red signal. 'Normalize' this number to allow for variations in the brightness of the scene, by dividing by the sum of the two signals. The resulting number is the 'normalized difference vegetation index' or N D V I. Here it is called simply the vegetation index, because it has swept the board as the way of distinguishing plants.

Humanitarian applications of remote-sensing satellites over Africa, described earlier, use the vegetation index to monitor effects of drought and look for the breeding grounds of locusts. And by grasping a whole piece of the Earth system, the vegetation index makes a decisive contribution to the new global geography of the era of satellites and computers. The analysis of how a leaf looks from space illustrates the physics that underpins remote sensing. By way of computer models, observations of plants from space plug directly into descriptions and forecasts of the interplay between living landscapes and the weather.

Despite the fact that individual plants and animals fall far below the resolution of the satellites, the vegetation index opens up remarkable prospects for monitoring ecological systems from space. And as farms, rangelands and forests come under detailed scrutiny from space, this chapter tells of practical applications in Europe and South America, and an international experiment on the Kansas prairie that verifies and consolidates the scientific base.

Indexing vegetation

*T*HE WATERGATE scandal was not the only worry in Washington DC in 1972. While Republicans burglarized the Democrats, commercial agents of the Soviet Union quietly filched a quarter of the US wheat crop from the open market at an artificially low price. During the Cold War food was an economic weapon, yet the USA was unaware of the dire state of the Soviet harvest that year. A demand went out to the US intelligence services and to the remote-sensing community for much better assessments of Soviet harvests.

Spy-satellite experts, more familiar with machinery than vegetation, set out to count harvested bales, while NASA and the US Department of Agriculture began using data from NASA's newly launched *Landsat* for direct observations of crops. It was one of the satellite's advertised purposes, and the vegetation index (NDVI) was invented for use with *Landsat*. Harvest-forecasters examined scenes of Soviet farmlands, and compared space images with ground studies in more accessible places. In 1977 the Large Area Crop Inventory Experiment (LACIE) succeeded in spotting a shortfall in Soviet wheat production.

Meanwhile, a biologist at Colorado State University was finding out why the vegetation index worked. This was Compton J. Tucker, always known as Jim. In greenhouses and fields, Tucker and his colleagues pointed light-meters at the foliage to measure visible and infra-red rays. They confirmed the signature of vegetation, and Tucker turned to the physics of leaves to explain it.

Facing:
Biogeography by satellite. From space observations of vegetation in Africa changing season by season (inset) pioneers of the technique mapped the zones of Africa (main image). These are deserts (pink), Sudan and Guinea zones (pale green and magenta), tropical forest (red), savanna (dark green) and semi-arid regions (buff). Blue areas are transitional.

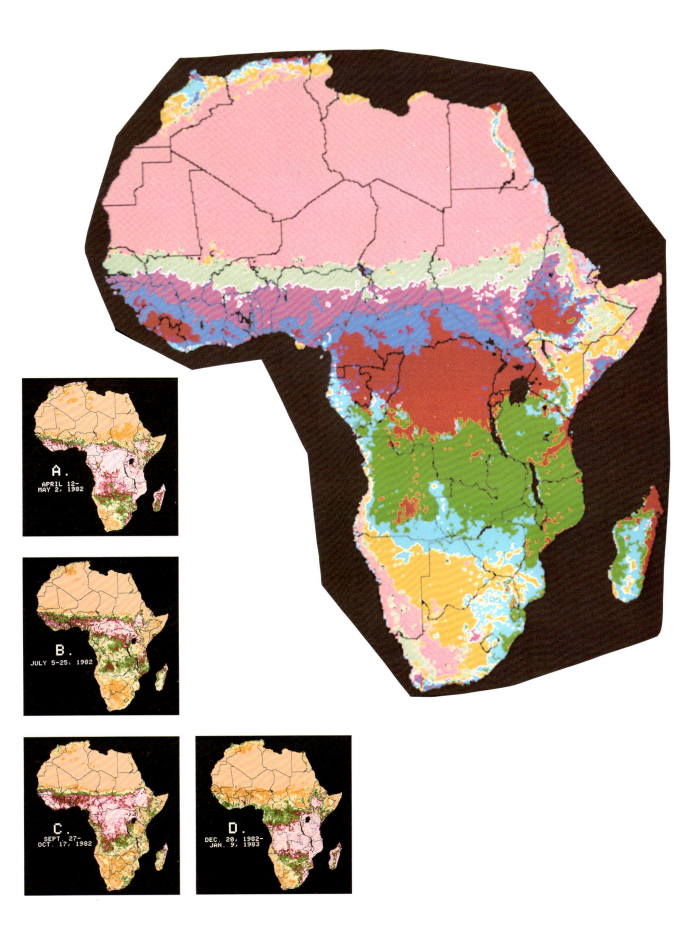

A.
APRIL 12–
MAY 2, 1982

B.
JULY 5–25, 1982

C.
SEPT. 27–
OCT. 17, 1982

D.
DEC. 20, 1982–
JAN. 9, 1983

For the most important chemical process on Earth, the photo-electric machinery of a leaf deploys molecular photo-cells and light-guides of great antiquity and efficiency. They trap photons of daylight and liberate electrons. These drive the reactions of photosynthesis that convert carbon dioxide and water into sugars and other chemicals, and release oxygen as a by-product.

A leaf catches the light with pigments, mainly chlorophyll, that reject a little green light. Yet that is not reason enough for the leaf to look dark green, close-to. It concentrates its pigments in small light-using units, dark green spots visible only in a microscope. Without special optical properties, a leaf should appear almost transparent, and be hopeless as a light-gatherer.

The look of a leaf depends on visible light ricocheting about inside it, until trapped by one pigment molecule or another. Tucker saw that a maze of air spaces, among the water-filled cells of the leaf, accomplishes this by scattering the light. Yet the same optical action makes the leaf a strong reflector of the near infra-red rays. These ricochet too, but the pigments ignore them and in the end they escape, mainly through the upper surface of the leaf. Nothing else mimics the leaf's abrupt switch, from darkness by red light to high brightness in the near infra-red.

When Tucker had understood how leaves and radiation interacted, he joined NASA in Maryland, at the Goddard Space Flight Center's Laboratory of Terrestrial Physics, to use the vegetation index in practical remote sensing from space. But he caused surprise bordering on consternation by saying, 'For most applications this is better achieved from meteorological satellites than *Landsat*!'

In 1979 a new weather satellite *NOAA-7* carried the first Advanced Very High Resolution Radiometer (AVHRR) into space, on behalf of the US National Oceanic and Atmospheric Administration – a rival of NASA often called 'the other space agency'. Despite its name, the resolution of the AVHRR was a measly 1 or 4 kilometres, depending on reception arrangements, as against the 80 metres of NASA's early *Landsats*. Yet AVHRR did observe in separate red and near infra-red channels, and its designers pointed out these could be used for vegetation studies.

The *NOAA* satellites had one huge advantage. To meet the needs of the meteorologists, they supplied copious and cheap data from every part of the Earth every day. Using AVHRR was therefore like holding a bucket under a gushing fire-hydrant. Jim Tucker made first a crusade and then a science of applying AVHRR to continent-wide observations of vegetation. When critics complained about the poor resolution, Tucker said, 'I want to do the whole world.'

In 1980, Tucker teamed up with a British geographer, John Townshend of Reading, to proclaim the virtues of AVHRR. They noted that the weather satellites' high frequency of observation was the best way of beating the weather. *Landsat* users could easily fail for a year or two to see a required piece of land, if it happened to be cloudy at each infrequent pass of the satellite. AVHRR promised continent-wide observations of vegetation month by month. Tucker persuaded Goddard's director to back him. In 1982 a research group was created, spelt GIMMS to look official, but pronounced Jim's.

The first complete portrait of a living continent painted with AVHRR was for Africa. When Tucker and Townshend mapped the vegetation index, season by season, they were able to distinguish broad areas of rain forest, grassland and so on, by the density of vegetation and its seasonal behaviour. They quickly produced a continent-wide image of vegetation zones similar to maps generated in a century of exploration by biologists and geographers. But the satellite saw real-time changes that ground-based teams could never chart. It observed effects of climate fluctuations and manmade alterations to plant cover.

This use of weather satellites for vegetation monitoring marks a U-turn, away from excessive reliance on satellites of the *Landsat* type. Consider the desert-locust application described in an earlier chapter. As soon as the first *Landsat* flew, in 1972, locust experts at the Centre for Overseas Pest Research in London tested its images as an aid to spotting vegetation in the Arabian Desert. The UN Food and Agriculture Organization (FAO) was impressed enough to pursue the possibilities of remote sensing for locust control as well as for early warnings of harvest losses due to drought, with famine-prone Africa as the prime theatre for both objectives.

Landsat images proved their worth for examining locust lairs and desert blooms in detail, and FAO still uses them for that purpose, together with images from the Japanese *MOS-1* satellite. But to cover the huge recession area of the desert locust would require detailed analysis of 700 *Landsat* scenes twice a month, with masses of information in each scene irrelevant to vegetation. Something was wrong with an instinctive belief of many remote-sensing specialists that the sharper the images, the better.

99

Jelle Hielkema, the Dutchman leading the remote-sensing work at FAO, heard about Tucker's use of AVHRR, on a scale so coarse that seven orbits of a NOAA satellite would scan the entire desert-locust recession area. Hielkema at once teamed up with Tucker to raid the tape archives and look with hindsight at the AVHRR view of vegetation in West Africa before a locust upsurge in 1980–81. They saw a telltale strip of vegetation 50 kilometres long in the locust-breeding zone of northeast Mali, precisely where the upsurge began in June 1980.

If the vegetation index from AVHRR did no more than paint unprecedented portraits of Africa and other continents adorned with plants, and reveal the broad changes from season to season and year to year, it would count as an astonishing innovation. Yet that was only a start. The vegetation index turned out to be a prime measure of the influence of plants in the Earth system.

This was far from clear in the early days. Some experts hoped that the vegetation index might measure biomass, the weight of plant tissue present in an area, but that was obviously wrong because forests disappeared out of season. Tucker was sure he was seeing chlorophyll, but in just what sense remained hazy until the observation of plants from space fused with efforts by others to make computer models of vegetation in action.

Beer is better for the progress of science than any amount of bureaucratic planning. In 1983, at a party, Jim Tucker met a young British scientist called Piers Sellers. Although working only a few kilometres apart, they were quite unaware of each other's existence. Sellers was enthralled by Tucker's vegetation images, and Tucker gathered that Sellers could help to settle the persistent arguments about what the images really meant.

While learning ecology at Edinburgh University, Sellers had grown impatient with its strategy of describing life in small patches and immense detail. Like Tucker, he wanted a broader view. At the school of geography at Leeds University, he worked on a regional scale, seeing how vegetation, rainfall and runoff interacted in river valleys. *Landsat* images came his way, but they showed the same accidental detail that Sellers had fled in ecology. All the while, he was learning physics from books. Computer models seemed the high road to global studies and, when Tucker met him, Sellers was modelling the interplay between vegetation and the weather, at the University of Maryland.

Facing:
The growth of plants on all the lands of Spaceship Earth, observed by satellite during the northern summer (top) and winter (below). The vegetation index confirms the stark seasonal contrasts. Each year, the north's abundant summer growth temporarily reduces the level of carbon dioxide in the atmosphere.

NOAA SATELLITE DATA, INTERPRETED AT NASA GSFC, USA

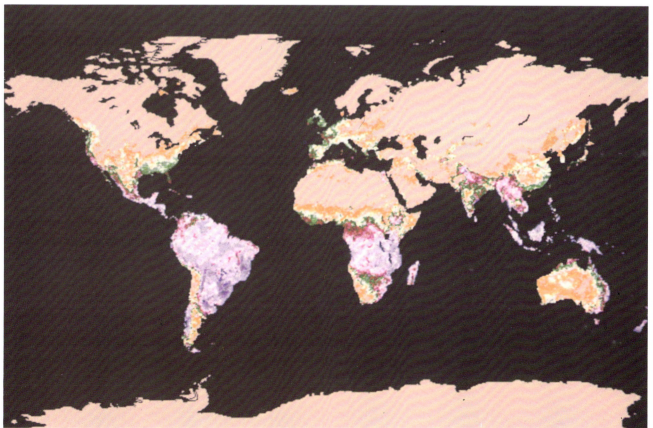

Landscapes by numbers

*T*HAT MATHEMATICAL physics can describe the wonders of a living landscape is not an easy idea to accept. The imagination flounders at first among geometric trees and algebraic herbs. But anyone indignant about science trampling the primrose into algorithmic mud should pause to compare two descriptions of a verdant scene.

> Ye valleys low where the mild whispers use,
> Of shades and wanton winds, and gushing brooks,
> On whose fresh lap the swart Star sparely looks,
> Throw hither all your quaint enameled eyes,
> That on the green turf suck the honeyed showers,
> And purple all the ground with vernal flowers.

John Milton, Lycidas, 1637

$$E_{d_i} = \frac{D_i}{z_d} \left(\frac{\psi_i - \psi_l - z_T}{\overline{r_{\text{plant}}} + \overline{r_{\text{soil}}}} \right) \rho_w$$

P. Sellers et al., 'A Simple Biosphere Model', 1985

As the only equation in the book, this should be seen as a picture of sorts. It matches a line of the poem and tells how plants in the green turf suck the honeyed showers. Its metaphor is of the form 'current equals voltage divided by resistance', though to decode it fully would be as officious as construing Milton's swart Star. Other mathematics proclaims the shady architecture of plants, and describes light filtering through forest foliage.

With 105 equations, Piers Sellers and his colleagues in Maryland 'let the vegetation determine the ways in which the land surface interacts with the atmosphere'. Their Simple Biosphere Model takes in conventional weather data and computes changes in leaf temperatures, the rain and dew wetting the leaves, and the wetness of various layers of soil.

By colouring the land, plants increase the local intake of solar energy. They act as brakes on the wind, and by fanning the air they promote the transfer of heat and moisture from the land surface to the air. Plants intervene in the transfer of water from rain to soil, and their shade reduces evaporation from the soil. On the other hand, plants consume water and expel water vapour through their leaves. This floral sigh, called transpiration, adds moisture and latent energy to the air, for making clouds and driving 'wanton winds'.

Leaves open or close their pores in response to the prevailing conditions. The pores (stomata) let in air carrying the carbon dioxide needed for growth, and let water vapour escape. Plants can, though, hold their breath by closing the pores. During droughts they forego growth in order to conserve water. Even in normal circumstances, plants do most of their growing in the morning and rest in the afternoon, when the air is drier and water loss would accelerate. Equations in the Simple Biosphere Model express the natural control of transpiration as a variable resistance to the passage of water.

The model copes with anything from Arctic shrubs to tropical forest. The American geographer A.W. Kuchler had defined thirty-two different vegetation regions in the world. The Maryland modellers found they could match thirty-one of them by combinations of just three entities: bare soil, ground cover of grass and herbs, and a canopy of shrubs or trees. And as the model deals as readily with farms and other manmade landscapes as with wild vegetation, it takes the human factor in its stride.

Howls of protest greeted the Simple Biosphere Model, when it was published in 1986. 'Far too complicated!' the meteorologists said, while ecologists called it 'a crass oversimplification', so Sellers and his colleagues thought it might be about right. The Japan Meteorological Service became the first to incorporate the model into routine computations. Meanwhile, Sellers had thrown in his lot with Jim Tucker.

The planet breathes

THE SATELLITES watch the grass growing. Piers Sellers' model tracks the same interactions between the living landscape and visible and infra-red photons that figure in the space observers' vegetation index. He showed Jim Tucker a theoretical proof that the index tells far more about life on Spaceship Earth than anyone had a right to expect. The chain of reasoning has five steps.

1. The vegetation index is related to the amount of radiation absorbed by the plants for the process of photosynthesis.

2. In a sense, it is related to the amount of chlorophyll exposed to daylight, which plants use for their growth.

3. The amount of active chlorophyll is a good measure of the rate of growth of plants.

4. The vegetation index is therefore also a measure of the rate at which plants take in carbon dioxide needed for growth.

5. Because a leaf cannot take in carbon dioxide without losing water, the vegetation index measures transpiration too.

Scientific papers by Sellers and Tucker explained all this in convincing mathematical forms. But a botanist might be puzzled especially by the boldest step, number 3. No plant can grow without chlorophyll, to be sure, but it does not use it non-stop, either. What about the resting of plants in the afternoon? What about the shutdown during a drought? A gentle answer is that any local variations in plant behaviour could be handled by tweaking a few numbers in Sellers' equations. A more strident answer is that local details scarcely matter. All plant communities at all places and all times use their chorophyll to much the same overall effect.

Swift confirmation that the vegetation index is a universal measure of plant growth came when Tucker calculated the average vegetation index across all the Earth's land masses, and its variations from month to month. The number doubles from January to July, when the large land masses of the Northern Hemisphere reach the peak of their growing season. A corresponding fall occurs in the amount of carbon dioxide in the Earth's atmosphere, because the growing plants gobble it up.

The seasonal variation in carbon dioxide had been known for more than 20 years. An observatory on Hawaii first saw the whole world breathing, when Charles Keeling instituted the first long-term watch on the world's carbon dioxide. The measurements showed an inexorable rise from year to year, but equally striking was the rise and fall in carbon dioxide each year, in obedience to the seasonal cycle of those dominant plants of the Northern Hemisphere. Later, a global network of carbon-dioxide sampling stations saw the same phenomena at many out-of-the-way places including the South Pole.

Tucker joined forces with carbon-dioxide watchers and found a good match with the global vegetation index, especially when they allowed a month's delay for the effects of vegetation on carbon dioxide to make themselves felt at the remote sampling sites. This result was strong evidence that the vegetation index was essentially measuring plant growth, with plants behaving alike, at least in their continent-wide averages. The differences in character between, say, tropical grasslands and northern forests, seemed irrelevant to the overall reckoning.

That left the link between the vegetation index and transpiration.

104

This could be tested only in an experiment on 'land surface climatology', along with other uses of remote-sensing satellites to observe the interactions of vegetation and the weather, in line with the needs of weather forecasters and climate modellers. That was why, in the late 1980s, the cowboys of Kansas found themselves in the midst of a science rodeo.

The FIFE experiment

MOST OF THE tallgrass prairie of the USA yielded to the plough long ago, but a pocket remains in the Flint Hills of Kansas, too uneven and stony for convenient farming. Nature, too, would abolish the prairie if it could. Had the Amerindians not burned it regularly to maintain a happy hunting ground thick with herds of buffalo (bison), the land would be forested. The tallgrass prairie is another of the world's 'wildernesses' that turn out on investigation to be human handiwork. The present incumbents, the cow-and-calf ranchers, continue to put the prairie to the torch.

So do the scientists of Kansas State University who manage Konza Prairie, a reserve within the Flint Hills. It figures both in the US National Science Foundation's network of sites for long-term ecological research, and in a worldwide network of special reserves designated by UNESCO. The presence of this strong scientific base drew NASA scientists to the Flint Hills for the FIFE experiment, a major field study of the interactions between plants and the weather, as observable from space.

It took place in 1987 and 1989. FIFE is a 'second-order' acronym in which FFE stands for First Field Experiment and the I means International Satellite Land Surface Climatology Project. In charge of the multimillion-dollar effort were Forrest Hall, a physicist at the Goddard Space Flight Center, and Piers Sellers. At NASA headquarters, a former astronomer Robert Murphy had strongly backed Jim Tucker's vegetation work and, when Sellers first sketched FIFE to him in the early 1980s, over a beer, he became the project's godfather.

Bridging different geographical scales was the essence of the task. At one extreme, weather systems straddle continents and the weather and climate models work with grid points about 200 kilometres apart. At the other extreme, a plant's interaction with the air occurs in leaf structures that need a microscope to see them. In between, satellites observe pixels ranging from tens of metres to kilometres in width.

Nature itself is a great averager. The wind blowing across the landscape scoops up influences of clumps of vegetation and patches of bare soil and feeds them indifferently into the global circulation of the atmosphere. So it is entirely reasonable to ask what the average density of vegetation, wind speed, cloud cover or rainfall over any area may be. But a deep understanding of the processes is needed to make a human reckoning of those averages accurate and meaningful.

Never before were so many satellite images collected for the study of one small piece of the Earth's surface: thousands from the *GOES* and *NOAA* weather satellites, and dozens from *Landsat* and *SPOT*. FIFE compared what the satellites saw with close-up measurements using instruments at ground level and in aircraft. By 1989, the fleet of research aircraft numbered eight. One came from Canada, and a NASA C-130 carried instruments from the Soviet Union.

Over an area 15 kilometres square, including the Konza Prairie reserve and adjoining ranches, the scientists scattered weather stations like confetti. Several times a day, weather balloons probed the upper air, while a laser beam scanned the atmosphere over the prairie, watching blobs of warm, moist air rising like invisible smoke to build clouds. Konza's hydrological stations measured stream flows.

Activity rose to a peak whenever a *NOAA* satellite passed overhead on a clear day. During a typical pass, the C-130 would be looking down from 5000 metres with its own array of remote-sensing instruments, while a helicopter would be doing the same, hovering at 300 metres. A small research aircraft with an elongated nose would sweep by at 150 metres, during the satellite pass, its instruments sniffing for puffs.

The prairie acts as a large leaf, drawing down carbon dioxide from the air, and releasing water vapour. These 'fluxes' move in turbulent puffs, as parcels of warm, moist air rise from the prairie, and downgoing puffs replenish the carbon dioxide. In 1987, the aircraft failed to register all the flows of water vapour, carbon dioxide and heat, as measured near the ground. As FIFE '89 confirmed, they were missing some big, slow puffs that carry a disproportionate share of the fluxes.

The prairie's input of water vapour into the atmosphere links to the vegetation index observed from space even better than expected. Apart from being a direct sign of the vitality of the vegetation and therefore of its likely throughput of transpired moisture from soil to air, the

Facing:
Homing on the range. A small region of Kansas prairie is seen by weather-satellite data coded red for vegetation. Successive images enlarge the scene of the FIFE experiment, which tested plant–weather interactions and their observability from space. The experimental area included the Konza Prairie, a reserve just south of the city of Manhattan. In the last image the pixels, about 1 kilometre wide, illustrate the typical resolution of a weather satellite. The yellow marks show some of the experimental sites on the ground.

106

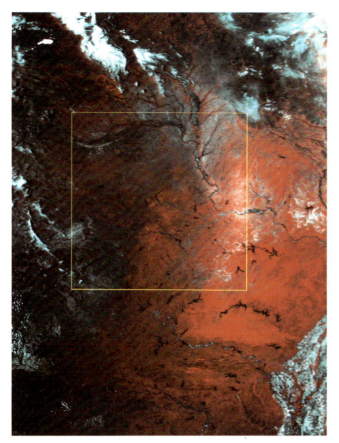
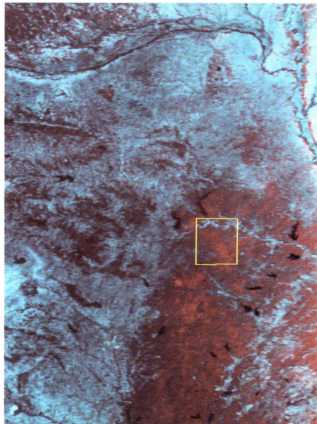
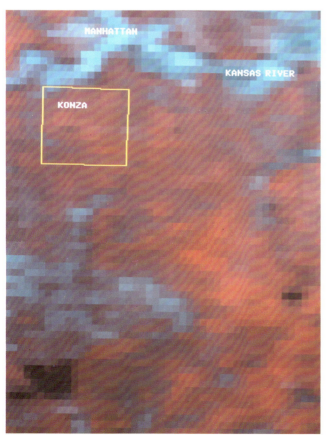

MANHATTAN

KANSAS RIVER

KONZA

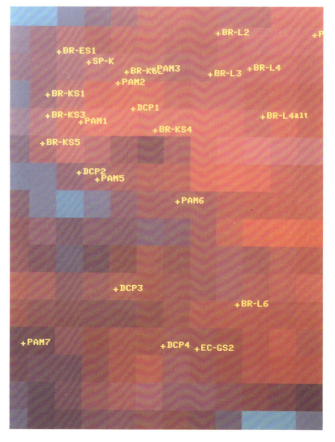

+BR-L2

+P

+BR-ES1

+SP-K

+BR-K6 +PAM3   +BR-L3   +BR-L4

+PAM2

+BR-KS1

+DCP1

+BR-KS3   +BR-L4alt
+PAM1

+BR-KS4

+BR-KS5

+DCP2
+PAM5

+PAM6

+DCP3

+BR-L6

+PAM7   +DCP4 +EC-GS2

Airborne observations of prairie vegetation, coded red, from June (top) through August to October. Note the persistence in tree-lined river valleys.

vegetation index is an indirect guide to soil moisture. The grass wilts in dry soil and flourishes in wet. So the direct evaporation from the soil into the air is yet another item linked to the vegetation index. And the input of water into the atmosphere follows so predictable a course from hour to hour that an observation at any one time during the day will tell you the rest.

As a matter of local interest, the burnt parts of the prairie showed a much higher vegetation index at the end of May than the unburnt parts, as the new shoots grew vigorously. The unburnt areas caught up, by the end of June, but their peak growing period lasted only 25 days, compared with 50 days for the burnt areas. The Amerindians were smart, in using fire to create and maintain the tallgrass prairie.

Strictly speaking, the FIFE results apply only to the prairie of eastern Kansas. 'Other places are different,' Sellers says, 'but not that different.' After FIFE, the International Satellite Land Surface Climatology Project aims to carry out experiments on plant–air interactions in other climatic settings. With self-assurance gained in Kansas, the scientists can plan simpler enterprises, using fewer ground stations and aircraft. On the desert margin of Niger in West Africa an experiment called HAPEX-II/SAHEL is set for 1992, with a major contribution from the French. Alberta in Canada will host a FIFE-like study of northern forests in 1993. Tropical forests and Arctic tundra will have similar treatment later.

'It really is a miracle!' Sellers commented to the author. He meant, not the scientific successes of the Goddard group, but the vegetation index as a botanical fact. No one has been able to think of any physical or evolutionary reason why pine needles, maize leaves and cactuses should all be reliably shiny in the near infra-red, and in such a strict proportion compared with red light that estimates of plant growth and transpiration are possible. Without that convenience on the part of Nature, the vegetation index would not work. The 10-year surge in science, from the launch of the first AVHRR instrument to the completion of FIFE, could not have occurred. Without the vegetation index, there would have been no transformation of the global geography of vegetation, from static maps of what grows where to a dynamic movie of a living planet seen from space.

T HE FRENCH *SPOT* and the American *Landsat* and *NOAA* satellites examine the farms of Western Europe in the MARS project that monitors agriculture by remote sensing. What grows where, and how much of it? Remote-sensing specialists of the European Community's Joint Research Centre (JRC) at Ispra in northern Italy coordinate the MARS project, initiated in 1987.

In a fertile continent with high-tech farming that always threatens to produce embarrassing gluts, the Common Agricultural Policy is meant to share crop-growing and animal-rearing fairly among the twelve member states of the Community, while using subsidies to maintain living standards for farmers and rural areas. Hitherto, they had to rely on agricultural statistics gathered by twelve governments, with variations in method, reliability and speed of delivery. There are also problems of fraud, and air surveys of olive trees, for example, are meant to discourage growers from misreporting tree counts.

One task of MARS is to make an annual inventory of the allocations of land to various crops. *SPOT*'s high resolution is best for delineating the rather small fields of Western Europe, while the greater number of infra-red bands makes *Landsat* better for distinguishing the crops. Pilot studies in France, Germany, Greece, Italy and Spain have tested the methods by comparing the space data with air photos and field-by-field verification of crop types on the ground. In one area, in the Loire valley southeast of Paris, identifications from *Landsat* data have been excellent for sunflower, rape and maize, quite good for vines and wheat, and poorer for barley and grass.

The MARS project also designates a grid of fifty patches, each 40 kilometres square, distributed across the Community countries. These are for rapid sampling across Europe using *SPOT* and *Landsat* to give an overall impression of areas allocated to the main crops, and their likely yields. Pilot studies are confined to a few of the sites in the early years. For comprehensive monitoring of the state of Europe's crops and predictions of yields, the MARS project uses low-resolution vegetation indices from the *NOAA* satellite data. A geographic information system supplies data on the physical and agronomic characteristics of Europe's farming areas. The observations of vegetation from space interact with computer models that predict crop growth.

Dutch scientists showed how to calculate the spreading of roots, the budding of new shoots, the increase in leaf area available to trap sunlight, or the filling of grain at the culmination of growth. The models emphasize factors limiting growth, with seasonal day-length the critical factor in Europe. Simplified versions for MARS apply the broad principles of such models to tracking crop interactions with the weather during the growing season. From the start of the season onwards, the growth models predict eventual crop yields on the basis of actual weather experienced so far and average conditions expected until harvest time. Peculiar weather may make a model erratic, but the current vegetation index can put it back on track.

Taking out the forests

MODERN FORESTRY and the scientific study of forests go hand-in-hand. In the northeastern USA, for example, the US Forest Service has made available to university scientists a tract of forest called Hubbard Brook, in the White Mountains of New Hampshire. The National Science Foundation has earmarked it as another of its special sites for long-term ecological research. Here, in the past few decades, details and principles of forest ecology have emerged from intensive studies.

Air photos show a row of small drainage areas, here called watersheds, that discharge their runoff of water in small streams leading down to the brook that gives the experimental forest its name. They define independent blocks of forest that scientists can modify experimentally by different felling regimes. In one watershed, for example, you can see forest left to Nature, where the toppling of trees creates holes in the soil in a natural mode of ploughing. In another, the scientists simulated a hurricane by felling all the trees and leaving them lying, to watch for a quarter of a century how opportunistic shrubs and trees spring up in the aftermath until the dominant species gradually reassert themselves.

Analysis of the stream-water tells a chemical story of what happens in each regime. A granite base to the forest prevents seepage, and allows the scientists to elucidate the workings of the forest as a chemical machine, and comment on the effects of commercial-style operations. The water is the forest's bloodstream, by which it exploits the energy of sunshine and the nutrients of the soil, to make trees. When trees are removed, the runoff increases, and excess nitrates in the water show that microorganisms in the soil are busy fixing new nitrogen from the air to make good the losses. Calcium is harder to replace. This element, used in building bark, has to come from the slow weathering of mineral grains in the soil.

Increasingly, computer models and large-scale geographic information systems help to illuminate the researches at Hubbard Brook. Hundreds of scientific papers on a small area of forest carry the word to forest ecologists worldwide, and boost fashionable studies in geochemical cycles in the Earth system. Effects of acid rain due to air pollution can be diagnosed. The forest managers of the US government and private industry too can drink deep from Hubbard Brook.

None of that solves a problem in human ecology very close to the experimental forest. A highway from Boston brings the vacationers in droves. At New Hampshire's resorts, trees fall to make ski runs and space for second homes for the city dwellers – who wish so dearly to enjoy the White Mountains, they threaten to spoil them. At a time when everyone is lamenting the large-scale destruction of tropical

Research on the northern hardwood forest at Hubbard Brook (above) focuses on the runoff. A data system (below) details the topography. The transfer of contours to a triangulated network allows individual gullies to be represented in perspective form and by steepness.

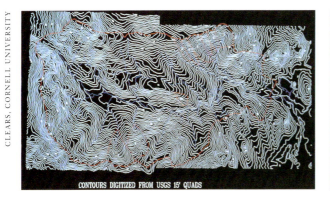

CONTOURS DIGITIZED FROM USGS 15' QUADS

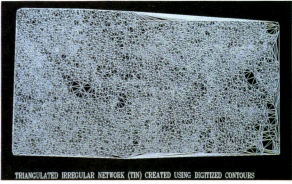

TRIANGULATED IRREGULAR NETWORK (TIN) CREATED USING DIGITIZED CONTOURS

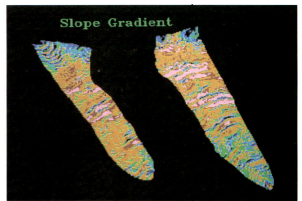

Slope Gradient

forests, it is only fair to ask: 'And what became of the forests that formerly clad Europe and colonial America?' The frontiersman who 'tamed the wilderness' to make it fit for cows and ploughs is an American folk-hero.

Nature itself is a great destroyer of forests. That must be part of any balanced view of the current crisis in the forests. Hurricanes, natural forest fires, volcanic eruptions, landslides and salt-water floods all exact a toll. Advancing glaciers make powerful bulldozers, and during ice ages, which are the climatic norm for the present stage of geological time, huge areas presently forested in Eurasia and North America disappear under ice sheets or become frigid deserts.

Human activities may now be affecting the world's forests more severely and rapidly than ever before, and remote-sensing satellites bear witness to the destruction. When the government of Finland quietly cleared large tracts of the state forests for ready cash, a remote-sensing expert Mikko Punkari unleashed a national scandal when he spotted the large-scale clearcutting in *Landsat* images.

In Germany the outcry at the decline of the Black Forest and other beloved playgrounds concerns not reckless felling, but poisoning by air pollution. Conifers on high mountain slopes are especially vulnerable. Satellite images can just about discern the damage, though it is better mapped from the air or the ground. Damage to trees by air pollution is a Europe-wide problem, and a map prepared for the UN is a grim document. Computer models at the International Institute of Applied Systems Analysis in Austria predict future levels of pollutants in Europe's air, and show how high a hill Europe has to climb, before its forests are safe again.

Umpires in space

*I*N THE TROPICAL forests, an acceleration in clearances during the 1970s and 1980s coincided with the appearance of remote-sensing satellites capable of observing them. Cleared areas are often conspicuous in large-scale images, either as rectangular blocks or as tree-like branches off main highways through the forest. A remote-sensing team at the Space Research Institute of Brazil (INPE) was quick to apply early *Landsat* images to assess recent deforestation throughout 'Legal Amazonia', an area defined in 1953, which is mainly forested but in-

112

cludes some savanna on its edges. The Brazilian team established a baseline for 1975, according to which 0.6 per cent of the area was deforested, not counting some very old areas of clearance associated with settlements going back to the colonial era.

During the 1980s Brazil found itself at war on two fronts. At home, the government tried to moderate the rate of clearances in the Amazonian forest, and police a frontier region as gun-happy as the old Wild West of the USA. Internationally, they had to deal with a rising chorus of criticism about the rate at which the forest was disappearing. In 1982, on the basis of INPE's figures, predictions by an American scientist P. M. Fearnside amounted to a forecast that 44 per cent of the Amazonian forest would be lost by 1988.

The Brazilians greeted such estimates with frank disbelief. There then followed a contest between calculation and remote sensing to try to establish the true facts. In 1988, Jim Tucker of NASA and Jean-Paul Malingreau at Ispra published estimates of percentage of land deforested in two parts of the Amazon basin, based on surface temperatures measured by the *NOAA* satellites up to September 1985. In an infra-red channel, cleared patches appear warmer than the surrounding forest because the cooling effect of transpiration has been lost. Manmade and natural forest fires show up as hotspots.

For the State of Acre, the Malingreau–Tucker figure was 3.45 per cent deforested, and 11.38 per cent for the State of Rondonia, where more than half the deforestation occurred between 1982 and 1985, according to the space data. The areas of 'disturbed' forest were much larger than the deforested area. And very high levels of deforestation were evident in the State of Mato Grosso, only part of which includes Amazonian forest.

In 1989, the World Bank published estimates indicating that 12 per cent of Legal Amazonia was already deforested by 1988. This was based on calculations from the state of affairs in 1980. By this time the Brazilians were growing very angry. Although the figure was far less than the Fearnside estimate, the fact that it came from the World Bank ensured it a place in international environmental folklore. The Brazilians appealed again to the umpires in space: the unblinking instruments of the remote-sensing satellites.

At INPE, Roberto Pereira da Cunha decided to make a 'wall-to-wall' assessment of the deforestation in Legal Amazonia. As he remarked, 'No one wants to do the dirty work of gathering the data. It is a very trivial task for scientists.' Trivial, but not unlaborious. Pereira's team assembled 234 *Landsat* scenes, and selected for close interpretation 101 images that showed evidence of deforestation. From colour composites of three wavelength bands the scientists outlined the deforested patches, and used a grid to measure their areas. Images for different years established rates of deforestation.

The most important conclusion was that there was no acceleration: deforestation was proceeding at a more or less steady rate. As for the total recent deforestation up till the end of 1988, INPE's answer was 5 per cent of the area of Legal Amazonia. Meanwhile, Fearnside had changed his forecast. His new figures indicated 7 per cent deforestation of Legal Amazonia by 1989 – a far cry from his 44 per cent figure of just 7 years earlier, and almost in line with INPE's figure. In 1990 Jim Tucker and Chris Justice of NASA broadly confirmed the Brazilian result by a similar large-scale use of *Landsat* imagery, but with a different technique, using only a single infra-red channel.

Climate modellers have looked at possible effects of deforestation on the regional climate. A saying 'The rain forest makes the rain' accords with meteorological theory, because transpiration from the trees vigorously recycles the available water. On the south coast of West Africa, ships run aground in the estuaries of the great rivers where the outflows are no longer enough to scour the seabed, perhaps because of the severe deforestation along the coast. Climate models testing the consequences of total deforestation in the Amazon basin have given variable results. Recent runs, including one using the vegetation–climate interaction model, suggest that rainfall in the area might decline to a level where the rain forest could not recover.

To deplore tropical deforestation without attempting to understand why it happens can smack of telling a drowning man to stop swimming because he is disturbing the fish. The tropical countries affected are drowning in international banking debts incurred in that very recent era when international opinion favoured development as rapid as possible, and environmental protection and financial caution were unfashionable.

Tropical hardwoods fetch good prices, and in the late 1980s the northern part of the island of Borneo was virtually mined for logs for the Japanese market (more than 10 million tons in 1987). Elsewhere, plantations replace the native trees with stands of profitable teak, rubber, oil palms and the like. Other forest areas disappear for the sake of

Manmade fires in the Amazon forest, seen from space.

Facing:
Brazilian study of huge inroads into a piece of forest, coded red, between 1973 (top) and 1987 (below).

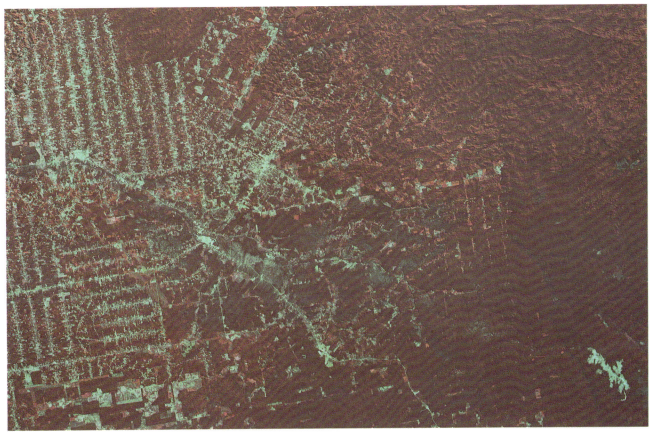

mineral extraction, charcoal production, ranching, plantations, and transport systems.

For families drowning in poverty, slash-and-burn cultivation, a farming technique of last resort, involves clearing a patch of forest, growing some crops and then moving on to let the forest regenerate. But more conventional farming practices aim at permanent conversion of forests to fields. These make the biggest inroads into the tropical forests, and the environment is likely to suffer more if they fail than if they succeed. Their prospects have to be judged case by case.

On the very edge of the Amazon Basin, in Bolivia, a zone of tropical forest somewhat drier than the rain forest is the scene of that country's most vigorous development. From the boom city of Santa Cruz a road and railway run eastwards towards the Brazilian border. Alongside them, and plainly visible from the air or from space, are large rectangles where the pioneers have carved new farms out of the forest. They are neither brash developers nor bewildered beggars, but diligent farmers, some of whom immigrated from distant lands to make a new life in the wide acres of 'underdeveloped' Bolivia. Soya is a prime cash crop.

In 1989 a Bolivian remote-sensing company, CUMAT, completed an environmental study of the area, using *Landsat* and *SPOT* images combined with field surveys. The possibility of mishap appears all too clearly in dunes made from dry, windswept soil in a district south of Santa Cruz city, which is also beset by unwonted floods and pollution by pesticides. The World Bank, which had been criticized about its role in deforestation, commissioned the study before deciding whether to back further agricultural and industrial development east of Santa Cruz. It deputed CUMAT to be its conscience, to see whether the farms in the forest should be encouraged.

'Yes, but . . . ' was the answer. Don't farm south of a line drawn on CUMAT's computer mapping system – the soil will be too dry. Even north of it, don't neglect the need for windbreaks to prevent soil blowing away. And don't be too single-minded about soya: vary the crops and rotate them, and apply fertilizers as necessary. The prescriptions do not treat the forest itself as inviolate, but try to help the farming match its setting well enough to prosper indefinitely.

The verdict from space on exaggerated predictions about the rate of loss of the Amazon forest prompts a cool look at a related matter: the extermination of species of animals and plants that accompanies deforestation. Whenever botanists and zoologists carefully examine

Facing:
Brazil's province of Pará seen in one of the mosaics of Landsat images made by NASA scientists to assess overall disturbance of the Amazon rain forest. Large areas of clearances appear in white, but even larger areas are mainly intact (dark grey). The Amazon River appears black. The compilation of 1990 uses 1988 Landsat data for a single infra-red channel. Each of the individual images is nearly 200 kilometres wide.

117

pieces of a rain forest, they soon discover many species previously unknown to science. But high rates of species loss, reckoned in species per day or per hour by some biologists, are based on guesswork. They assume that there are some millions of species, far more than the total number of species in the world so far catalogued (around 1.6 million). A further assumption is that most species occupy small areas, so that any destruction of any part of the rain forest wipes out entire species. Finally, high estimates for the rate of forest destruction are used to arrive at pessimistic figures.

What is often lacking from public pronouncements on the loss of rain-forest species is any perspective on Nature's own, highly creative vandalism. In forests left untouched by human beings and undisturbed by hurricanes and natural forest fires, 'biodiversity' diminishes with the passage of time. The number of species present declines of its own accord, because some species prevail over others. Natural disasters give the former diversity the opportunity to reappear. And dozens of episodes of severe deforestation, associated with the ice ages of the past few million years, created the present diversity of rain-forest species.

The repeated reduction of forests to small enclaves by volcanic eruptions is responsible for the enormous numbers of unique species found in Hawaii. Animals cut off from their kin evolve so freely and so fast that biologists can track changes in the DNA of the genes, from one forest pocket to another. Drastic changes of climate have had a similar effect in rain forests around the world. Only 20,000 years ago, in the coldest and driest phase of the most recent ice age, the planet's stock of true rain forest was far smaller than now, despite the undoubted depredations of recent human activity. The surviving species of the rain forests were all huddled in a few isolated refuges. Zoologists have traced the particular refuges occupied by certain lizards, birds and butterflies in the Amazon region at that time. So far from any mass extinction resulting, the refuges were species-factories.

Human action on the tropical forests probably is extinguishing many unidentified species, especially among those that Nature has already marginalized to the verge of extinction. But the same damage no doubt gives fresh opportunities to other species and perhaps even acts as midwife for new species. In any case, a new ice age is due to begin during the next 1000 years or so. Left to itself, Nature will wipe out huge tracts of forest and many expendable species, and allow new ones to evolve.

To query deforestation rates and the assessment of species loss is not

118

to condone any mindless misuse of tropical forests. But objective experts, including Ghillean Prance of London's Kew Gardens, see the gap between destruction and conservation narrowing at last, at least in Brazil. It is high time to refocus concern on the human beings.

Those who suffer amid the current depredations on the tropical forests include dispossessed forest tribes, poor peasants trying to scratch a living from often unsuitable soil, and would-be agroforesters who see immense natural resources being ignored if not laid waste. Many have already perished as a result of manmade changes in the forests and the gun law that sometimes enforces them. The survivors want a little room in the forests to live out their lives and perhaps do better for themselves. If scientists and environmentalists in other countries are to comment, they had better be sure of their facts and theories, and not play polemical games with other people's lives.

The myth of the marching Sahara

*T*HE BRAZILIAN forest was not the first place where remote-sensing satellites had to correct far-fetched assertions about rates of change. 'Desertification' was a term bandied about by world-watchers at the end of the 1970s as much as 'tropical deforestation' 10 years later. A widespread belief among some scientists and many environmental pressure groups was that the terrible droughts afflicting Africa were linked to an inexorable southward march of the Sahara Desert. There was even a number set against this phenomenon. The desert was said to be advancing at 5 or 6 kilometres a year.

A grim meteorological scenario described a self-sustaining mechanism of desert-making. Bare ground absorbs less sunlight than grassy or wooded land, and so releases less heat into the air. For want of updrafts to encourage cloud formation and rain, newly denuded land can be expected to remain bare, and so become an extension of the desert. Such reasoning encouraged the idea of an advance of the Sahara, and predictions that huge areas of Africa, including one or two entire nations, would be barely habitable by the end of the 20th Century.

The verdict of the space observations was that the marching desert was a myth. The vegetation-index images of Africa generated by Jim Tucker's group at Goddard, from *NOAA* satellite data, almost settled the issue by the mid-1980s. They showed an apparent southward shift

119

of the desert margin in the drought years of 1983–84, with a huge belt across Africa depleted of vegetation. But in 1985, when the rains were much better, the vegetation returned at once to the denuded areas. Indeed, by generating an image of Africa showing the difference between the vegetation from 1984 to 1985, the Goddard scientists delineated Africa's problem zone called the Sahel in a strikingly simple way. The image conveys the salient fact that the characteristic of the

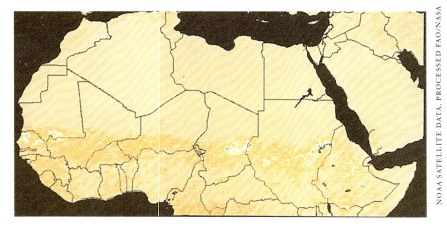

The variability of vegetation at the southern edge of the Sahara desert picks out the Sahel as a drought-prone zone of erratic rainfall. To make this image, scientists subtracted 1984 vegetation data from those of 1985, a better year.

NOAA SATELLITE DATA, PROCESSED FAO/NASA

Sahel is not so much its low rainfall as its highly variable rainfall.

There was nothing imaginary about the long succession of droughts that afflicted Africa in the 1970s and 1980s. Babies with limbs as thin as pencils, amid the skeletons of dead herds: television conveyed the agony of mass hunger all too vividly. The harrowing events lent urgency to using the vegetation index in FAO's operational Artemis system, monitoring Africa for 'food security' planning as well as locust-hunting. The famines also forced experts to think more clearly about the causes and consequences.

Incursions of a southwest monsoon from June to October brings rain to the Sahel of West Africa. Travel northwards from, say, the coastal lagoons of the Ivory Coast into Mali and you will pass through a succession of zones: tropical forest, a cultivated forest zone, open savanna with scattered trees, the Sahel with baobabs, mimosas and other drought-resistant trees and shrubs, and finally the desert. These zones merge into one another, and the mean yearly rainfall diminishes from 1900 millimetres near the coast to less than 200 millimetres in the Sahara. The Sahel has 500 to 200 millimetres, but these averages conceal the variability in the monsoons from year to year.

In the early 1980s, Dutch scientists combined their powerful crop-growth computer models with field studies of herding and farming in Mali. They concluded that the real problem zone was not at the desert's edge or in the Sahel proper, but on the edge of the better-watered zone, at the 500-millimetre rainfall line. And here the limiting factor in plant growth is not the variable rain, but a lack of nitrogen and phosphorus in the soil. Plant growth could be five times greater before the variable rainfall would make much difference.

The scientists have put a big question mark against policies that favour the settled farmer against the wandering herder. When the rains come to the drier areas, the livestock of free-ranging herders forage plants whose protein content is far higher than anything available in the wetter areas. Lasting damage to the land occurs at the 500-millimetre line and southward. Here the herders moving south in the dry season or in a failed wet season, looking for grazing, collide with other people trying to farm and keep cattle in settlements pushed as far north as possible. Overintensive use of land and consequent erosion by wind and water ensue. Even further south, land degradation occurs as a result of promiscuous clearing of trees to grow crops, typically by burning. And here high rainfall is the problem, because it attacks the unprotected ground and washes away the soil.

The forces of Wasteland are not yet mounting a frontal assault on habitable territory along the desert's edge. Instead they wage an insidious guerrilla war far behind the lines, taking out small areas in comparatively well-watered places. Perhaps one day these will grow and merge into a devastated landscape. Meanwhile the task is not to monitor an advancing desert front, but to detect many relatively small areas of degraded land dotting the continents like measles. *Landsat* or SPOT, or remote sensing from the air, are better suited to finding degraded patches than the NOAA satellites are. Many local studies are under way in Africa, notably by remote-sensing specialists from France and the European Community.

'Desertification' turns out to be so slippery a concept that the term might be better avoided. Even so, the fear that much land may be degraded and thrown permanently out of production lies close to the heart of current concerns about global change. Scientists of the UN Environmental Programme resolved to assess 'desertification' worldwide, by 1992. They needed a quick method of finding small wastelands anywhere. For suitable experimental landscapes and the remote-sensing expertise to evaluate them, they looked to East Africa.

121

DESERTIFICATION HAZARD, BARINGO

N ↑

- ☐ None
- ☐ Slight
- ☐ Moderate
- ■ Severe
- ～ Rivers
- — Roads

'Desertification' hazards near Lake Baringo, Kenya, assessed in a space-air-ground study. Hatchings indicate the risk.

Facing:
A Landsat image of Kenya's rift valley shows degraded land near Lake Baringo, top left. The lake itself is discoloured by soil, as compared with the black Lake Bogoria to the south. Well vegetated scarps, red in the image, border the valley.

Degraded land in Kenya

WITHIN THE living memory of the old folk, the grass grew tall beside Lake Baringo in Kenya's rift valley, and you had to watch out for charging rhinos. Scrubby bushes have replaced the grass, and in and around clusters of homesteads in the Njemps Flats south of the lake, large slabs of soil lie brown and bare to the equatorial Sun. Cattle, sheep and goats have so nibbled and trampled the ground that it is smooth enough to parade a regiment.

In the dry season the winds raise dust storms from the barren soil and scatter a choking red-brown powder far and wide, like a cool volcano. Water erosion in the wet season aggravates the degradation of the land. Running water tunnels under the hard surface, through the softer subsoil. When the tunnels collapse gullies form, creating the strangely sculptured barren ground typical of badlands. The streams carry the silt into Lake Baringo, the most beautiful of the rift valley. It has changed colour from blue to ruddy brown, and is becoming shallower.

What has happened in the Baringo area may be fairly typical of local land degradation in many places across Africa and around the planet. Kenya is not in the Sahel, and the climatic setting is different. Nevertheless, in the far north, lack of rain creates a small near-desert in the rift valley, and the rainfall increases southwards. Near Lake Baringo, the herding life of the drier areas runs up against farming.

The UN Environmental Programme chose the Baringo area as one target for its pilot study of rapid methods of assessing and mapping 'desertification' worldwide, by remote-sensing methods. It commissioned the work from the Kenyan government's Department of Resource Survey and Remote Sensing (KREMU). Clues to the rate at which the vegetation had degraded came from comparisons of current aerial surveys with old air photos going back to the time when Kenya was still a British colony. Computer models provided a foil for interpreting, underlining or enhancing data from space and ground surveys.

The models simulated water erosion, wind erosion, the capacity of the rangeland for carrying livestock, degradation of vegetation, and human populations and settlements. The major features identifiable from space were the state of the soil and the state of the vegetation. On summary maps of degraded land and areas at risk, the Njemps Flats, with its large denuded patches, was confirmed as one of the worst-affected places.

KREMU reported at the end of 1989 that remote sensing could indeed identify degraded land and areas at risk. Whether the methods tested at Baringo will successfully meet the needs of the global study of 'desertification' remains to be seen. Meanwhile KREMU's own work continues, as the Kenyans seek to extend the surveys to cover all parts of Kenya at risk.

Here, as with so many other topics and places in Earth-system science, the human factor proved to be at least as important as the physical or biological. Why did the people of Baringo allow some of their lands to become degraded enough to be identifiable from space? And what can be done to put matters right?

Untended flocks are the first oddity that a visitor to Baringo notices, as sheep, goats or cattle browse and wander as freely as their wild herbivorous cousins. Traditionally the children should be minding the animals, but they are at school. Pastoral people whose herds were the prime focus of their cultures now have competing priorities, like education. By tradition, a man was judged rich or poor according to the size of his herds, especially of cattle or camels. Eight cows would buy a wife. A fisherman was by definition very poor, however bountiful his lake.

Mobility was the key to success, when herders moved their animals between desert and semi-desert, and between high ground and low ground, according to the seasons. Fire helped to maintain good grazing. In the 20th Century, British colonists barred the herds from important areas of dry-season grazing. In post-colonial times, the pastoralists found their lands and their lives caught up in arable farming. The herds of cattle dwindled and the once-despised sheep and goats became more important.

'Pastoralists know how to survive, but here changes have been imposed on them and their systems have broken down.' So says Elizabeth Meyerhoff, an anthropologist by training, who lives in the Tugen village of Kampi ya Samaki beside Lake Baringo and works among the local people. She sees them caught up in the thrust towards 'development' from the Kenyan government and international agencies, whereby schooling, health care, irrigation schemes for farming, and so on, are meant to make people settle down.

In the traditionally egalitarian pastoral communities herding was highly organized, whereas now it is lax. The elders who formerly dealt with environmental issues have lost control, as more and more decisions are taken by the government and others. Amid social apathy, the homesteads aggregate into village-like clusters without adequate grazing for the combined herds. Overgrazing thwarts regeneration and the land deteriorates from year to year, over widening areas. Firewood is hard to come by.

Yet with care and skill the new wastelands of the Njemps Flats can become a rain-fed garden. Just beginning to show up in the high-resolution satellite images of Baringo are patches of a healthier colour near the lake. Since 1982 the Baringo Fuel and Fodder Project has won the consent of the villagers to borrow, fence off and replant hundreds of hectares of degraded land. Murray Roberts, who grew up beside Lake Baringo, initiated the project with seeds from his mother's garden.

To trap the rain, create a chessboard of low banks. In each of the enclosures, after rain, plant saplings of fast-growing species from the project's nursery, and sow drought-resistant grasses. Use a solar-powered electric fence to protect the area from domesticated and wild animals. But this is no nature reserve: the trees are meant to be used. Mesquites, for example, from South America provide firewood and timber for construction, and leaves and pods for feeding livestock. Local thorn trees spring up spontaneously on the restored land, with nutritious pods, and their wood serves for making charcoal or beehives. The grass of the reclaimed areas can be used for thatching houses, as well as for fodder.

At first the communities doubted if their badly degraded plots would ever support vegetation again. Now anyone can see the difference between thriving trees and the parade-ground barrens nearby. The project points the way to a possible new way of life: agroforestry. A lush, grass-floored forest of mesquites and acacias can be managed in ways compatible with traditional herding, and with a renewed sense of communal control over the community's life and landscape.

Ecology from space

*T*WO DEFINITIONS. An ecologist means in this context none of the political or sentimental people who usurped the name of a fledgling science before it had even taken wing, but a biologist who examines the complex interplay between plants and animals large and small, and between them and their physical environment. An ecosystem is the theatre where the natural drama unfolds. It may be a pond, a prairie, a

125

forest, or the whole globe. Ecologists count species and populations and trace the flows of energy from the eaten to the eater. They marvel at the adaptations of species to their environments and rejoice in the manifest differences between ecosystems.

Ecologists now have to adjust to the idea that plant communities of all kinds are very similar machines. The computer models of plant–weather interactions and the satellites that sense their growth see them all smoothly slipping into whatever gear suits the local climate and day-to-day weather. For the conventionally-minded, there is worse to come. The vegetation index observed from space is a good guide to the abundance and character of animal life in all wild ecosystems.

To those preoccupied with the dramatic wars and symbioses among highly individualistic species, in the Arctic tundra or the African savanna, this idea may seem as crass as trying to judge a play from an air photo of the theatre. Who dares to generalize about alluring fruits and repellent thorns? Or lump together in a ledger the reptiles, miserly with their food energy, and warm-blooded birds and mammals that squander it like gamblers?

The answer is that mathematically-minded ecologists are finding the plot of the natural drama to be strangely unoriginal and repetitive in all its settings. Joel Cohen in New York and Robert May in Oxford are two of those who seek, and find, simple principles and rules among the bewildering complexities of real life. Discoveries that they and their colleagues have made provide the theoretical underpinning for ecology from space.

Biology has already experienced one transition from arm-waving to an exact, all-embracing science, in the discovery that all heredity is conveyed in a simple four-letter chemical code. The related finding that all organisms from mushrooms to whales are cousins, and rely on rather limited choices of biochemical tricks of great antiquity, makes a certain predictability in ecosystems unsurprising.

From deserts and Arctic tundra, through salt marshes and grassland to tropical forests -- when S. J. McNaughton and his colleagues at Syracuse University in the USA compared the data gleaned by ecologists from all these settings, they found striking consistencies. The rate of production of animal tissue is always about one-thousandth of the rate of production of plant tissue observable from space. Yet the rate of consumption of vegetation by animals is far greater when the vegetation is luxuriant than when it is sparse. In some deserts, 99 per cent of vegetation lives and dies without entering any animal mouth, while in tropical grassland the animals overlook less than 50 per cent of it.

Why then is the proportion of plant growth converted into animal tissue no greater in the Serengeti than in the Sahara? A growing animal converts about 10 per cent of its food into new tissues, but an adult merely renews what it has. In the tropical grassland, the food goes into building larger, longer-lived animals (wildebeests, elephants and the like), the zoological equivalent of mature trees. So the biomass of plant-eating animals is much higher. According to the new McNaughton rules every doubling of the vegetation index, as derived from satellite data, increases the mass of the animals by a factor of nearly three.

This gives answers about real ecosytems that are accurate to within a factor of ten, as compared with the herbivorous biomasses reported by ecologists in the field. That may seem very rough indeed. But from one kind of ecosystem to another, across a huge range of plant-growth rates and geographical settings, the rules work well. The discrepancies arise among ecosystems of the same type, and some may be due to errors or inconsistencies of observation. Real variations may reflect damage to ecosystems by natural or man-induced pollution, trampling or over-grazing. To be right globally with no greater error, across a 200-fold range in plant productivity from tundra to tropics, and a 3000-fold range in animal biomass, is something of a triumph, for a first shot at ecology from space.

As for the snakes, vultures and lions – the scavengers and predators that feed on the tissue of other animals – it seems only a matter of time before they too figure in the inferences from the vegetation index. The mathematical ecologists are finding simple rules about the proportions of 'basal', 'intermediate' and 'top' animal species, the linkages between them, and the numbers of individuals in each range of physical size. The theories have to accept that living nature is 'fractal' in its geometry, so that a square metre of soil or bark is in a real sense far larger for a beetle than for a rhinoceros.

So far from diminishing the human appreciation of ecosystems, ecology from space and the comparisons between ecosystems which it stimulates should help to make it more sensitive and rational, not least about the human factor. Tropical forests have recently been regarded as the quintessence of life on Earth, and tropical grassland as a poor relation. If the criterion is the sheer number of different species supported by the ecosystems, then the forests score very high, with their vast numbers of small species. But the species-count is not the only test of natural vigour. Tropical grassland comes top for larger animal species, as well as for the fraction of plant material used by animals.

This chimes with another very recent discovery about tropical grasslands. Ecologists had grossly underestimated the productivity of the grass because they failed to take account of the roots and recently dead material. In the late 1980s an international team led by David Hall of London University made careful measurements in four continents and found that tropical grasslands are about *four times* more productive than experts had imagined.

Elephants and other large animals helped to create the East African grassland by bulldozing trees. When human beings had evolved there, and mastered fire, they used it to maintain and extend the grass of their hunting ground. In the better watered, less degraded regions of the rift valley, where the wildebeests and lions still roam in parks, herders nearby keep up the tradition of burning the land.

Who will condemn that gross and deliberate human assault upon Nature that helped to create one of the world's most treasured ecosystems? And who will still mock the herders who prefer to graze their cattle and sheep in an approximation to the old order, instead of 'settling down' to farm the land and satisfy other people's prejudices about development?

CHAPTER 5

The Slosh of the Seas

*T*HE REVOLUTION in ocean
science worked by satellites and computers promises to rival what happened in weather forecasting. Taking in large areas of ocean at a glance, the satellites can observe in hours or days phenomena that seafarers took centuries to map. They see variations in the life of the sea, not as surely as the vegetation index narrates the course of life on land, but far better than before. And Japanese fishing vessels use space observations of sea-surface temperatures to help them find the fish.

Designers of space vehicles put baffles in their tanks to prevent excessive sloshing of liquid fuels, and the continents play a similar role in the salt-water tank of Spaceship Earth's global ocean. Their shorelines restrict and guide bulk movements of sea-water. Nevertheless, differences in sea-level associated with currents and submarine waves still occur, together with eddies large and small, and great risings, sinkings and sub-surface currents that have emphatic effects on life, by sea and land. Satellites and computer models are only beginning to master these phenomena of the deep ocean.

Geographers often give the oceans short shrift, even though any globe shows the oceans and contiguous seas occupying more than 70

129

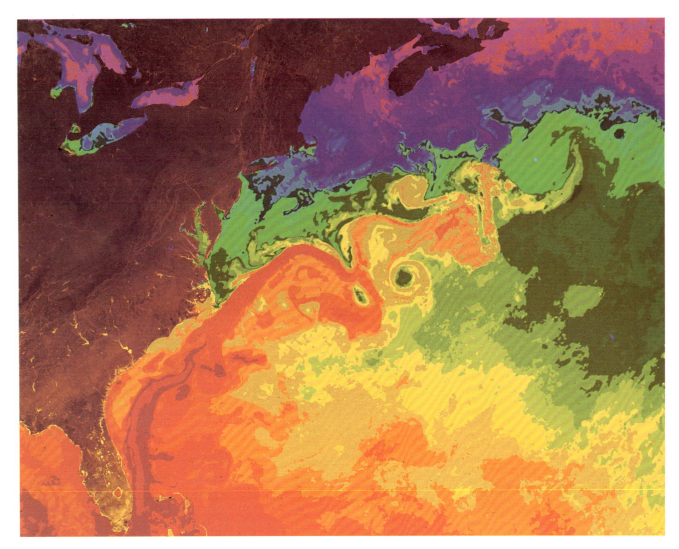

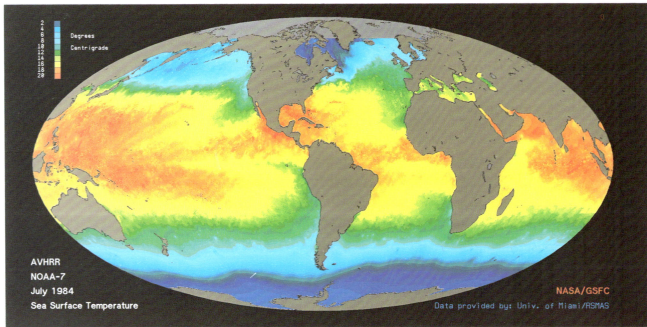

AVHRR
NOAA-7
July 1984
Sea Surface Temperature

NASA/GSFC
Data provided by: Univ. of Miami/RSMAS

Degrees
Centigrade

2
4
6
8
10
12
14
16
18
20

per cent of the Earth's surface. A popular undergraduate textbook of geography devotes only 1 per cent of its pages to the oceans and oceanic islands. There is rough justice by the old way of thinking, because geography is about people, and the islanders are few in numbers.

Yet even leaving aside geopolitical issues about naval activities or the ownership of the ocean floor, everyone's existence depends on the performance of the oceans as a huge piece of the Earth system. Life first flourished in the sea, where it oxygenated the atmosphere, converted surplus carbon dioxide into limestone rock, and blundered ashore only during the last 10 per cent of Earth history. About a quarter of all life's activity continues in the ancestral brine. The oceans are the primary source of all rain, their currents help to warm high-latitude lands, and they act as a thermostat during fluctuations of weather and climate.

The Polynesians who inhabit the world's largest geographical feature, the Pacific Ocean, peopled its scattered islands in prehistoric canoe voyages, sailing against the prevailing wind. They relied on a great seesaw in the oceanic weather to make progress eastward. When warm water sloshes across the wide Pacific, El Niño causes wayward weather all around the world. If oceanographers and meteorologists can make sense of the Polynesian wind, and the odd behaviour of the Great Warm Pool of the western Pacific, claims to understand the Earth system may seem less fanciful.

Follow a Japanese boat

AFTER THE wholesale conversion of the human species from hunter-gatherers to farmers, metalworkers and insurance salespersons, fishermen are the last big group of hunters left. The ocean fish-catch ranks behind beef, but far ahead of mutton and pork as a source of protein for the human diet. For Japan and several other nations and regions, fish and seafood are basic to the cuisine and the culture.

Yet the oceans remain the greatest wilderness on the Earth, where human influences are still comparatively slight. Even the overfishing of certain fish and whale species is less severe than the overhunting by which Stone-Age men extinguished most of the large, naive game of the Americas and Australia. Marine birds and mammals eat more fish than human beings do, even though the electronic fish-finders rival the dolphin's sonar, and satellites the eye of the albatross.

Facing:
Sea-surface temperatures from space, with warmer colours denoting warmer water. The upper image shows the Gulf Stream in the western Atlantic. Patches of untypical colour reveal warm-core eddies north of the Gulf Stream and cold-core eddies to the south of it. In the global image below, cold upwellings west of South America and Africa are important features.

131

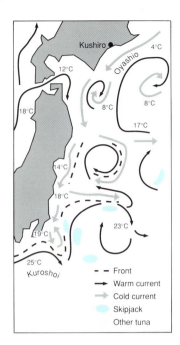

Fish-hunting by satellite. Sea-surface temperatures off Japan (above) are routinely interpreted (diagram) to show where the fish are likely to be abundant.

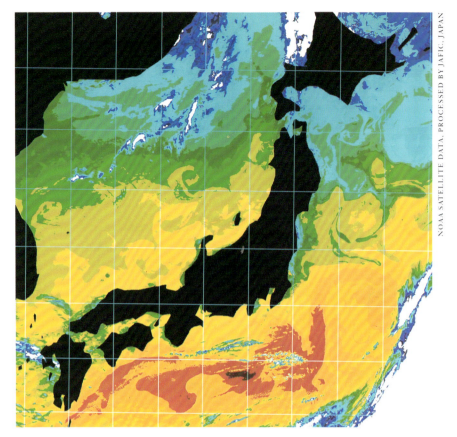

NOAA SATELLITE DATA, PROCESSED BY JAFIC, JAPAN

Anyone can pick up data from the American *NOAA* weather satellites as they pass overhead four times a day, normally to generate images of the cloud patterns over the local region. If you are the skipper of a high-tech Japanese fishing vessel striving for sealane credibility in the 1990s, you may want a fancier receiver that ignores the clouds as far as possible and uses the satellite signals to generate a map of sea-surface temperatures. It gives broad hints about where the fish may be.

With 200 such temperature mappers installed in Japanese deep-sea fishing vessels by 1989, and thousands of boats without the equipment receiving the real-time satellite maps by fax, this is the first substantial use of remote sensing from space by non-scientists. The Japan Fisheries Information Service Center in Tokyo pioneered the technique as a service to its industry. Besides faxing the satellite maps, JAFIC also gathers and distributes reports on sea temperatures from the fishermen themselves, together with news of catches landed.

The sea-surface temperatures off Japan relate to the oceanic saga of nutrients needed for life. Marine organisms tend to sink when they die, taking with them precious atoms of nitrogen, phosphorus, and the like.

The nutrients are soon exhausted in the sunlit zone near the surface. In coastal waters, rivers may bring fresh supplies, but a broad ocean soon becomes almost barren unless nutrient-rich water can well up from its depths. Sunlight represses the upwelling by creating a lid of warm, buoyant water near the surface. The circumstances in which upwelling succeeds play a dominant part in oceanic life worldwide, and in the hunt for fish off Japan.

Just northeast of Japan's most populous island, Honshu, two great currents meet. The cold Oyashio Current, heading southwest, encounters the warm Kuroshio Current heading northeast. Where they meet, fronts form between the two bodies of water, like the warm and cold fronts between air masses. Vertical motions in the water, equivalent to updraughts and downdraughts in the atmosphere, stir the sea and bring nutrient-rich water to the surface.

Skipjack tuna and saury (a relative of the Atlantic's skipper) are the main fish catches in the region, together with the invertebrate flying squid. The species are fastidious. Each prefers a particular water temperature in degrees C: 13–15 for squid, 14–18 for saury and 18–20 for skipjack. But the abundance of the various species depends on contrasts in temperature, with the fish concentrating at the fronts, on the warm or cold side depending on which temperature is more to its liking. So you hunt for saury on the cold, Oyashio side of a front, and for skipjack on the warm, Kuroshio side. The fishermen have long associated their richest hauls with fingers of water of the appropriate temperature protruding into the other current.

The sea-surface temperature maps from satellite data show that the meeting of the Oyashio and the Kuroshio Currents creates compact patches of warm or cold water. So far from being a simple line, with fingers, the front is accompanied by strings of eddies. Each warm patch is enveloped by a cold ring, 50–100 kilometres in diameter. This is an eddy swirling clockwise, just like an anticyclone in the atmosphere (in the Northern Hemisphere at least). Around the cold patches, warm eddies revolve widdershins, in the watery equivalent of hurricanes.

Japanese fishery scientists were aware of the importance of fronts and eddies long before the advent of remote-sensing satellites, and before ocean scientists in other parts of the world realized they had overlooked these features. That oceanic eddies were not generally recognized until recently is another reminder of the human capacity to miss the point about the Earth system. If an Asian geographer failed to notice the

133

Himalayas, that would be less of an oversight than the oceanographers missing the eddies. They contain far more energy of motion than the Kuroshio and all the other large current systems that gyrate around the ocean basins. And the eddies play a vital part in pumping nutrients into the surface water. If you are a skipjack tuna, a smart place to be is in the neighbourhood of a warm ring, at just the distance from the cold centre where the temperature reaches a comfortable 19 degrees. Amid a rich growth of marine plants, there will be plenty of small fish to eat.

And if you are the skipper of a tuna boat, seeing such a ring in your onboard display of sea-surface temperatures, from the latest pass of the satellite, you may consider altering towards it. J A F I C offers other indications for other species, here and in all the major Japanese fishing grounds. The rings persist much longer than the storms and anticyclones of the air, but they are mobile, like the fronts that spawn them. What could be niftier than a satellite display that spots them for you?

The only thing wrong with this story is that the fishermen in question hardly need the help. By their own proverb: 'If you want to find fish, follow a Japanese boat.' Deep-sea fishing in the waters off Japan has been going on for 10,000 years. Modern sonar fish-finders can speed the work once a promising fishing ground has been selected, but knowing where to go depends on intuitions about the sea's mood, which have not yet disappeared from the high-tech wheelhouse.

A fisherman senses the changing qualities of the water that affect the populations of marine plants and fish. Like a hunter on land, he studies the habits of the species he pursues. He watches the fish-hunting seabirds that act as unpaid scouts. 'Shiome' is the Japanese fisherman's name for an oceanic front that gathers the schools of fish. Fog is often a sign of a transition from warm to cold water. If no thermometer or satellite is available, your finger will do to judge the temperature of the water. Smell it and taste it too, if you like, but experienced eyes can judge the water by its hue.

The colour of the sea

*T*HE 'GRASS' OF the oceans, on which other living things from shrimps to whales depend directly or indirectly for their sustenance, consists of minute plants. Sample any bucket of water from near the sea surface, and a microscope will unmask the plankton or 'wanderers':

free-floating, drifting organisms with a variety of science-fiction-like forms. The plants of the phytoplankton coexist with miniature animals of the zooplankton, which are the first to graze, and the first to be eaten by predators. Eggs of fish and other animals drift with the plankton.

The small marine plants absorb the energy of sunlight in pigments and use it to combine carbon dioxide and water into living tissue, releasing oxygen. This is just like the behaviour of plants on land, except that the carbon dioxide comes from the water, not the air, along with essential nutrients including nitrogen and phosphorus. As in a pasture on land, the productivity of the sea is limited by the fertility embodied in those nutrients, although the plants never lack water.

While a pasture on land remains recognizable all the year round, the phytoplankton appear and disappear with the changing seasons, or sometimes just in the course of a generation, which lasts about half a week. Marine biologists can monitor the blooms in any one part of the sea, most conveniently in coastal waters. But when they cruise the wide oceans in slow ships, hoping with fine-mesh nets and water samplers to count the plankton and so gauge the biological productivity of the sea, they are trying to catch quicksilver on a fork. While they observe in one place, conditions are changing at the previous station. Currents move the wandering organisms, storms stir the sea and replenish nutrients, and the lilliputian world of the plankton enacts its cyclical dramas of reproduction, growth, ingestion and decay. Obliging merchant ships and fishing vessels have for long helped in such work, but there are huge areas that commercial shipping scarcely visits.

At the price of much seasickness and disruption of family life, scientists gradually acquired an approximate overview of life in the oceans. But when big businesses or poor countries enquired politely about the potential of fisheries, for example, or how conditions varied from place to place and season to season, the marine biologists' answers were vague. Other environmental scientists, trying to mesh the parts of the Earth system together, asked the biologists: 'How much life is there in the sea? How much carbon dioxide does it mop up each year? Where does the carbon finish up?' Without the excuse that the sea is a big place, the want of firm answers to such elementary questions might have been embarrassing.

The colour of the surface water of the sea has always been a guide to biologists as well as fishermen. The transparent blue of the eastern Mediterranean and many parts of tropical oceans denotes apparently

135

barren water with very little plankton in it. The murky grey-green of the North Atlantic and North Pacific is an unmistakable sign of abundant life. Most marine plants are green, by virtue of the chlorophyll that they share with green plants on land. Near the coast, silt carried by rivers or sediments stirred up from the seabed discolour the water with one of the many shades of mud. Abrupt changes of colour, across a perceptible line in the water, can occur at the edges of currents, fronts and eddies, both inshore and in mid-ocean.

Nearly 70 years ago a British marine biologist, Alister Hardy, was flying over Europe's continental shelf, trying to spot shoals of fish from the air. The muddiness and choppiness of the sea defeated him, but he did see a remarkable colour change.

In flying from Plymouth to the western mackerel grounds we passed over a sharp line separating the green water of the Channel from the deep blue of the Atlantic; it ran on a slightly irregular course from the Lizard to the southwest as far as we could see to the distant horizon . . . If these marked colour changes can be correctly interpreted we may in the future find aircraft being used to make rapid surveys of the surface conditions in relation to fisheries.

The colour change at the mouth of the English Channel is now interpreted as a front in the sea, marking the onset of a vigorous churning of the water of the English Channel as strong tidal currents encounter irregularities in the seabed and the shoreline. The churning begins out in the Atlantic, at the edge of the continental shelf, but the strong currents suddenly intensify it. The cold, nutrient-rich water coming from below cools the sea-surface and makes it more fertile. A research ship exactly straddling the Channel front can collect from the bow and the stern different species of arrow worms that favour different temperatures of water.

A simple device called a Secchi disk, a white-painted circle of metal for lowering over the side of a research ship until it disappears, has long been used to measure the transparency of surface waters. It also gives a more precise impression of the local colour of the sea: for example, the milky colour of coccoliths or the 'red tide' of a pathological dinoflagellate bloom, to mention changes from the usual green.

Around 1970, oceanographers and other specialists, mainly in the USA, began thinking about how to use a satellite to observe marine plants by their effects on the colour of the sea, and so assess the productivity of huge areas of the sea. Their calculations led to the Coastal Zone Color Scanner, which observed the colour of the sea from space from

1978 until 1986 – much longer than expected. Now the marine biologists are waiting impatiently for American and Japanese replacements for CZCS, because it was like a Secchi disk as big as the Earth.

CZCS flew in *Nimbus-7*, the highly successful experimental remote-sensing satellite that took part in the discovery of the Ozone Hole as well as revolutionizing the study of life in the sea. Despite its name, CZCS did not loiter at the coastal zones, but peered at all parts of the ocean. Indeed it gave more reliable results concerning the colour of the deep oceans than for the muddied waters offshore.

The scanner looked for the green chlorophyll of marine plants, using sensors for three wavelengths of visible light, in the blue and green parts of the spectrum. As in all remote sensing, the gulf between a simple aim and its execution had to be bridged by careful thought about the look of the Earth from space. For a start, the blue glow of the atmosphere produced far stronger signals in the wavelengths of interest than anything in the sea could do. Fortunately the sea looks black by red and infra-red light, so what a satellite over the ocean sees at these wavelengths is almost pure atmospheric scattering. By adding red and infra-red sensors to the CZCS, the scientists could work out how much to disallow for the atmosphere, in the critical blue and green.

The radiance of the sea itself comes from light entering the sea, going down some tens of metres and being scattered back out into space. Scattering by the marine plants themselves gives to the light the characteristic tinge of chlorophyll. Measurements of pigment concentration and the colour of sea water, made at sea and in laboratories ashore, enabled scientists to interpret the sea colour seen from space as a measure of chlorophyll in the ocean surface water.

Plankton that bloom in the spring

DURING ITS 8-year operating life, the Coastal Zone Color Scanner on *Nimbus-7* sent data for 68,000 scenes, each covering 2 million square kilometres. A few areas of the ocean remained stubbornly cloud-covered during the 10 per cent of the satellite's operating time allotted to the CZCS. The need to patch together cloud-free views from different days for adjacent parts of the sea produced an artificial blotchiness in the images. But otherwise, the instrument faithfully observed marine life and its changes, all over the world.

A low Sun lighting the ocean and atmosphere in the morning and evening confused the interpretations so much that many observations had to be disregarded. A new way of processing the data to cope with that difficulty has recently doubled the amount of information about chlorophyll recoverable from the CZCS tapes. Incurable problems include wide variations in the relationship of pigment to sea colour between the various species of marine plants. Another is the invisibility of plants below a certain depth in the water, where the light becomes too dim to see from space but not for the plants to live.

Despite these drawbacks, the scientists concerned consider that uncertainty even by a factor of two is very much better than no measurement at all. And with a pixel size of 1 kilometre, at a million pixels a minute, the CZCS was equivalent to millions of research ships making slightly sloppy measurements. If landlubberly biologists were limited to seeing life by the bucketful or netful, and then could lift their eyes to behold prairies and forests plainly for the first time, their gratification would be scarcely greater than the marine biologists' with CZCS.

The most stunning products are maps of the world showing seasonal changes in marine life, published by NASA in 1989. The Goddard Space Flight Center, working in collaboration with the University of Miami, produced them by combining CZCS data over periods of three months. Look at them as objectively as if they were new close-ups of Mars or Jupiter. They are the very stuff of the new global geography. While there is no discouraging mismatch between the CZCS reported and what 100 years of seagoing biology made out, there are things to see in the CZCS images that no one knew before.

One surprising discovery was the extent and intensity of the spring bloom in the North Pacific and North Atlantic Oceans. This corresponds with the spring blooms long known in coastal waters in temperate latitudes, after the storms of winter have churned and re-fertilized the water by bringing nutrient-rich deep water to the surface. The bloom in the northern oceans occurs in April, more suddenly than the gradual awakening and growth of seasonal plants on land. Some claim that this spring bloom in the northern oceans is the largest signal of life in the Earth system.

In the waters around Antarctica, a feeding ground of the great baleen whales that were hunted to near-annihilation in the 1950s, the summer bloom stands out clearly in the CZCS composite. In a remarkably simple food chain, the marine plants support shrimp-like krill and the

Facing:
Seasonal life in the North Atlantic observed from space. The Coastal Zone Color Scanner detected pigments of marine plants in the surface waters, at concentrations ranging from low (purple) to high (red). The seasons are spring (top left) summer (top right), autumn (middle left) and winter (middle right). The springtime bloom is remarkable. The last image is a composite of year-round data for 8 years.

138

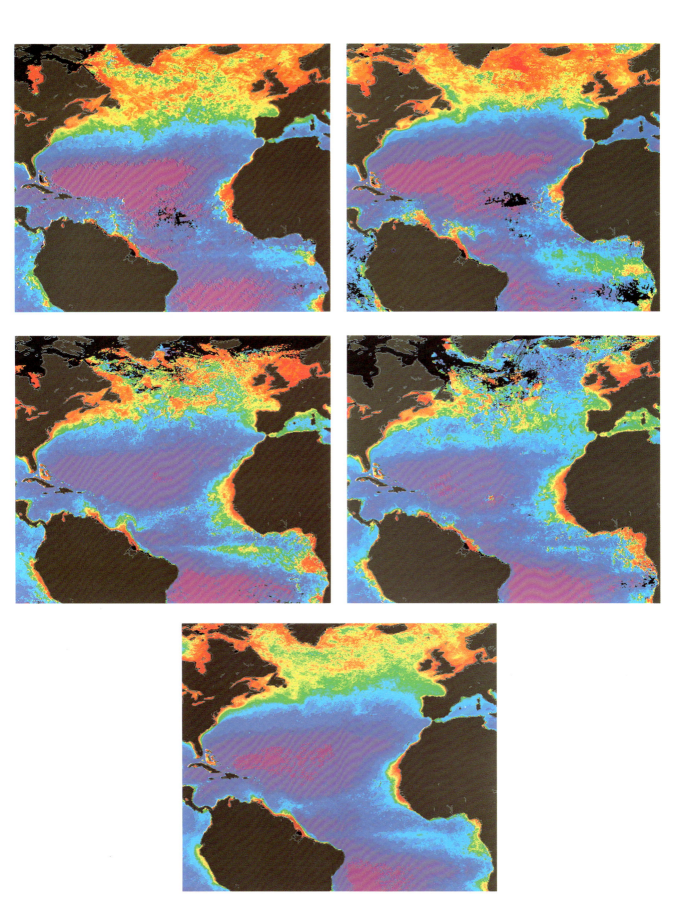

whales eat the krill. With the whales' decline, the seals have boomed.

On the other hand, the productivity of large areas of the tropical oceans seems to remain low, in accordance with an orthodox view that they are the deserts of the sea. By analogy with satellite observations of vegetation on land, the greenness of the sea is a rough guide to the primary productivity of plants turning carbon dioxide into tissue. Without the natural photo-cells associated with coloured pigments, the Sun's energy is running to waste in the blue oceans. A lack of essential nutrients is to blame. Some biologists nevertheless believe that ocean nutrients and the biomass may be underestimated, if most of them are locked up in marine animals and fish, rather than the water itself or in the plants of the plankton.

Reverting to those awkward questions – how much life in the sea, consuming how much carbon dioxide? – the marine biologists can now feed results from the CZCS into computer models that link the amount of plant pigment to the rate of plant growth. Other models, based on what eats what, and when corpses sink, have to establish how rapidly the

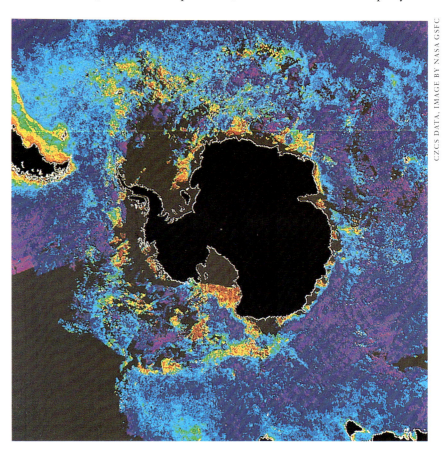

CZCS DATA, IMAGE BY NASA GSFC

The satellite's view of the summer bloom in Antarctic waters. The red and yellow patches are concentrations of marine plants, and the grey areas close to Antarctica are sea-ice.

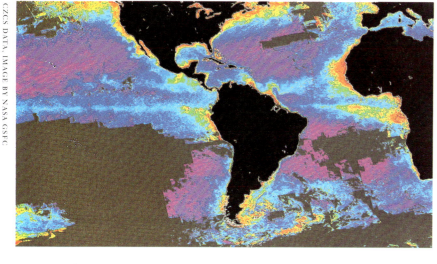

CZCS DATA, IMAGE BY NASA GSFC

The Equator from space. A fertile band extends westwards from South America along the not-so-imaginary line.

life of the sea removes carbon dioxide from the surface water in the form of an organic rain into the depths of the sea. The answers still contain much guesswork, and so far from abolishing the need for oceanographic cruises, the success of CZCS gives them added point.

The world's great fishing grounds show up vividly in the CZCS maps, as regions where abundant marine plants support fish in plenty. Upwelling is the key, because of the nutrients it delivers to the surface. Off Africa's west coast, for example, prevailing winds push the surface waters away from the shore. This action siphons up nutrient-rich water from below the surface layer near the coast, which feeds the plankton blooms plainly visible to the CZCS in space. Rich deposits of phosphorus ore on and off the African shore, made from dead marine organisms, testify to many millions of years of such activity. Besides the African and European fishermen who flock here, long-haul boats from the Soviet Union and Japan come to fill their holds with African sardines. Similar upwelling occurs on the west coast of South America.

In the last quarter of the year, long tongues of fertile water stretch westwards from the upwellings off Africa and South America. They reach far across the tropical Atlantic and Pacific. The line of fertility in the Pacific is particularly striking, not least because it runs exactly along the Equator for a quarter of the way around the world. The Equator is usually considered an imaginary line defined by astronomers. But an astronomer on the Moon, equipped with the equivalent of the CZCS, would see the Equator as a real green line stretching from Ecuador, the country that named itself for the Equator, as far east as the mid-Pacific island group of Kiribati.

141

The oceans in three dimensions

*T*O THE EXTENT that life concentrates mainly at the sunlit surface, and there lays out its pigmented photo-electric traps for the light that energizes growth, the oceans resemble the surface of the land. In all other respects they are much more like the air, being fluid and emphatically three-dimensional. As in the atmosphere, the laws of physics rule, but the saltiness (salinity) of the sea takes the place of humidity in the computer models. These divide the ocean into grid-boxes and compute the flows on the surface and at various depths. Global ocean models are poor, though.

The eddies in the oceans (10–100 kilometres wide) are much smaller than depressions and anticyclones in the atmosphere (1000–5000 kilometres wide) and a hundred times as much computing power would be needed to match the quality of global models of the atmosphere. The best results so far have come from models of parts of the ocean – for example, a US–German model of the North Atlantic which 'captures' the eddies of the Gulf Stream.

Observations of the oceans are also much inferior to those for the atmosphere. Oceanic research rightly looms large in plans for the coming decade, to try to fill an abyss of ignorance concerning the principal fluid at the Earth's surface, which is 300 times more massive than the air and on average about 4 kilometres deep. At the ocean's surface, satellites work wonders in observing winds, waves and sea-surface temperatures. With radar altimeters, they can also measure the height of the sea-surface accurately enough to detect humps in the water, about 1 metre in elevation, associated with major ocean currents. Like an anticyclone in the air, the excess pressure of a hump of water supports a circulation going clockwise in the Northern Hemisphere and counterclockwise in the Southern.

The main humps in the sea adjoin the powerful Western Boundary Currents that flow away from the tropics along the eastern margins of the continents. These show up in another way in the radar-altimeter measurements, as scenes of great variability in sea-surface heights, because of the eddies associated with them. The currents in question are the Kuroshio off Japan, the East Australian Current, the Somali Current off southeast Africa, the Brazil Current, and the Gulf Stream off the eastern USA. These great rivers in the oceans, transporting tens of millions of tons of warm water every second, help to redistribute heat

Facing:
The Southern Ocean modelled by computer. The chart, from the British FRAM model, depicts the great eastgoing Circumpolar Current around Antarctica. Colours denote the total flow occurring between a given point on the chart and the northern (outer) boundary of the model. The abrupt blue – yellow – red transition off the tip of South America, (left) corresponds to an intense eastgoing current there. The blue, purple and white region near South Africa (top right) is the westgoing Agulhas Stream, strong and warm.

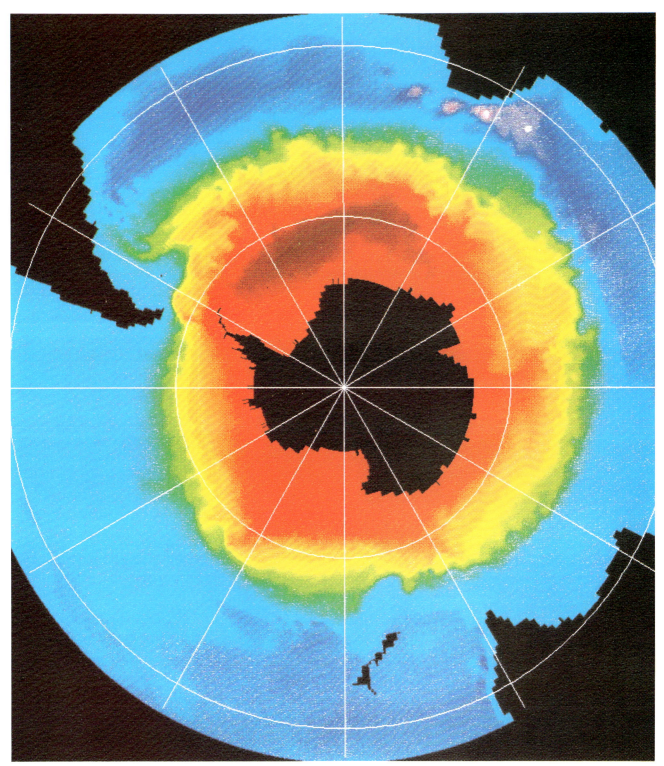

FRAM MODEL © NERC, UK

from the tropics towards the Poles. Yet the Western Boundary Currents are poorly understood, and the global computer models represent them imperfectly.

The greatest current of all flows clockwise around Antarctica, supported by a slope in the sea, downwards towards the southern continent. This Circumpolar Current helps to keep Antarctica in deep-freeze by acting as a barrier to warm water. The Institute of Oceanographic Sciences in Britain coordinates work by university scientists on a computer model of part of the global ocean, which represents the Circumpolar Current particularly well. The Fine Resolution Antarctic Model (FRAM) shows that warm eddies can in fact sneak across the current and make Antarctica a little warmer than it would otherwise be.

The FRAM model covers the oceans south of Latitude 25 South (about the southern tip of Madagascar) which represent almost 40 per cent of all the world's oceans. The grid points for computation are roughly 27 kilometres apart and at thirty-two levels down to the ocean bed. The model seems to give a realistic impression of the ocean at all depths and most places. It demonstrates, for example, how encounters between the Circumpolar Current and shallow regions promote the formation of eddies, and how the eddies help to restrict the speed of the main current. But to simulate a year in the life of the ocean in the FRAM model takes about a month on a supercomputer, which indicates why comprehensive ocean modelling is going to be a long, hard task.

Salient features of the deep ocean are already known to oceanographers from their seagoing explorations. Water becomes denser when it cools; also when it becomes saltier as a result of losing part of the water, by freezing or evaporation. The dense water sinks, and slowly travels great distances far below the surface. Warm, salty outpourings from the Mediterranean Sea and the Dead Sea can be traced at intermediate depths in the Atlantic and Indian Oceans. But the polar regions dominate the oceans by filling them all with chilly, dense water.

Except for the uppermost 1000 metres or so, the temperature of ocean water is lower than 5 degrees C even in the tropics. Greenland sharks feel quite at home off the Californian coast in 2-degree water 3000 metres down. Radiocarbon dating tells oceanographers how long has elapsed since the water deep in the oceans was last at the surface. The 'age' of the deep water of the Pacific is about 1600 years, while in the North Atlantic it is much younger, at 350 years or so. The one goes

Facing:
Ocean currents by computer and from space. The uppermost chart is a detail from the FRAM model which traces strong, deep currents computed for the Drake Passage between South America and Antarctica (white weakest, red strongest). The currents flow in the directions pointing away from the dots. The other images are space observations of the turbulent Agulhas Stream, heading westwards past the southern tip of Africa. The middle image shows variability in the sea level detected by a radar altimeter in space (pink no variation, black most). The lowermost image is of sea-surface temperatures observed from space.

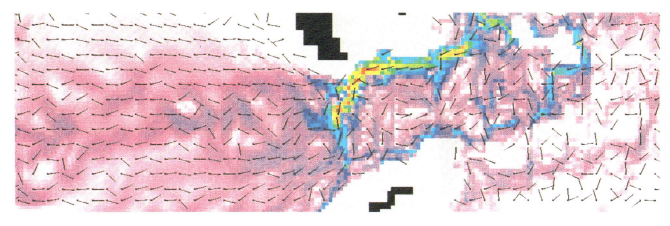

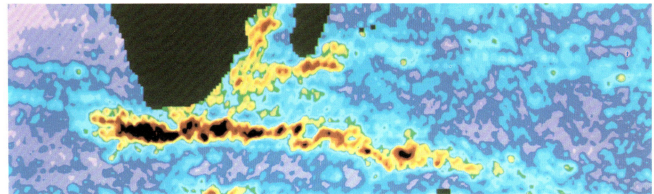

AVHRR N7 JUN 1 83

SOUTH AFRICA

AGULHAS C.

21

22 C

19

20

355

back to late Roman times; the other was 'breathing' the atmosphere of the North Atlantic around the time of *Mayflower*'s voyage. These dates give an impression of how slowly the ocean works, but they are averages only. New deep water is forming continually.

Antarctica probably makes most of the deep water, beneath the pack-ice of the Weddell Sea (south of South America) and the Ross Sea (south of New Zealand). The other principal source is the North Atlantic, the North Pacific being strangely unproductive of deep water. The North Atlantic Deep Water turns out to be especially important for the Earth system. It originates from pack-ice factories lying east and west of Greenland. It flows southwards to the Southern Ocean and then migrates eastwards all around the world, supplying the Indian and Pacific Oceans with some of their deep water.

The deep-water flow out of the North Atlantic is balanced by a flow the other way of shallower, warmer water from the Pacific and Indian Oceans, into the Atlantic. This warm water travels westwards from Indonesia, around South Africa and thence across the South Atlantic to the Gulf of Mexico, where it helps to nourish the Gulf Stream of the North Atlantic. The FRAM computer model has helped to confirm the theory that the Agulhas Stream off South Africa, fed from the Indian Ocean, generates warm eddies that carry the warm water westwards, past Cape Agulhas and the Cape of Good Hope. The South Atlantic is unique among the major oceans, in transporting heat towards the Equator, instead of away from it.

The production of North Atlantic Deep Water is tightly coupled to climate and climate change. By sinking at its formation sites and letting warm surface water slosh northwards to replace it, the North Atlantic Deep Water conspires with the Gulf Stream to keep Europe much warmer than places at similar latitudes in Asia and North America. If the North Atlantic loses some of its saltiness, as happened in the event called the Great Salinity Anomaly, in the 1970s, this impedes the sinking and leaves cooler water on the surface. The knock-back effects may be widespread. Apart from a cooling over much of the North Atlantic surface, warming occurs in the South Atlantic and Indian Oceans, possibly because the flow of warm water towards the North Atlantic is impeded. The Great Salinity Anomaly may be implicated in the droughts that afflicted Africa in the 1970s and 1980s.

146

*E*UROPEAN EXPLORERS thought that the coconut palms, so conspicuous on the shores of many oceanic islands, were natural vegetation. Botanists imagined coconuts floating from island to island, and seeding themselves. A snag about that idea is that the prevailing winds and currents of the tropics would drive the coconuts westwards. So how could they have found their own way eastwards across the Pacific, from their origin in Southeast Asia? The modern opinion is that prehistoric voyagers transplanted the coconuts.

That explanation transfers the problem to the voyagers, and especially to the Polynesians who inhabit the most far-flung islands. How did *they* sail across the Pacific, against the prevailing winds and currents? The archaeologist Thor Heyerdahl argued that they came from South America with a favourable wind, but archaeological, botanical and linguistic evidence all points the other way. Molecular-genetic findings confirm the Asian origin of the Polynesians.

A Samoan folk-tale tells of the arrival of the coconut from an island to the west. A chief from Fiji, magically transformed into a giant eel, begs a Samoan girl to cut off his head and plant it. Its fruit will quench her thirst, and every time she drinks she will kiss him. Fanaafi Le Tagaloa of the University of Western Samoa thinks that the story means that the coconut came from Fiji when Samoa had already been inhabited for some time. There is no such tale for the other Samoan staples (taro, breadfruit, bananas, sugar cane) nor for the traditional animals (chickens, pigs, dogs).

That older package of plants and animals presumably came with those who 3000 years ago first discovered Samoa. This group of volcanic islands lies far out in the Pacific, and was probably the origin of Polynesia. Some of the discoverers' descendants continued eastwards by sailing canoe to find and people many more islands. The Polynesian Triangle with corners at Hawaii, New Zealand and distant Easter Island is a sector of the world more extensive than North America, but accessible only by sea or air.

Many tourists now fly to the Polynesian islands, to envy the idyllic life. Many young Polynesians, whose ancestors arrived by canoe, now leave by jet plane in search of another life in the USA or New Zealand, and money to send home to their relatives. Contrary to the European myth of noble savages, and Margaret Mead's canard about free love,

Samoans share the usual virtues and vices of the human species. They are jolly puritans, much given to flowers and dancing, who preserve a strict and ancient social order based on village chieftainships.

At other times and in other places, the Polynesian social order has been autocratic, cruel and warlike. It laid Easter Island to waste in a frenzy of statue-making. In more benign modes, as in Samoa today, it entwines culture and agriculture in the concept of *aiga* that unites the family, the village and the land. *Taboos* (another Polynesian word) may be as important for protecting the environment as for formalizing sexual and religious prohibitions.

Chiefs hold the land in trust for the people, who are their relatives and potential successors. They oversee the allocation of land to individuals, and the first call on the land is for the nutrition of the village. Stocks providently set aside prove their worth in disasters like the hurricane (cyclone) that assailed Samoa in 1990. Surplus land can grow cash crops for sale in the local markets or to exporters. Ceremonies cement the social relationships and every day is Christmas in Samoa. Gift-giving redistributes wealth and exerts power. The more you give away, the bigger man you are. The Western value system that rates a person by what he keeps for himself is something that South-Sea islanders have to try to master, for dealing with foreigners.

For 3000 years, the Samoans maintained their culture and agriculture without external help, the coconut eel excepted. Their Asian crops and animals displaced much of the pre-existing wildlife, but that was a hundred generations ago. The Samoans made room for European-style plantations during the colonial era, and continue to develop and modernize them for the sake of export revenue. This is achieved without evident hardship, in a land where the most serious nutritional problem is obesity.

A team from the New Zealand Department of Scientific and Industrial Research recently used air photos, ground surveys and a geographic information system, for an agronomic report on Western Samoa. When its experts compared the soil data with land use, they were bemused by the large areas of inherently productive land that remain unexploited either for village gardens or for commercial plantations.

Until very recently such a state of affairs was called 'underdevelopment', and was a matter for blame rather than than praise. But in the 1990s, when the rest of the world anxiously counts its hectares, the superfluity suggests that the Samoans are in better shape than many more 'advanced' nations, to face the next 3000 years with confidence.

The Christmas wind

HOWEVER THEY rate as gardeners, as navigators the Polynesians come top of anyone's class. Without instruments but with senses keenly tuned to the stars and the sea, colonizing expeditions more purposeful and dangerous than those of any modern astronauts set off into the blue in sailing canoes. Starting first from Samoa, and then from later settlements away to the east, they would seek out undiscovered islands to make new homes, or perish in the attempt. Once settled, they navigated freely between known islands.

Two centuries ago in Tahiti, the Polynesian pilot-priest Tupa'ia drew for Captain James Cook a chart of seventy-four scattered islands, from Fiji and Samoa in the west to the Marquesas northeast of Tahiti. The distance between these extremes is 5000 kilometres. The chart is not entirely accurate and the pilot admitted that his father had known more islands than he did. But Tupa'ia answered the riddle of how the Polynesians sailed east, against the prevailing east wind. Cook wrote:

Tupia [*sic*] tells us that during the months of November, December and January westerly winds with rain prevail and as the inhabitants of the islands know very well how to make proper use of the winds there will no difficulty arise in trading or sailing from island to island even though they lay in an east and west direction.

'Westerly' to a sailor, in this context, does not necessarily mean a wind blowing directly from the west. It can be from the north or south even, as long as the absence of an easterly component allows a sailing canoe to proceed eastwards without tacking. In 1986, in a project masterminded by Ben Finney of the University of Hawaii, a replica of a Polynesian canoe sailed eastwards from Samoa to Tahiti. It took 44 days, against Tupa'ia's estimate of 30 days, but then the Hawaiian expedition used a dubious west wind in July, not at Christmas.

The Earth system engineers the Polynesian wind during a damaging change in the weather of the Pacific Ocean. South American fishermen call it El Niño, the Christ Child, because it often sets in at Christmas. Its effects are felt all around the world, via the changes long known to meteorologists as the Southern Oscillation.

The scene shifts back to the west coast of South America where an upwelling of cold water, rich in nutrients like phosphorus and nitrogen, fertilizes the sea. The marine plants and the fishes that feed on them flourish mightily in the cold water. The birds that eat the fishes paint the cliffs white with their droppings and corpses, which humans mine as guano, for fertilizing their fields. The upwelling occurs because the prevailing southerly winds push the surface water of the sea away from the land. This detaches from the coast the northgoing Humboldt Current, and lets deep, cold water rise to take its place.

Every year around Christmas the fishermen of Peru and Ecuador are accustomed to warm, infertile water flooding the surface of their prime fishing ground, in the seasonal event that gives El Niño its name. Usually the warming is only 1 or 2 degrees C, and the fishery is back in business by March. But every few years a strong El Niño lasts much longer, and covers a much wider area. With a slick of water ranging up to 10 degrees warmer than usual, Nature devastates the ecology of the eastern Pacific. From a visit to Ecuador's Galapagos Islands during a severe El Niño, the author's abiding memory is of a fluffy carpet of starved sea-bird chicks.

In 1970, Peru's anchovy catch of 12 million tons made it the world's greatest fishery. By 1983, after three severe El Niños in 10 years, the catch had fallen to less than half a million tons. The 1982–83 El Niño was particularly severe, and it was blamed, rightly or wrongly, for unusual weather in many parts of the world. El Niño is now one of the most intensively researched phenomena of the climate.

As to what triggers a strong El Niño event, theories on offer range from a conspiracy of hurricanes, to volcanic eruptions on the seabed. Most attention focuses on the Great Warm Pool, which is the warmest region of the world's oceans. It embraces the island of New Guinea north of Australia, and sprawls eastwards for 2000 kilometres or so across the Pacific, with a temperature of 28–30 degrees C. The hot ocean, driving moist air upwards, creates abundant clouds and rain in the western Pacific and Southeast Asia.

The Great Warm Pool is usually self-sustaining, because the updraft it creates sucks in air from the east, so maintaining the prevailing easterly winds and currents that keep feeding it with warm water. At El Niño time the warm water of the western Pacific moving towards South America threatens this normality. In mild cases, the warm water sloshes eastward only for a brief period. But it is easy to see why the situation can worsen, to create a severe El Niño event.

150

The contrast in temperature between the hot western Pacific and the cool water off South America is the chief driver of the prevailing winds from the east, and these in turn shore up the normal contrast in sea temperatures. Once the easterlies falter, the central and eastern parts of the ocean begin to warm up. The loss of the east wind and the warming can then become a runaway process, with what the modellers call positive feedback. The air–ocean subsystem thus seesaws from the normal state to El Niño. To explain how normality returns, after a severe El Niño, is just as much a challenge to the theorists as explaining the onset of the event.

Images and models of El Niño

*T*HE SATELLITES observe El Niño well, especially its changes of sea-surface temperature. The images show the classical disappearance of the tongue of cool water that normally stretches westwards into the Pacific from equatorial South America. They sometimes also display the Great Warm Pool growing and intensifying in the western Pacific, before the event. Then its sprawl across the Pacific becomes more pronounced, as a long tongue of warm water protrudes eastwards. Sometimes separate pools form, at the tip of the tongue.

Data from below the ocean surface have to come mainly from ships and buoys, and are much sparser. The radar of the US *Geosat* satellite spotted an underwater wave, called a Kelvin wave, travelling eastwards across the Pacific during a strong El Niño event. Theorists had offered the Kelvin wave as a mechanism for transporting warm water eastwards and for repressing any upwelling of cold water.

In the ordinary weather-satellite images, an eastward shift of clouds from Indonesia into the central Pacific is readily apparent during a severe El Niño event. Indonesia and other parts of Southeast Asia are deprived of rain, and satellite images of the vegetation index show that growth is plainly less abundant than usual. A southward drift of cloud-clusters, in the convergence zone where the trade winds of the Northern and Southern Hemisphere meet, alters the rainfall patterns in the South Sea islands. The warm-water spillage eastwards favours hurricanes, and also a succession of depressions shooting off across Mexico towards Europe.

The Tropical Ocean Global Atmosphere (TOGA) study is a key part

The apparent impact of a severe El Niño event in eastern Asia. There was a widespread reduction in plant growth (middle image, April 1983 – April 1984) as compared with the preceding and subsequent years (first and last images).

Facing:
Sea-surface temperatures in the eastern tropical Pacific observed from space for the Novembers of 1982 (above) and 1983 (below) during and after a severe El Niño event.

of the World Climate Research Programme, and it attempts to reproduce El Niño in computer models. Some of these have computed the reaction of the atmosphere to the known changes in sea-surface temperatures, others the response of the sea to the known changes in the winds. Ocean models show the sectors of the normal westgoing currents reversing and going east. This fits with the idea that the water of the Great Warm Pool can itself move eastwards across the Pacific, but does not necessarily rule out an alternative theory that the central and eastern parts of the ocean warm up locally.

Fancy underwater events like Kelvin waves may not be necessary to explain El Niño's surface effects, but may explain changes below the surface. The most important concerns the thickness of the surface layer of the ocean, above the 'thermocline' that separates it from cold, deep water. In a normal year the surface layer is shallower in the eastern Pacific (about 100 metres, compared with 200 metres in the west) but in a severe El Niño it has much the same thickness (150 metres) all across the ocean. This 'flattening of the thermocline' suppresses an equatorial undercurrent that normally flows eastwards along the thermocline in the opposite direction to the surface current. Oceanographers have noticed that undercurrent disappearing during El Niño.

Models that couple the atmosphere and the ocean together do not rely on known data but attempt to create simulated El Niños afresh, with the hope of eventually forecasting real events. Some simplified models can generate the basic seesaw. The most elaborate of the coupled air–ocean computer models wrestling with El Niño are at Princeton in the USA, Bracknell in England and Hamburg in Germany.

Severe El Niño events probably affect the whole planet, but precise connections with, say, droughts in the Sahel or harsh winters in North America are hard to verify. More certain is an effect on global levels of carbon dioxide. The plants that suffer from diminished rainfall, in Southeast Asia and perhaps elsewhere during an El Niño event, fail to absorb their normal quota of carbon dioxide needed for growth. As a result the amount of carbon dioxide in the world's air increases.

For about a year, during a strong El Niño, the rise in carbon dioxide due to natural causes temporarily exceeds the manmade input due to the burning of fossil fuel. This is despite activity in the oceans affected by El Niño, which cuts their emissions of carbon dioxide. In a normal year the equatorial ocean pumps a surplus billion tons of the gas into

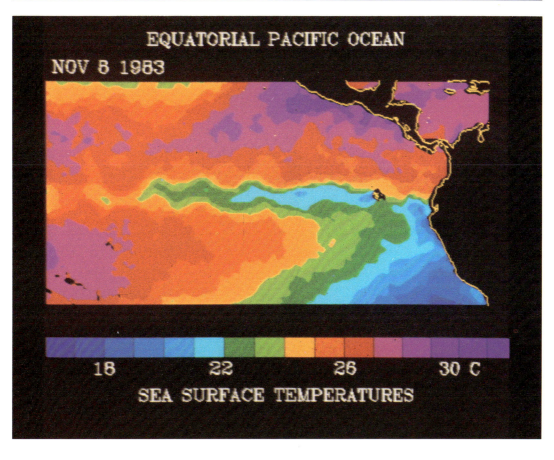

EQUATORIAL PACIFIC OCEAN

NOV 8 1982

18   22   26   30 C

SEA SURFACE TEMPERATURES

EQUATORIAL PACIFIC OCEAN

NOV 8 1983

18   22   26   30 C

SEA SURFACE TEMPERATURES

the air, and the eastern Pacific is by far the largest source. In an El Niño year its contribution falls virtually to zero, for want of upwelling water, which is rich in carbon dioxide. Yet when scientists carefully subtract seasonal effects and manmade injections from the global carbon dioxide record, they confirm that the carbon dioxide increases.

A rare, heavy form of carbon, carbon-13, helps to distinguish the roles of physical processes and living organisms in the fluctuations of carbon dioxide. Living things prefer the ordinary carbon-12 and the proportion of carbon-13 is lower in them than in the air or seawater. Carbon-13 data confirm that the carbon-dioxide pulse associated with El Niño is due to a growth failure of plants on land. The carbon dioxide that they fail to use for building new tissue more than compensates for the interruption of injections from the El Niño ocean.

The new European ERS-1 satellite may have the opportunity to measure wind speeds and directions over the tropical Pacific before, during and after an El Niño event. It is often the case, in efforts to understand the Earth system, that key information may be very scarce, especially from lonely parts of the world like the tropical Pacific. That is certainly so for the winds of El Niño. The US *Seasat* made worldwide wind measurements by radar observations of the waves, and ERS-1 has similar equipment. For the first time, meteorologists and climatologists may acquire a comprehensive picture of the prevailing easterlies giving way, at the end of the calendar year, to the Polynesian 'westerlies' commended by Tupa'ia to Cook. This annual seesaw will then either swing gently back by March, or lurch into a severe El Niño event.

CHAPTER 6

Running Water

THE PLUMBING of Spaceship
Earth is known in a sketchy fashion, but no one can swear to the sizes
of the pipes that deliver fresh water to its various compartments. When
water evaporates from the huge reservoirs of the oceans it leaves its salt
behind, and this natural distillation creates a great division in life between marine organisms that are adapted to salt water, and organisms
on land and in rivers that need fresh water.

Availability of water is often the limiting factor for life on land.
Human beings are bags of water, stretched out by bones, in which the
chemical operations of action and thought can proceed. Unless that
water is continually renewed people die – sooner than of hunger. Plants
too need moist soil from which to draw essential water, and the driest
places are deserts.

Great river systems in North America, southern Asia and Soviet
Central Asia tell very different stories of a human love–hate relationship with running water. The last of them concerns the most conspicuous manmade change in the appearance of the Earth from space, where
contempt for people and natural systems has condemned a great lake to
become a salt desert.

SATELLITES LOOKING down on the Mississippi river observe a writhing snake that the US Army has been trying to tame since 1824. Its name means Big Water in the language of the Algonkian Amerindians, and it carries the runoff from a large piece of North America into the Gulf of Mexico: 18,000 tons of water per second on average delivered to the sea. The Mississippi itself flows southward from the uplands near the Great Lakes. The Missouri tributary, coming from the west, brings water from the Rocky Mountains and the Great Plains, while the Ohio drains the inland slopes of the Appalachian mountains to the east. Like a endlessly branching tree, every tributary has tributaries of its own, until wet soil on a remote hillside is nourishing barely visible runnels.

Water and gravity erase mountains grain by grain, patiently trying to turn the world into a flat swamp where water might find tranquillity at last and gravity would have nothing left to do. Swift water propelled by gravity scours the land and rivers carry fine particles of rock and soil, held in suspension for as long as the speed of the current allows. In the last ice age the Mississippi rushed straight down a canyon to a lowered ocean. When the sea rose, the river switched from a scouring to a plastering mode, as currents slackened and gravity commanded them to drop their load. Now the Mississippi, often 2 kilometres wide, meanders in ostentatious sweeps across a flat alluvial flood plain created by its own silt. Although geographers characterize the Mississippi as a 'mature' river, or even 'old' as in *Old Man River*, the present plain is only about 5000 years of age, roughly contemporary with the pyramids of Egypt.

Today the Mississippi river system is a highway carrying 400 million tons of commerce a year on 20,000 kilometres of navigable waterways, mainly in barges. The rivers bring water to homes, farms and industries along their banks, where people are more likely to work in a chemical plant than in the traditional cotton fields. The work of the US Army Corps of Engineers, which started with clearing logs that impeded navigation, has evolved into an endless attempt to constrain the power of a great river to human needs.

Zigzagging currents make and move sandbanks, but walls that protrude into the stream can force the main current to follow a chosen course, while dredging keeps the channel clear for the barges. Flood-

A huge working model of the Mississippi computed flows in a complex river system.

Facing:
The Mississippi basin, in part of a space mosaic of the USA.

ALBERS EQUAL AREA PROJECTION
MOSAIC OF FIFTEEN AVHRR IMAGES
24 MAY, 1984 - 14 MAY, 1986

water slowing as it overtops the banks builds natural raised banks, or levees, to remind the Mississippi of its present path. The engineers strengthen the levees and increase their heights, or replace them by manmade levees following different lines. Reservoirs, spillways and pumps give the Corps of Engineers a certain control over the river. Nowadays satellites and computers help to guide the work of dredgers and bulldozers.

Landsat images and air photos merge with digitized maps and data in a geographic information system for 1000 kilometres of the lower Mississippi flood plain. It monitors long-term changes in land use beside the river, including loss of trees that help to stabilize the banks. The landforms help to define habitats for fishes and birds, which river works can sometimes improve. Oxbow lakes left by abandoned meanders make excellent refuges, and aquatic playgrounds for human beings.

The most important data from space are not images but real-time signals relayed by satellite from instruments at water level. Data stations automatically measure the height, speed and water quality of the Mississippi and its tributaries. Other stations record rainfall. At the River and Reservoir Control Center at Vicksburg in the State of Mississippi, measurements from nearly 300 stations, harvested in a computer, give an hour-by-hour picture of the state of the rivers. The Ohio river is the tributary watched most warily. It brings rainwater and snowmelt from a large part of the northeastern United States and supplies half the Mississippi's total flow.

Water-control managers use the system to help them decide when to issue flood alerts, or take emergency action to redirect the flow. In theory, they are supposed to be able to cope with a flood of a quarter of a million tons of water every second, exceeding the worst flood on record, which in 1927 devastated farms and towns across 60,000 square kilometres of the flood plain. One option, to let the river spill to a second line of levees set back several kilometres behind the normal banks, was opposed during floods in 1982–83 by lawyers acting for people living in the designated floodway. Another possibility is to open huge gates (completed in 1986) to allow more of the Mississippi to flow down its shortcut to the sea, the Atchafalaya river.

The complex dynamical behaviour of a natural river system under human management defies any simple analysis. Computers now model the flows of the Mississippi, but half a century ago work started on a

158

giant hydraulic model. It simulates the Mississippi and its tributaries with water flowing through 13 kilometres of scale-model rivers. Five minutes' operation of the model corresponds to a day in the life of the rivers. Some 30 years' work went into building and running the model at Clinton, Mississippi, to create a library of knowledge about river management.

Of all the world's great river systems, the Mississippi is thus the most comprehensively studied and conscientiously run. Yet the writer William Faulkner, who lived in the State of Mississippi and knew the river also as a sometime rum smuggler in the delta, likened it to a mule that will work for you for 10 years for the privilege of kicking you once. In the 1980s the Mississippi was still confounding the engineers, first with severe floods, and then with drought that left barges stranded in abnormally low water.

That some problems of river management may defy any clear-cut engineering solution is most evident at the Mississippi's outlets to the sea. The US government and its engineers, having elected long ago to take charge of the river, must now choose between keeping a great city in business or saving a valued tract of coastal territory in the delta of the Mississippi.

River water slows down terminally when it reaches the sea and drops the last of its sediments. Normally these fall on a shallow seabed and gradually create a delta of new swampy land where mangroves grow and birds on the migration route called the Mississippi Flyway find a convenient stopover. During the last 5000 years the Mississippi has changed its outlet six times. Whenever that happens, old parts of the delta become vulnerable to erosion by the sea, especially during hurricanes. A new delta normally makes up for the losses, but not now.

The USA is losing more than 100 square kilometres of its territory each year, from the Mississippi delta. Extraction of oil and water from underground in the delta region causes subsidence that lets sea water flood the ground of the delta and kill the plants. More fundamental is the fact that where the main channel of the Mississippi now reaches the sea, from a slender 'bird's-foot' delta, the offshore seabed is too deep for the sediments to be able to build new land.

Without the attentions of the Corps of Engineers, the Mississippi could have put itself back in profit as a delta-maker, by changing its main outlet to the Atchafalaya shortcut. Although only 30 per cent of the Mississippi flow is allowed down the Atchafalaya, except during floods, it does a creditable job of land-building. Yet the engineers feel compelled to go on forcing the greater part of the water to hold its present course below the Atchafalaya branchpoint, to enable New Orleans to continue to function.

This cosmopolitan city of jazz, home for a million people, is one of the world's great ports. French settlers founded New Orleans near the Mississippi's outlet to the sea, as a place to load oceangoing ships with goods rafted down the river. That was nearly 300 years ago, and the city's raison d'être has not changed. Allowing the Mississippi to abandon New Orleans would cause an economic disaster. In present thinking that outweighs the environmental problems of the delta and of the French-speaking Cajuns who made their home there.

The satellite images exhibit the engineers' dilemma. They show the port installations of New Orleans, and the mangroves thriving in the meagre new lands at the mouth of the Atchafalaya river 150 kilometres to the west. In other parts of the delta, grey patches represent areas sterilized by salt water as the sea claims back its domain. And at the main exit from the Mississippi bird's foot, used by the shipping, streaks of sediments run to waste in the deep water of the Gulf of Mexico.

Startling ignorance about water

*R*IVERS LOOM large in human life chiefly because they are the handiest source of fresh water, for drinking, watering crops and running industries. Most cities have sprung up on the banks of rivers or lakes. Waterwheels driven by streams were the mainstay of industry from Roman times until the 19th Century, and even now they generate a significant share of the world's electricity. The supply of clean water is taken for granted in rich countries, but many women in the Third World spend several hours of every day of their lives fetching water from impure sources that makes their families ill. Waterborne diseases kill at least 5 million people a year and debilitate many more.

All of the water on land originates from the oceans, and the wind delivers it in the form of vapour or clouds. The water descends as rain and starts a complex series of processes that include re-evaporation and more rain. (For 'rain' read rain, hail, snow, dew or rime – all the means by which water precipitates from the atmosphere.) Many of the world's farmers rely on rain falling directly on their fields, in rain-fed agriculture as opposed to irrigation systems. The transfers of water between the oceans, the air and the land, and back to the ocean, start with the evaporation from the oceans, each year, of about a metre of water (1300 millimetres). As the oceans are almost 4 kilometres deep on average, only a very small part of the Earth's water stock takes part in the water cycle.

Most of evaporated water returns directly as rain falling on the oceans, and the rest comes back in runoff from the land, mainly via the rivers. The runoff equals the amount of water delivered to the land from the oceans, by wind and rain, which may be roughly 7 per cent of the oceans' evaporation. The land's sub-cycle of evaporation and rain makes its total rainfall about three times greater than the input by the winds off the oceans, perhaps averaging about 700 millimetres a year on the land masses.

These figures are impressionistic only. About the water cycle, a crucial piece of the Earth system, human knowledge is startlingly defective. Ignorance about evaporation, clouds and the amount of rain falling on the Earth's surface is so pervasive that the true rainfall figures could be twice as great, or half as great, as those given in textbooks. The greatest uncertainty is in the 'firebox' of the tropical oceans, which powers the global weather machine. Methods of judging rainfall from space depend mainly on sightings of clouds with cold tops. Snow and ice lying on the ground are better observed, by satellites.

Rivers ought to be the easiest part of the water cycle to monitor, yet few runoffs are measured with anything like the precision of the Mississippi. Climate modellers need to know the runoffs, to balance their books concerning the water cycle, and also to take account of the behaviour of oceans as rivers reach them. This is where the main loop of the water cycle completes itself. The fresh water created by the original distillation from the ocean surface returns to mix with the salt sea. But the mixing is not instantaneous, and films of fresh water cover the sea surface at the mouths of rivers. They are especially important in the Arctic Ocean, where fresh water from the northern continents freezes more easily to form sea ice than the salt water would.

Efforts to compute and observe the interactions between rain, plants and soil moisture are also urgent. The soil divides into a thin top layer from which direct evaporation is possible, a root zone where the plants extract water, and an underlying zone where water moves down under gravity or upwards by diffusion. All this is only one phase of the water cycle on land, which altogether is the special concern of the science of hydrology. The processes are easier to sketch in a computer model of a drainage basin than to observe accurately in real life.

Snow and ice, for example, can bottle up water in the winter and release it to the soil and the rivers during a thaw. Rivers and lakes receive some rain water directly on their surfaces, and also evaporate highly variable amounts of water back into the air. Rain water can run horizontally over or through soil, or percolate underground. Vegetation influences the behaviour of the water. Ground (underground) water tends to form a layer of saturated soil or rock at a level called the water table. Whether it is a metre or 100 metres down, the water table defines how deep a well must be, to tap ground water in a simple way.

Sometimes the ground water reemerges in springs, or seeps directly into rivers. Sometimes it settles in deep-lying reservoirs. In desert regions, such reservoirs may be unreplenished for thousands of years, and their contents are called 'fossil' water. At any stage in the water cycle on land, the water may be relatively pure, or contaminated with various loads of living organisms, salts and other chemicals. Add to all such natural processes the human interference with rivers, soil and vegetation, and it may be unsurprising that the numbers describing the water cycle are vague, to put it politely.

The realism of numerical models is always a stringent but legitimate test of the state of knowledge of pieces of the Earth system. In the mid-1970s, climate modellers tried to predict the runoff of water from the land, region by region, from the known pattern of sea-surface temperatures. The resulting map was wrong enough to be comical, with some deserts awash and the Mississippi and great rivers of Asia running dry. It would not be worth mentioning but for two reasons: the models have not greatly improved, and the main errors arise early in the water cycle, with the computing of rain.

Hydrologists complain that they were not consulted about the design of the present generation of remote-sensing satellites. They would like to be able to measure the extent of all freshwater bodies, rivers and lakes, with a resolution of 30 metres, and their heights to an accuracy of 5 centimetres – and to do so daily. That is a tall order, and flooding under a canopy of vegetation, such as happens annually in the Amazon Basin, might require long-wavelength radar for its detection. Automatic data-collection platforms at water level, as on the Mississippi, radioing information via a satellite if appropriate, may be a surer,

162

quicker and cheaper way of achieving this degree of monitoring.

For both agriculturalists and hydrologists, the water content of the upper layers of soil is a key quantity. The activity of plants, as measured by the vegetation index, is a proxy indicator of soil moisture, which can also be roughly calculated from rainfall estimates and surface temperature measurements. For direct measurements, remote-sensing hydrologists look to microwave radio emissions from the Earth. Dry soil radiates strongly at short radio wavelengths, but the signal is weaker, the wetter the soil.

The US experimental satellite *Nimbus*-7 carried a Scanning Multichannel Microwave Radiometer that looked slantingly at the ground and sensed the Earth's emissions. It gave measures of soil moisture, but with enough confusion from vegetation for Bhaskar Choudhury at NASA's Goddard Space Flight Center to advocate a 'microwave vegetation index'. And the poor resolution inherent with microwaves meant that small patches of ground drenched by torrential rain were overlooked, if the surroundings were dry.

Satellites of the *Landsat* and *SPOT* type, or surveys by aircraft, can help hydrologists and geologists to find ground water for wells. This is a high priority for remote-sensing experts in India, for example, with their *IRS-1* satellite. Sometimes it is a matter of reading the geology of the landscape, sometimes of spotting water near the surface that either reveals its presence by vegetation or breaks the surface briefly in a wet season. But the ground water's replenishment, by infiltration through the subsoil, is a crucial matter often left to guesswork.

Much easier to observe are long-term effects of the water cycle in remodelling the land. The gnawing power of water is apparent in deep canyons incised in rising ground, and more suddenly in landslides. Its building power is evident in every flood plain and delta. Landforms and watercourses often stand out clearly in satellite images. 'Before and after' observations can show a single storm or flood of exceptional violence altering the landscape more drastically than a century of quiet erosion and deposition.

The redistribution of material and nutrients is an endless refreshment of the land, and some accounts of soil erosion fail to distinguish between natural and manmade erosion, and between destructive and creative effects. One farmer's erosion can be another's new fertile field. China's Yellow River (Hwang Ho) was always literally yellow with silt carried from a loess plateau of windblown dust deposited during the ice ages. It was always China's Sorrow, too, because of its terrible floods and changes of course. Deforestation in the loess plateau has accelerated the erosion and aggravated floods downstream. The fact remains that the dense population of northern China thrives on the fertile yellow silt smeared across the farmlands by every flood.

An ever-changing map

EUROPE'S RHINE river flows through a rift valley in its prettiest section. It goes to the sea by another arm of the same system of rifts, into which pour the water and silt of the Rhine and other rivers, including the Maas (Meuse) and the Schelde. The very name of The Netherlands means the lowlands, and the Dutch rendered a delta of islands and sandbanks habitable and fertile by many centuries of effort. The Netherlands stands out in satellite images as the most comprehensively engineered patch of the Earth's surface.

The famous Dutch canals and dykes are an intricate system of water management conceived long before computers. The emblematic windmills pumped water from manmade fields into canals flowing at a higher level, before modern machines took over. Towns rose on piles that reached to the firmer sands of the delta. More than a third of the country is below sea-level. Disastrous sea-floods during storm surges kept drowning people and ruining the soil with salt, until the Dutch fenced off the sea with dams and storm barriers. The result is an artificial coastline. A barrier enclosed the former Zuiderzee in 1932. After a storm surge in 1953, a Delta Plan to seal off other estuaries was put in hand and completed in the 1980s. Barring a large rise in sea-level, the Dutch can put away their waders.

For Asia's Dutchmen, the Muslim Bengalis of Bangladesh, wet feet are still normal. About 116 million of them inhabit the Ganges delta, built by Nature in another rift valley leading to the sea. The Ganges itself, sacred to the Hindus of the big neighbour, India, drains the southern slopes of the high Himalayan mountains. The Brahmaputra river, bringing twice as much water, comes in a U-bend from the north of the Himalayas to join the Ganges in Bangladesh.

The Brahmaputra changes its name to Jamuna, and the combined Ganges–Brahmaputra is called the Padma. A third river, the Meghna, carrying almost as much water as the Ganges, joins it near the sea. It

Facing:
The Dutch Delta from space.
Manmade sea-barriers protect a
prosperous land of farms, ports
and cities created on the
low-lying mudbanks of multiple
rivers. Dutch scientists used
different Landsat channels to
depict the rivers and the land.

164

LANDSAT DATA, PROCESSED BY NATIONAL AEROSPACE LAB. (NLR), NETHERLANDS

Floodwater in Bangladesh darkens a weather-satellite image of September 1988 (top). Two months later (second image) the rivers were more normal.

Facing:
Changes in a Bangladeshi river mapped by SPOT. A remarkable composite shows a 30-kilometre section of the Jamuna river, alias the Brahmaputra, before the 1988 floods (dark blue) and after (light blue). Unaltered channels appear grey. The abandoned dark-blue channels represent new land, points and islands, while the light-blue channels were lost to habitation and cultivation.

pours in from the hills of the India–Burma border and from the Meghalaya plateau, which overlooks Bangladesh and receives the world's heaviest rainfall – up to 12,000 millimetres a year.

The Himalayas are still trying to rise, and ice, water and chemical weathering keep trying to tear them down. As a result, the world's highest mountain range supplies billions of tons of silt a year to the rivers of Bangladesh. Like Holland until recently, Bangladesh is vulnerable to storm surges from the sea. A hurricane (cyclone) in the Bay of Bengal in 1970 killed about 300,000 people, mainly by drowning. Great dams on the Dutch model might reduce this risk, which can only become greater if the sea level rises. But Bangladesh is one of the world's poorest countries. In wealth per head, the average Dutchman is as rich as seventy-five Bengalis.

River floods are an annual event in Bangladesh, when rainfall and snowfall on the Himalayas and the eastern hills peaks in the monsoon season, June to September. In about one year in three the runoff grossly overloads the rivers of Bangladesh and causes severe and widespread flooding. And perhaps once in 100 years an exceptional flood puts most of the country under water. This last happened in 1988.

Like the Dutch of bygone times, the Bengalis are thoroughly adapted to the wet life in the Ganges Delta. Rice is the natural choice for their main crop, and fish and shrimps provide most of their protein. Their buildings stand on natural ridges, artificial mounds or stilts. Roads and railways run on embankments, but boats serve for transport as well as fishing. The only way to cross the major rivers is by ferryboat.

The flood of 1988 covered 62 per cent of Bangladesh, and largely submerged even the capital, Dhaka, where city slickers had forgotten how to cope with water. It was the worst flood since instrument records began. Exceptional rainfall in the northeastern corner of the Indian subcontinent was the cause of the trouble. The Brahmaputra–Jamuna peaked at the end of August at the highest level ever noted, and the Ganges and Meghna also stood very high a few days later, competing with the Jamuna for the outlets to the sea. The levee on the right bank of the Jamuna burst for a second year running.

Clouds cleared to let *NOAA* weather satellites see the Bangladeshi flood in September 1988, when it was just past its peak. The images showed the very rainy northeast of country under open water, which is usual in late summer. More to the point, a temporary lake 200 kilometres long and 70 wide filled much of central Bangladesh along the

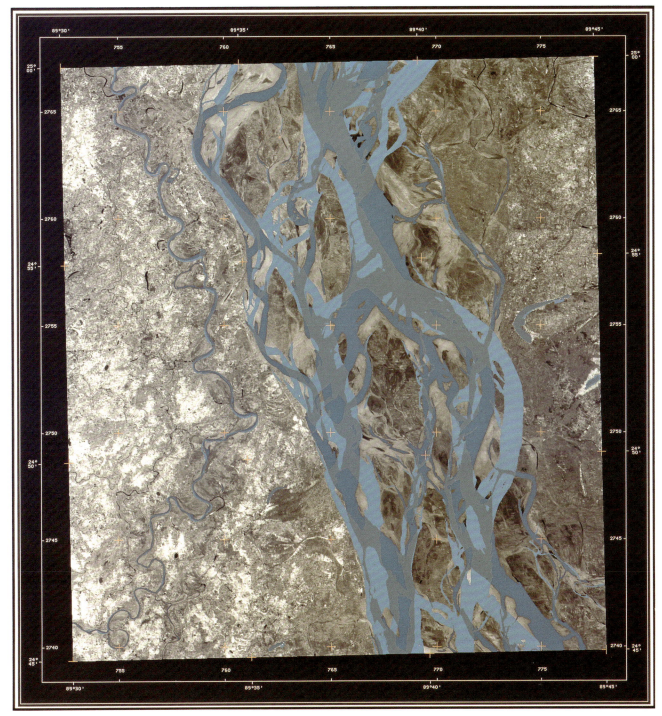

route of the Brahmaputra–Jamuna. The government reported that the 1988 flood damaged or destroyed 7 million homes, along with 1200 bridges and culverts, 14,000 kilometres of roads and railways and 2000 kilometres of flood embankments. The official death toll was 2000, out of 45 million people directly affected. If the rural Bengalis did not have plenty of aquatic common-sense and agility, the figure would have been far higher. But their government faced massive costs for relief operations and repairs to the nation's infrastructure.

What about food? According to official figures, 13 per cent of the year's rice crop of Bangladesh was lost in the 1988 flood – dire indeed, if true, for a poorly nourished country. But what the rivers destroy they make good with bountiful water for other harvests. A British geographer, Hugh Brammer, reappraised cereal production in Bangladesh for 1987–89, years affected by severe flooding, and concluded that it was no lower than for the preceding flood-free year, 1986–87. Bumper crops in regions outside the worst flooding, plus replanting of flooded areas when the water recedes, help to replace the crops drowned or swept away. Production of rice, and wheat too, increases in the dry season following a severe flood.

The real price of the floods is paid by the many farming families directly ruined by the loss of their crops and livestock. In some cases they lose even their land. The land is in any case divided and redivided into small parcels, with a typical farming household having a piece the size of a tennis court. The least fortunate 40 per cent of the rural population has no land at all, and must scrabble for a living on banks and temporary islands of the rivers and estuaries of the delta. Every flood changes the channels, and a shift of 100 metres can dispossess dozens of families.

The remapping of Bangladesh from space, after the 1988 floods, is one of the most notable applications of the *SPOT* remote-sensing satellite. In the past, the absence of up-to-date maps showing recent river changes made it all the harder to plan river defences, transport routes and relief operations to cope with the next severe flood. The French Institut Géographique National joined with Spot Image and the Bangladeshi government's own remote-sensing experts and water engineers, to use *SPOT* for the purpose. In comparisons with older satellite images and conventional maps the changes due to the floods of the late 1980s show up clearly.

International agencies and half-a-dozen rich countries have been

168

bombarding Bangladesh with offers of help and often contradictory technical proposals. The most urgent needs are for earlier warnings from India on the state of the big rivers, better telecommunications with Bangladesh's own river and rainfall gauges, and rain radars in the wet hills. UN agencies are developing a computer model of the river system to help predict floods, while Denmark sponsors a more detailed model of local impacts.

Better warnings may save lives, but only large-scale engineering works can make much difference to the extent of the flooding. Reservoirs to trap excess water would require too much land. The priority for new embankments is bound to be the protection of cities, power stations and other expensive installations. No one imagines that Bangladesh, at its present state of development, can prevent floods or stop the rivers varying their courses. Indeed, the *SPOT* team is standing by to repeat the remapping after the next flood. Meanwhile, on new-formed river banks and temporary islands exposed by the falling water, patches of vegetation in the *SPOT* images show where Bangladeshi families grow a little rice on ground that will disappear in the next flood.

Pollution by fertilization

*T*HE FERTILE silt of the Nile, spread by annual floods, created Egypt's prosperity in the days of the pyramid-builders. The conqueror Alexander sited Alexandria on the coast of the Nile delta. Satellite images of Egypt show a long ribbon of farmland following the Nile through the desert, and fanning out in the delta. Away to the south, a manmade lake more than 300 kilometres long straddles the Egypt–Sudan border behind the Aswan High Dam, completed in 1970.

The full reckoning of Egypt's gains and losses from the High Dam is complicated and unfinished. But it does reduce the Nile's flow and traps nearly all its silt. Adverse effects are evident where the Nile reaches the Mediterranean Sea. One is subsidence in the unreplenished delta. Another is a severe impact on marine life and fisheries in the eastern Mediterranean. These relied on natural chemical nutrients washed from the land and delivered by the Nile to the open sea.

As life on land is restricted by water supplies, the sea's fertility is limited by nutrients. The plight of Egypt's coastal fishermen is a telling demonstration that the water cycle is partly a nutrient cycle. The

LANDSAT DATA, PROCESSED BY JOINT RESEARCH CENTRE, EC

Slime from space. On the northern Adriatic Sea, the green mucilage that afflicts Italian beach resorts in hot, windless summers was well observed by Landsat in July 1989. European Community oceanographic models link the slime to the route of effluent from the Po delta, upper left.

fertilization of the sea by the rivers is a necessary natural process – a point worth remembering, when cases arise of overfertilization of the sea by human action.

Tourists visiting the beaches of Italy's east coast to laze in the summer sunshine have in recent years encountered a repellent green slime. It is a biochemical product, originating at the bottom of the Adriatic, that can smear the sand and paint ankles green. The exact origin of the slime is still debated. It can occur naturally, especially in fine summers, but nitrates and phosphates running off Italy's farms down the Po river, notably in the form of untreated pig manure, probably aggravate the problem by nourishing blooms of algae. Human sewage from the coastal resorts themselves makes its contribution.

The geographical setting does not help. Most of the world's coast-lines are washed by wide, deep oceans, with a great capacity for absorb-ing, diluting and disposing of chemicals. Water pollution is usually severe only in inland waters, estuaries and coastal seas immediately adjoining the sources of pollution. But the Mediterranean is a land-locked ocean. A collision beween Eurasia and Africa has left it as a bottle with only a narrow neck to the Atlantic, through the Gibraltar Strait.

More than 100 million people live on the Mediterranean shores, in seventeen countries and 120 major cities. And Italy's east coast is in a bottle within a bottle: the Adriatic Sea, a narrow and shallow flooded valley between Italy and Yugoslavia. The collision between Italy and Switzerland built the nearby Alps, and downwarping created a valley leading into the Adriatic. Here the Po river carries water from the Alps and chemicals from the farms and cities of the Po's own flood plain.

The European Community's Joint Research Centre at Ispra in northern Italy uses remote-sensing satellites to study pollution in the Adriatic. Sea-surface temperatures from weather satellites help to show the flows, but the most useful images were from the now-defunct Coastal Zone Color Scanner of the US *Nimbus*-7 satellite. The scientists processed them to show algal blooms, and tongues of silty water emerging from the delta of the Po displayed the route of nutrients leaving the river.

Interpreting the satellite data goes hand in hand with making computer models of the Adriatic. These simulate the circulation and turnover of water in the constricted sea, and predict the dispersal and fate of chemical contaminants in the living marine system. The winds of winter and normal summers stir the sea and disperse the contaminants quite quickly, but in a particularly calm summer the fresh warm water from the Po forms a nutrient-rich layer on the sea surface. This is the breeding ground of an explosively growing, fish-killing mix of algal species whose eventual decay seems to give rise to the green slime.

The slime is a warning against relying on averages. In typical weather, the Adriatic bears its burden of nutrients without truculence. In the rare still air of a hot summer it hits back. The tourist industries of Italy and Yugoslavia have suffered badly, as beach-seekers switch to unslimed destinations. Saving money by not dealing properly with pig manure and human sewage has cost a fortune in the end.

Hyperfertilizing chemicals are not, of course, the only pollutants that rivers deliver to the sea, nor is the Adriatic the only landlocked sea. Europe has more than its share of these, with the Black Sea, the Baltic Sea and the North Sea all exposed to the effluents of densely populated and highly industrialized nations. The North Sea, fed by the Rhine and many smaller rivers, has for long been polluted by the seven nations on its shores and by others upstream on the Rhine and Elbe rivers.

The North Sea is now the subject of environmental crusades and intensive scientific research, including remote-sensing similar to that used in the Adriatic. The research helps to show who is to blame for the toxic chemicals, radioactive pollution and untreated sewage that join the oil slicks and polluted rain in a sorely mistreated puddle. Up till now, the villain has often been Britain, perhaps because islanders are too easily accustomed to using the sea as a dustbin.

Salt is the chief natural contaminant acquired by rivers in washout from the land: mainly common salt, sodium chloride, but also other salts that reflect the geology of the region. Problems created by the traces of salt in inland waters have plagued water managers since prehistoric times.

The fall of the first civilization

*A*BOUT 8000 YEARS have passed since people living near what is now the border between Iraq and Iran discovered that they could enlarge the area of their croplands by digging ditches to carry water. Geographically the place was an inducement to the first experiments in irrigation, because it is an area of alluvial fans. These are like sloping inland deltas, made by branching rivers where the mountains meet the plain – in this case, the Zagros mountains and the Mesopotamian plain. Trenches cut sideways from the streams easily led water to new fields. The early farmers freed themselves from dependence on intermittent river floods or unreliable rain.

More than 2 million square kilometres of the Earth's land suface is now irrigated. Although that is only 1.5 per cent of the total land area, it includes important concentrations of population, in China, India, Egypt, California and elsewhere. Techniques of draining waterlogged land are like irrigation in reverse. Canals for transport and aqueducts for urban water supplies are variations on the same hydraulic tune, and ditch-digging and redigging has occupied countless human hours for eight millennia. The results are often plain to see on satellite images, as grids and networks of lines across the landscapes. Conspicuous modern emblems of water management are clusters of circles in the desert made by rotary irrigation systems, typically fed from wells.

'Making the desert bloom' is an honourable objective that has motivated gigantic human effort. The Great Manmade River project in Libya, in the desert of North Africa, is a contemporary example.

It taps large underground lakes of fossil water beneath the Saharan sands. Phase 1 of the project draws on 270 wells located around 500 kilometres inland, in eastern Libya. From 1992, pipelines 4 metres in diameter and totalling 1900 kilometres in length will deliver 1.5 billion tons of water a year to towns, farms and industries near the Mediterranean shore. Fossil water is a nonrenewable resource, like the oil that makes Libya rich enough for a manmade river, and the pipelines will run dry in about 50 years.

Globally, irrigation seems likely to increase greatly, to help feed the growing world population, and perhaps also to cope with regional threats of drier soil in a greenhouse warming. Irrigation systems can, though, go badly wrong. This happened slowly for the first hydraulic civilization, Sumer, and faster for a large irrigation scheme in the valley of the River Indus in Pakistan initiated in the 19th Century by British engineers, and most rapidly for a major irrigation enterprise in Soviet Central Asia. For modern geographers concerned with the interaction of human social and political systems with the environment, irrigation is a prototype.

Sumer in Mesopotamia (modern Iraq) occupied the flood plain of the Tigris and Euphrates rivers, downstream from the alluvial fans of the early irrigation trials. With irrigation ditches and newly invented ploughs, the Sumerians created food surpluses that made possible the rise of cities, beginning about 3800 BC. Wheels and writing were two other major innovations in Sumer, which was also a setting for profound social change.

Digging and maintaining irrigation ditches, and sharing the water and the produce equitably, called for a high degree of organization. At first this may have been achieved by more or less democratic means, but a gulf grew between primary producers and administrators. This quickly led to the invention of modern civilization: that is to say, to taxation, class distinctions that enabled the rich and privileged to give orders to the poor, and chronic warfare sponsored by a ruling warrior caste – all sanctified by organized religion. It was in Sumer and nearby Egypt, around 3000 BC, that rulers first succeeded in taming human beings en masse, at much the same time as donkeys were domesticated.

With its network of canals and cities, Sumer prospered for 2000 years, because the Sumerians were intelligent irrigators. They knew that success depended on preventing the irrigated ground from becoming waterlogged. In an arid environment, evaporation of water from the soil leaves traces of the salt that the water carried. The salt hardens the soil and eventually poisons the crops. Cautious application of irrigation water, combined with good drainage, can prevent waterlogging. The Sumerians also used deep-rooted weeds as natural pumps to draw water out of the soil and transpire it to the air.

Eventually, though, excessive seepage into the ground and a general rise in the level of underground water began to cripple Sumer. One explanation on offer is that, in strife between cities, cutting off water supplies was a favoured stratagem, and this led to the hurried construction of new, hydraulically superfluous canals. In a slow decline, lasting 700 years, the build-up of salt in the soil led first to a replacement of wheat by barley, and then to shrinking yields of barley. The proud cities of Sumer became villages and the Babylonians conquered them.

Several large areas of the Earth's land masses have 'internal drainage'. The rivers make lakes and inland seas in the lowest parts of the terrain. The water then has nowhere to go but up into the air by evaporation, the only way to close the loop in the water cycle. Natural and manmade contaminants of the water, which in other circumstances would be washed out to sea, are then simply dumped by the evaporating water.

A natural product of internal drainage and the evaporation of water is often a very briny lake, like the Dead Sea in the Middle East where fishes cruising down the Jordan river face sudden death. Wholly dried-out salt lakes make playas like Bonneville Salt Flats in Utah. Intermittent rewetting can keep a playa extremely flat, so that record-breaking car drivers esteem the Bonneville Flats. And without the redemption of an outlet to the ocean, mismanaged irrigation in a basin of internal drainage can create a manmade salt lake, as the Soviet Union has been demonstrating.

How not to irrigate

FROM THE AIR, the Aral Sea in Soviet Central Asia looks at first sight like a tidal estuary at low water, with sandbanks rising above channels and runnels. But, as an inland sea, the Aral never had a tide worth mentioning, and the present ebb has a terrible finality. Beside channels dry except for forlorn puddles, grey-white swirly ribbons of salt decorate the sandbanks. A broad grey-white band, stretching along the eastern shore until it disappears in a haze of airborne dust and salt, denotes a new salt desert created by evaporation at the margin of a shrinking sea.

The name of the Aral means 'sea of islands' and the islands have grown much larger as the level of the sea has fallen. Around the former shore, villages that were lapped by the water of the bountiful Aral now stand high and dry, like so many Arks on Ararat. The most haunting image of all, whether from the air or the ground, is the fishing fleet of Muynak stranded more than 20 kilometres from the water's edge. The once-abundant fishes are in any case extinct, in a new Dead Sea.

An astronomer on the Moon would see the Aral Sea shrinking, like an eye closing, as the most visible change to the planet caused by current human action. Atlases that show the Aral as the fourth largest lake in the world, and about the size of Ireland, are out of date. That was the situation in 1960, when the Aral covered 63,000 square kilometres. By 1990 it had lost about two-thirds of its water and more than 40 per cent of its surface area. The changes were plain in satellite images from the 1970s and 1980s, and geographers were unsurprised.

Melted snow from the high mountains of Central Asia comes down two rivers, the Amu Darya and Syr Darya, that have no outlet to the ocean but run through a desert towards the Aral Sea. They used to deliver 55 billion tons of water a year to the lake, and every year the same amount evaporated from it. The Aral moderated the severe desert climate, which swings from Saharan summers to Siberian winters.

The desert of Central Asia was dreaded by travellers on the old Silk Road that linked China with the Middle East and Europe from classical times onwards. Leaving the cities of Samarkand and Bukhara behind them, the westbound caravans laden with silk for Roman flirts or medieval matrons crossed the Amu Darya river and struggled through the Karakum Desert. There, sand-storms and large mobile sand-dunes, propelled by strong winds, routinely buried roads and villages.

To protect a railway, Russian geographers in Czarist times created a research station at Repetek, an ancient resting place for the caravans. The Repetek station, surrounded by dunes in various states of mobility and stabilization where camels still wander, is now world-famous as a centre of desert research. Its climatic records show temperatures touching 50 degrees C in summer and 30 below zero in winter.

The scientists at Repetek documented Nature's way of halting the dunes, with desert-proof saxaul trees spreading large roots to find the water table that lurks even under the desert sand. They developed tricks of their own, to shelter pioneering grasses and shrubs with small fences, or to put down mats to stop the wind picking at the loose sand. They showed how overgrazing by animals of the desert herders, or excessive cutting of the saxaul for firewood, could set the dunes marching again. But the desert researchers were powerless to stop destabilization on a grander scale.

Soviet engineers drew off the water of the two rivers supplying the Aral Sea, for growing cotton in the desert. When Lenin himself declared to the republics of Central Asia immediately after the Russian Revolution, 'What you need most is irrigation,' it was not a particularly original thought. Some 30,000 square kilometres of desert land was under irrigation in 1917. In feudal times, long before the Russian Czars conquered them, the Central Asian peoples had used their rivers to irrigate an area approaching 100,000 square kilometres. This was not very small compared with the 150,000 square kilometres of the 1980s. Ancient methods of managing water included underground galleries for drawing off the fresh water that floats on top of salty water in the desert water table.

Although Soviet builders of dams and canals dismissed such techniques as 'primitive', even the Sumerians could have given them a tip or two about the hazards of seepage and salt. In the unrelenting drive for more cotton, farmers drenched the fields with water without ensuring adequate drainage. Many canals and ditches were left unlined, causing waterlogging. Even without the destruction of the Aral Sea, salt accumulation and sheer waste of water would have made the Central Asian works an object lesson in how not to irrigate.

The most spectacular feature of the Soviet irrigators' empire is the Karakum Canal, which diverts 10 billion tons a year of Amu Darya water 1100 kilometres westward, into the Karakum Desert. But many lesser irrigation schemes together removed even more river water. In 1974 the Syr Darya ran dry at its outlet to the Aral Sea. In 1982 so did the Amu Darya. Exceptional precipitation sometimes revives the rivers, but otherwise the supply of water to the Aral has ceased. No computer model is needed to predict that the Aral can only evaporate into the desert air, leaving its salt behind.

Fishing boat stranded on the dried-out southern shore of the Aral Sea in Soviet Central Asia.

Facing:
The Aral Sea's decline charted in a composite of space images. In 1960 (light blue) the lake was as large as Ireland. By 1973 (mid-blue) it was beginning to diminish noticeably. By 1989 (dark blue) the Aral had lost much of its former area, and the fish were extinct.

*T*HIS OUTCOME is no sad mistake or miscalculation. Copying Sumer's authoritarian rule better than its irrigation skills, Soviet rulers sentenced the Aral to death, in a great hydraulic gamble on the 'white gold' of cotton. Lowering the level of the Aral Sea was also seen as a means of increasing the hydroelectric potential of the rivers, by the additional height, or 'head', through which the water dropped. As the planners meant the sea to disappear by 1980, it has lasted longer than expected.

Soviet climatologists managed to veto the most grandiose scheme of the water engineers, who wanted to divert the flow of two Siberian rivers towards the region north of the Aral Sea. The water of another was to be redirected south and west towards the Black Sea. More than 1000 billion tons of water flows yearly from these rivers into the Arctic Ocean. Why not use it to irrigate new farmlands and perhaps even rescue the Aral Sea? As the climatologists pointed out, the rivers' fresh water nourishes the sea-ice of the Arctic, and interfering with them could have drastic effects on the global climate.

The facts about what was going on in Central Asia were for long suppressed, even though they could not be hidden from the vigilant satellites. As recently as 1986, Soviet specialists were boasting to colleagues from the Third World of how they were making backward areas prosperous 'using the latest achievements of science and technology'. Desert researchers had to encode their criticisms as positive statements. One expert wrote in 1980: 'The area surrounding the Aral Sea can be considered an excellent example of desertification processes.'

Not until the Gorbachev era were scientists and journalists able to expose the horrors of the Central Asian disaster. The scientists brought out their own series of images from Soviet remote-sensing satellites that chronicled the Aral Sea's decline. They pointed to the ominous grey strip down the Aral's eastern shoreline, and to clouds of dust visible in some satellite images.

The irrigation planners had failed to take account of the strong winds of the region, that cause sand-storms and keep sand-dunes on the move. Now, from the edge of the Aral, they raise salt-storms and build salty dunes. The air of Central Asia, always dusty, has become laden with salt. Blowing across the deserts, oases and irrigated cotton farms, even to the mountains 700 kilometres away that are the source of the Amu Darya and Syr Darya, the Aral salt adds to the problems in the fields, and attacks the respiratory tracts of animals and human beings.

The want of imagination about the salt-storms and other environmental effects of creating a new salt lake in the heart of Asia was matched by indifference to the fate of non-Russian ethnic groups whose territories abutted on the Aral Sea. The journalists found the lives of 35 million inhabitants of Central Asia blighted by hydraulic mismanagement. Hardest hit are the Kara-Kalpak people whose only homeland is the southern shore of the Aral Sea. A generation ago, their life was modest but wholesome. They grew melons, rice, cotton and silkworms in the Amu Darya delta, grazed cattle and sheep on the desert margin, and hunted the fishes of the sea.

Any trickle of water coming down the river is now not only salty but polluted with pesticides and other chemicals. When the wind blows off the new salt flats, breathing is difficult. In a geographically absurd gesture of apology, the Soviet authorities send fish overland from Arctic and Pacific ports, to be canned in a factory that was built for the Aral's own fish. The Kara-Kalpaks' infant mortality rate is the highest in the Soviet Union, with one in ten babies dying before its first birthday. The red flowers of salt-resistant solianka bushes, growing wild, are emblems of a people's lost hope.

Despite a standstill in irrigation schemes, the Aral Sea now loses the uppermost metre of its water by evaporation every year. To stabilize the Aral at its 1990 level would require an immediate supply of 35 billion tons of water a year. The water engineers offer 21 billion tons by 2005, in a scheme where billions of roubles would go to correct the loss of water by seepage in the irrigation ditches and collect the runoff from irrigated fields.

In a land ruined by misrule, the Central Asian republics have joined the clamour by the Soviet Union's ethnic minorities to win at least partial independence. Some commentators thought that the republics would hold back, until the Russians had paid for clearing up the mess along the Amu Darya and Syr Darya rivers and at the Aral Sea. Evidently that now seems less important than the wish to regain local control of the environment.

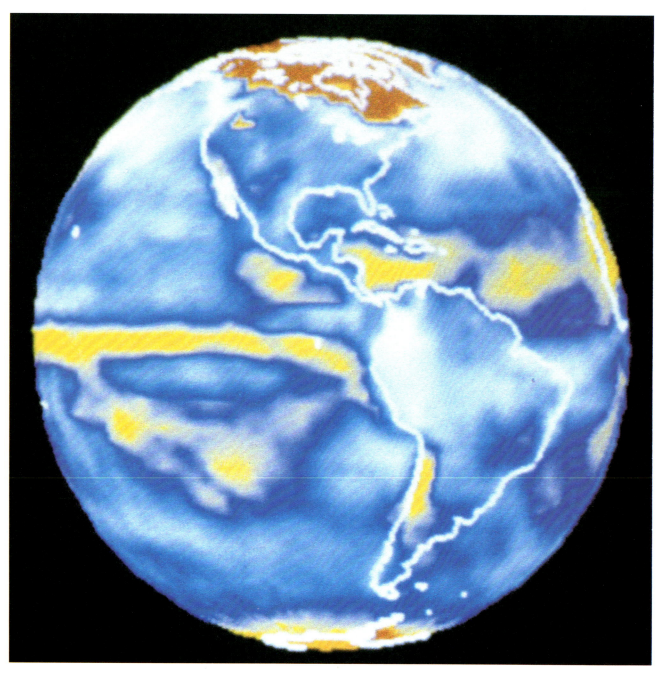

ERBS AND NOAA-9 DATA, ANALYSED
AT UNIV. CHICAGO

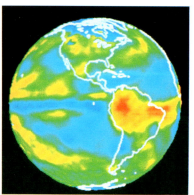

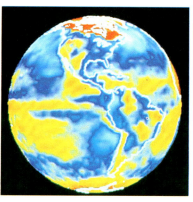

CHAPTER 7

The Watchkeepers

Nothing in the Earth system is as simple as it looks. This concluding chapter reverts to the space-ship's air-conditioning system, and to the proposition that the climate is about to change. Computer models of climate predict a warming due to human activity. In the creation of the new global geography, it falls to the climate modellers to draw in all the pieces of the Earth system that they can handle, and see how they interact. Scientifically speaking, this is strictly work in progress.

International controversy about the 'greenhouse warming' happens to be fierce in the 1990s. The particulars of that debate are largely avoided here, in favour of seeing the issues in a more durable frame-work of knowledge and ignorance. The discovery of a 'sink' for carbon dioxide in the Northern Hemisphere illustrates how false certain cherished assumptions about the Earth system can be. The same research contradicts the most pessimistic suppositions about the role of tropical deforestation in the greenhouse system. The appropriate stance in respect of the Earth system and environmental prescriptions is humility.

There is plenty to be humble about, not least concerning the

Facing:
Cooling effects of clouds observed in the Earth Radiation Budget Experiment. In the large image, for April 1985, blue and especially white regions experienced cooling due to the reflection of sunlight from the cloud tops. Greenhouse-like warming due to trapping by clouds of radiation from the Earth's surface (far left) is greatest in the yellow and red regions. The third image (near, below) shows the combined effect: cooling in blue and white regions and warming in yellow and red regions. Globally, the cooling outweighs the warming.

comprehensively confusing signals sent to the poor countries from the rich ones. The unofficial watchkeepers of Spaceship Earth, people leading their lives and interacting with their environments over the millennia in all parts of the world, can sometimes be smarter than the experts. An archaeological discovery in Bolivia is an example, and the book ends with a remark on ecocolonialism.

The enigmatic clouds

*T*HE FATE OF the human part of the Earth system during the coming century is written not in the stars, but in the clouds. They are the leading actors in the drama of weather and climate. In monsoon zones and semi-arid lands the most fervent prayers are those for rainbearing clouds. An airline pilot in a computerized cockpit will override the autopilot to weave through temporary Himalayas of high-rise clouds that could toss his jumbo jet about like a paper dart.

Cloud-watching is now back in fashion among meteorologists, whose recent predecessors were fixated by pressure charts and seldom looked out of the window. A generation of would-be modifiers of the weather literally carried a torch for the clouds, in the form of silver-iodide smoke generators. These supplied promising-looking clouds with small nuclei on which ice crystals could form and supposedly cause the cloud to drop its rain. The US Air Force used the technique in the Vietnam War, in the hope of bogging down enemy supply columns in mud.

In any attempt to understand the global climate, never mind to forecast changes, clouds are doubly crucial. Regionally, their behaviour governs the distribution of rainfall. Globally they could exert an overall warming or cooling effect, depending on their character and distribution. An International Satellite Cloud Climatology Project is a key element in current climate research. It attends to the physical characteristics of the clouds, as discernible from space, and the monthly and annual averages for cloud cover that it generates give a vivid impression of the world's climatic zones.

The rather shapeless clusters of clouds around the tropics show where warm, moist air is soaring into the upper air. The cloud-free zones of warm deserts, at the northern and southern edges of the tropics are regions where the air subsides and grows warmer – the very

182

opposite of a recipe for making clouds. The Poles are also largely cloud-free for the same reason, and surrounded by icy deserts.

Between the desert belts and the polar regions, in the great middle zones where warm, moist air meets cold, dry air coming from the far north or south, the most characteristic cloud pattern is that of a swirling depression. A wedge of warm air between cold air masses makes thick masses of clouds at its edges, called fronts. A mid-latitude depression usually marches eastwards, guided by a jet stream. This is a narrow belt of very strong winds in the upper air that zigzags around the world from west to east. The westerlies borrow their circumpolar whirl from the Earth's rotation, while the winds in a depression make a similar whirl on a smaller scale.

The monsoons, the chief modifiers of the pattern of zones, are readily apparent in seasonal space images of clouds. India and China, the countries with the largest populations, lie nominally in the desert zone, and have dry winters. But in summer huge masses of monsoon clouds cover them, as the Asian land mass warms up and draws in moist air from the south. Lesser monsoons occur in other parts of the world.

When the world is warmer or cooler than at present, the zones of climate shift. In an ice age the cold, dry polar zones enlarge, squeezing the other zones towards the Equator. Monsoons weaken and rainfall generally diminishes. In warmer episodes, the polar zones shrink, the other zones shift towards the Poles and rainfall intensifies. But the overall pattern of tropics, warm deserts, westerlies and polar deserts persists. It is always complicated locally by the geography of sea, land and mountains. Warm ocean currents supply moisture and heat to the atmosphere in otherwise chilly places, like the Gulf Stream that warms Europe. Mountains help to create the displaced desert zones of Asia and North America.

Clouds deserve to be watched with a child's sense of wonder. There are warm and cold clouds, wet and dry clouds, low and high clouds, layered and heaped clouds, fluffy and streaky clouds, disorderly and patterned clouds, and fog, thunderclouds, tornadoes ... not to mention the famous cloud no bigger than a man's hand, and the one that always looks like a camel.

When moist air cools it makes clouds by condensation of water droplets (fluffy clouds) and freezing of the water into ice crystals (streaky clouds). The cooling can be due to an encounter with cold sea or land that forms fogbanks. More commonly, buoyant air rises, ex-

183

pands, and so cools. Layered clouds are often a lid on a layer of cold moist air, held down by a layer of warm dry air above. Strong up-draughts of moist air make heaped clouds. These become self-sustaining, when heat released by condensation spurs the air to rise faster. The best rainmakers are tall heaped clouds that form ice particles at their cold tops. Most rain is melted snow, which is why remote-sensing specialists use cold cloud tops as a guide to rainfall.

The most telling space observations concerning clouds so far are those that established the pattern of their warming and cooling actions. The white top of a cloud reflects sunlight into space and prevents it warming its patch of the world, while the grey bottom of the cloud acts as a blanket, preventing heat radiation escaping from the Earth's surface. It is not self-evident, which action is more important.

In October 1984 the Space Shuttle *Challenger* launched a remote-sensing satellite called ERBS, as part of the Earth Radiation Budget Experiment. It measured incoming sunlight, visible light reflected from clouds and the Earth's surface, and thermal infra-red radiation leaking into space from the top of the atmosphere. Similar instruments flew also in the NOAA weather satellites. By 1989, data from ERBS and NOAA-9 had been analysed to show that clouds exert an overall cooling action on Spaceship Earth.

This natural effect of clouds is several times stronger than warmings predicted for the 21st Century by a manmade enhancement of the greenhouse effect. And it is only the difference between two much larger effects of clouds – their warming and cooling actions. The cooling effect, taken alone, runs at more than ten times the warming predicted for a doubling of carbon dioxide in the atmosphere by human action. A 10 per cent change in this effect could therefore slash or double any predicted greenhouse warming.

In their skyscreening and rainy roles, clouds thus seem to dominate the Earth system, yet they need feedbacks from other parts of the system, even to form readily. Small salt particles carried into the air by sea spray often help water vapour to condense to liquid droplets as the air cools. Sulphurous agents put into the air by volcanoes and marine organisms can also promote cloud formation. Mountains create clouds, and a thousand textbooks say that the rising ground forces the air upwards, to chill and condense its moisture into clouds. But when meteorologists put serious numbers to this process, they do not work out. Something else must be happening on the misty mountain-tops.

A CLIMATE MODEL is a dream in a supercomputer. As a program for computing day-to-day weather runs its course, reckoning the changes grid point by grid point around the planet, the electronic tempests and jet streams rippling through the electronic atmosphere gradually lose touch with reality. Petty errors multiply until the simulated weather systems no longer even approximate to what the weather will really do next week. The weather model is kept awake by continual sensory inputs – updates on what the real weather is doing. In a climate model, a similar program runs almost unhindered far into the future.

If, cantering through the model's year 2001, the computer conjures up a drought in Europe or a hurricane in Vietnam or a blizzard in Antarctica, these are not real events, but have the verisimilitude of a dream. Europe does experience droughts sometimes, Vietnam knows strong winds, Antarctica has to receive its quota of snow. The computer reports its averages and variations in weather – region by region, month by month, decade by decade. The results should roughly resemble the present climate. To make them better, the modellers attend to changeable features of the Earth system that weather forecasts can take for granted and climate models cannot: seasonal sea-surface temperatures, soil moisture, vegetation, and so on.

The modellers can set the computer dreaming of an ice age or, more fashionably, of a world warmed by manmade greenhouse gases in the atmosphere. Water vapour and carbon dioxide are the most important natural greenhouse gases. Like a greenhouse, they let sunlight in but impede the escape of heat from the Earth's surface into space. Without the natural greenhouse effect the Earth would be a dead ball of ice.

What will happen if human activity doubles the carbon dioxide in the air? Were there no feedbacks at all, no changes in other parts of the Earth system, the greenhouse warming could be calculated by fairly simple physics. It would mean an increase in the global mean temperature of 1.2 degrees C. But in a warmer world, more water evaporates from the ocean, and this water vapour itself adds to the greenhouse effect. Ice in the polar seas would tend to melt, allowing the sea to absorb more of the Sun's heat. These immediate knock-on effects would increase the global warming to 3.4 degrees.

The primary task of the computer models is to see how realistic weather systems operating in a greenhouse world could govern regional changes and affect the overall warming. All of the main climate models use the same physics, and make similar simplifications and assumptions. Yet in an auction in the late 1980s, three leading models in the USA and one in Britain gave five different answers for the eventual increase in the global mean temperature in degrees C, expected with a doubling of carbon dioxide.

National Center for Atmospheric Research, Boulder	3.5
Geophysical Fluid Dynamics Laboratory, Princeton	4.0
Goddard Institute for Space Studies, New York	4.2
Meteorological Office, Bracknell, England (1987)	5.2
Meteorological Office, Bracknell, England (1989)	1.9

There were similar variations in the expected increase in rainfall, in a greenhouse world. For any geographer, the most disappointing feature of the models is their failure to agree on regional changes, beyond a general edging of zones towards the Poles. The monsoon rains of China and India may become more generous, but the models tend to dump the extra rainfall in the oceans, and let huge areas of land dry out.

The main reason for the differences lies in the way the models handle clouds. The big cutback in the temperature rise predicted by the British Meteorological Office came about when the modellers distinguished more clearly between shortlived cold clouds made of ice particles and more persistent wet clouds made of water droplets. The cut from 5.2 to 1.9 degrees C for the predicted warming seemed to bear out the longstanding suspicion that clouds can strongly influence the severity of any climate change.

The oceans will moderate any warming in the short run, just as they moderate the difference between winter and summer by being slow to warm up or cool down. But two decades of modelling have left the oceans hard to handle. Typical climate models of the 1980s reduced the average depth of the ocean from a real 4000 metres to a token 50 metres or so that mimicked the seasonal behaviour of the sea.

A new generation of model experiments traces the development of the warming over simulated decades, as greenhouse gases increase according to various scenarios. In 1988, the New York (GISS) model predicted a gradual warming from 1958 to 2030 of 2.1 degrees C with unrestricted increases in greenhouse gases and 1.4 degrees with restrictions. In these experiments, the ocean had an active slab at the surface and a large heat capacity below to represent the deep ocean.

186

The Princeton modellers have for long led the efforts to deal with the global oceans adequately, and in 1989 they coupled a model of the atmosphere to an ocean model with twelve levels and realistic geography. The effects on the forecast of global warming by increased carbon dioxide are striking. Antarctica and the oceans of the Southern Hemisphere remain much cooler than in the standard predictions, because of a strong upwelling of deep, cold water close to Antarctica. The North Atlantic also stays relatively cool because rainwater on the ocean prevents warm surface water flowing in from the subtropics.

The weaknesses of current climate models in respect of clouds and oceans arise even before other pieces of the Earth system, like icecaps, vegetation and volcanoes, are incorporated properly. To say so is not to criticize the dedicated modellers, who are pushing at the limits both of their supercomputers and of human knowledge.

The Great Northern Absorber

*A*NOTHER UNCERTAINTY concerns the very origin of any greenhouse warming: the sources and sinks of manmade greenhouse gases that determine their build-up in the atmosphere. Emissions of carbon dioxide from fossil-fuel combustion were running at 5.3 billion tons a year during the 1980s. Guesses about inputs due to forest clearances ranged from 0.3 to 2.6 billion tons a year. As the annual increase of carbon dioxide in the air was less than the inputs, at about 3 billion tons, the Earth system was mopping up 2.6 to 4.9 billion tons a year.

A belief repeated in dozens of pronouncements on the greenhouse effect was that the missing carbon dioxide was absorbed mainly by the oceans. The analysis by Inez Fung of NASA's Goddard Institute of Space Studies and her colleagues, published in 1990, showed that this could not be true, and pointed instead to the existence of a mysterious Great Northern Absorber of carbon dioxide.

The global carbon cycle is yet another example of a seemingly boring set of 'facts' that generations of students tried to remember for their exams, but are now the subject of feverish research. The skeleton of the carbon cycle remains intact. Plants by land and sea take in carbon dioxide when they grow and give it back to the air when they respire or decompose. Reservoirs of loose carbon exist in the air, the soil and sea-water, and other carbon is assimilated into the Earth's crust as

187

carbonate rocks and fossil fuels. But the numbers defining the trades in carbon between different parts of the Earth system are hotly debated.

Much as a person might trace a gas leak by the varying intensity of the smell from room to room, Fung uses a computer model of the atmosphere to sniff out the sources and sinks of carbon dioxide. Her 'nose' is a gas analyser at Boulder, Colorado. There, NOAA scientists test flasks arriving at regular intervals from a worldwide network of air-sampling sites, scattered from northern Canada to the South Pole and mainly located on oceanic islands. Pieter Tans, working on the University of Colorado campus, was Fung's collaborator on this aspect of the work.

A lungful of air at the South Pole is almost the same as a lungful in the Arctic, but not quite. Mixing takes time, and slight differences in carbon-dioxide levels in the flasks arriving from a score of sampling sites give clues to where the air must be gaining or losing carbon dioxide. The overall global pattern shows somewhat higher levels of carbon dioxide in the air of the Northern Hemisphere than Southern Hemisphere. The game was to use the climate model at the Goddard Institute in New York City to juggle with gains and losses, so as to construct a geography of carbon dioxide that matched the observations.

Fung and her colleagues mapped the sources and sinks in the oceans, using data from research ships collated by Taro Takahashi of the Lamont-Doherty Geological Observatory, New York. The sea is a sink of carbon dioxide if the concentration of the gas in the air is higher than in the surface water, so that the carbon dioxide passes into the water. If the concentration is higher in the water, the flow of carbon dioxide is the other way, and the sea becomes a source.

The main year-round oceanic source of carbon dioxide is the equatorial ocean, with the eastern Pacific by far the most important region. The waters around Antarctica emit carbon dioxide in winter. The North Pacific is almost neutral in effect, with its summer emissions of carbon dioxide almost balanced by its winter absorptions. In the North Atlantic in late summer the inputs and outputs are in balance, but in winter and spring the same ocean becomes a powerful absorber. The rest of the oceans, and especially the large mid-latitude oceans of the Southern Hemisphere, inhale carbon dioxide all year round, with their capacity usually peaking in summer.

Yet the overall rate at which the oceans remove carbon dioxide from the atmosphere must be much less than experts had supposed. The chief sources of carbon dioxide from fuel combustion are in the North-

Facing:
Tracking carbon dioxide. The first map shows emissions from the use of fossil fuels in 1987 (least white, most brown and purple). In the middle map, differences in carbon-dioxide concentrations between ocean and atmosphere (January-April) are mapped from seagoing observations. In blue regions, carbon dioxide tends to pass into the ocean, and to pass into the air in yellow-purple areas. The third map shows absorption of carbon dioxide by plants on land during their growing seasons (least grey, most blue).

JAN–APR

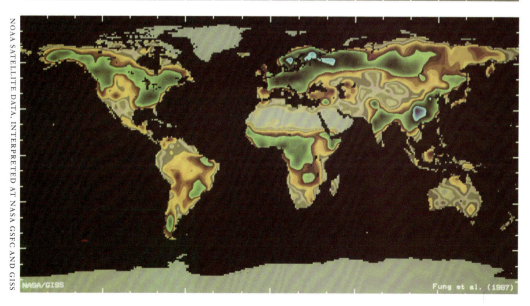

NASA/GISS

Fung et al. (1987)

ern Hemisphere. The chief oceanic sinks are in the Southern Hemisphere. The difference between the amounts of carbon dioxide in the northern and southern air is not as great as it should be, if the excess were flowing 'downhill' from one hemisphere to the other. The most that the flask data and the sniffing computer allow is an absorption by the oceans of 0.7 billion tons a year.

The rest of the absorbed manmade carbon dioxide, some 2 billion tons, must therefore be disappearing on land. And the global geography of carbon dioxide requires that the unknown sink must lie in the middle zone of the Northern Hemisphere, close to the main sources of fossil-fuel emissions. Is a growing spree in progress somewhere in the forests of North America, Europe or the USSR? Is undecomposed carbon-based material accumulating in the soil or in river estuaries? For the time being, what the Great Northern Absorber may be is anyone's guess.

The conclusions of Fung and her colleagues will have to be verified by new experiments, like any other good physics. Ecologists will build towers in forests and sample the estuary sediments in search of the absorber. Oceanographers will lurch about in the Roaring Forties of the southern oceans to confirm that the uptake of carbon dioxide by the sea ocean is really less than expected. One challenge for the international ocean-flux research programme now in progress is to see why wind-tunnel experiments ashore may have given the wrong answers about effects of wind-speed on the flows of gas between air and sea.

This research on sources and sinks of carbon dioxide also sets an upper limit to the contribution from deforestation in the tropics. A strong source of carbon dioxide near the Equator would contravene the observed geographical pattern of atmospheric carbon dioxide, gradually declining from north to south. The net carbon dioxide injected from tropical forests can be only about 1 billion tons a year, at most. If the more pessimistic estimates were correct, and the destruction of these forests were releasing 2.6 billion tons a year, then other plants in the tropics would have to be reassimilating most of the carbon dioxide right away, in extra growth.

PART OF THE story's strangeness is that, 30 years ago, the climate was something you looked up in geography textbooks and atlases. It was a fixed characteristic of a place, like the mountains and coalfields. As the life and administration of nations are set as much by the climate they inhabit as by their territory, there is more than a hint of anarchy in the idea of a changeable climate. Governments see it threatening their authority, as well as the wellbeing of their peoples. When 19th-Century scientists wanted to alert colonial rulers to the harm they were doing by destroying tropical forests they found that likely effects on the local climate were the surest point for commanding attention.

Nature keeps changing the climate, quite apart from anything that human beings may do. Even this idea displeases governments. Pioneer investigators of past climate changes, like Hubert Lamb in England, found official backing for their research hard to sustain. When Lamb pointed out that in recent centuries, in a 'little ice age', the Thames river at London often froze in winter, or that a thousand years ago the English climate was warmer than today, few listened. Even historians were sceptical about the idea that climate changes could have provoked some of the political upheavals of the past.

Least of all did anyone worry about ice ages. Geologically speaking, modern humans live in a warm interval in a glacial phase of the Earth's history. Although the last ice age ended only 10,000 years ago, that was regarded as reassuring. The characteristically planed, scored and lake-filled landscapes left behind by the ice sheets in Canada and Europe show up well in satellite images. But geologists said that only four ice ages had occurred in the past 2 million years or so, with long warm intervals between them.

Physicists investigating the atomic composition of marine fossils discovered that ice ages were far more frequent than the geologists had supposed, and the warm intervals far briefer. Corroboration on land came from multiple layers of wind-blown dust (loess) created during ice ages. The new account also explained the comings and goings of the ice. Wobbles of the Earth's axis alter its attitude in its orbit around the Sun, and changes occur in the shape of the orbit. Computable rhythms arise, in the intensity of sunshine falling on different parts of the world at different seasons of the year. Left to itself, Nature would already be easing the planet towards the next ice age.

191

In 1987 a French-Soviet team announced the most important reconstruction so far of changing conditions during an entire ice-age cycle. A Soviet thermal drill had driven into the ice sheet at the Vostok base in Antarctica, and extracted a core of ice. It reached down more than 2 kilometres into the ice sheet. As an ice sheet consists of a pile of unmelted snow that accumulated year by year, to probe into the ice is to take a journey in a time machine and recover *les neiges d'antan* (François Villon's 'snows of yesteryear').

The Soviet core goes back 160,000 years, to the end of the last ice age but one. The changing temperatures, as the Earth passed through a warm interval, plunged into a new ice age with fluctuating temperatures, and then emerged from the chill into our own warm interval, are clearly recorded by the proportion of heavy hydrogen atoms (deuterium) in the frozen water at different levels in the Vostok core. Air bubbles trapped in the ice reveal changing proportions of carbon dioxide in the air, closely matching the temperature fluctuations.

During the warm intervals, carbon dioxide makes up 280 parts per million of the air's volume. In the chilly trough of an ice age it is low, at 200 parts per million. But the fall in carbon dioxide did not occur until about 10,000 years after temperatures began to plummet, at the start of the last ice age, so it was following rather than leading the trend. Subsequent fluctuations in carbon dioxide were sometimes in step and sometimes out of step with temperature variations, until carbon dioxide and temperatures soared together during the onset of thawing at the end of the most recent ice age.

Since then, there have been many lesser fluctuations in climate, some due, perhaps, to small variations in the intensity of the Sun itself. And scientists have begun to wonder whether any of them were manmade climate changes. For example, could Noah's Flood, a sharp warming and sea-level rise about 2900 BC, be linked to the large-scale deforestations that occurred during the spread of early agriculture?

In the 1970s, leading climatologists were worrying about a global cooling that began around 1940. But by then the global temperature was already turning upwards. It wiped out the post-1940 decline in a few years, and has gone on climbing. Many climatologists now postpone any concern about an imminent cooling and instead expect the greenhouse warming to occur, largely as a result of the human appetite for fossil fuels — coal, oil and natural gas.

During the past 200 years, since the Industrial Revolution, the carbon dioxide in the air has increased by 25 per cent. Bubbles of air trapped in glacier ice show the historical trend, and the meteorological observatory in Hawaii has monitored the increase since 1958. Most of it seems to be due to the use of fossil fuels. It is a big change for an atmospheric component intimately involved both in the spaceship's life and in its climate.

At nearly 360 parts per million of the air (1990) the carbon dioxide already stands far higher than any level recorded in the 160,000-year Vostok ice core. There the carbon-dioxide concentration peaked at about 300 parts per million during the last warm interval before our own, at a time when lions and hippopotamuses lived in England.

Carbon dioxide is not the only greenhouse gas increasing as a result of human activity. Smaller in abundance but, molecule for molecule, more potent in their effects, are methane from rice paddies and the guts of cattle, and nitrous oxide from artificial fertilizers and the use of fuels including firewood. The chlorofluorocarbons (CFCs) blamed for damaging the ozone layer are also highly effective greenhouse gases.

Bert Bolin of Stockholm was concerned about the greenhouse warming from the early 1960s, but he was largely ignored, until interest grew rapidly during the 1980s. Greenhouse concerns were an important factor in the launch of the Global Change programme (IGBP) in 1986, by the International Council of Scientific Unions. By 1988 the computer models of the climate were giving roughly similar predictions for the warming, and politicians came under intense pressures to take the greenhouse issue seriously.

At the end of 1988, the World Meteorological Organization and the UN Environment Programme initiated an Intergovernmental Panel for Climate Change with working groups on the scientific assessment of climate change, on impacts of climate change, and on policy and response strategies. Bolin was overall chairman of the panel. The Swedish meteorologist whose ideas had been scorned for 20 years found himself cast in the role of chief scientist to the planet.

An anti-industrial revolution?

'*W*E HAVE NO minority report,' said the chairman of the scientific working group of the Intergovernmental Panel on Climate Change. John Houghton, chief executive of Britain's Meteorological Office, was stressing the high degree of consensus achieved among nearly 400 active scientists, reviewers and delegates from thirty-nine countries. Weighing their words, Houghton and his colleagues declared themselves 'certain' that the increase in greenhouse gases will enhance the natural greenhouse effect, resulting on average in an additional warming of the Earth's surface. Water vapour, the main greenhouse gas, will increase in response to global warming and further enhance it.

The scientists expressed other conclusions on a descending scale of conviction, exemplary in its clarity. That immediate reductions of 60 per cent in emissions of carbon dioxide, nitrous oxide and the CFCs would be needed to stabilize those gases at present levels was something that 'we calculate with confidence'. On the other hand, it was 'based on current models, we predict' that the global mean temperature would rise by about 1 degree C by 2025 and 3 degrees before the end of the 21st Century. This was in the case of a 'business as usual' scenario without controls on emissions of greenhouse gases, which also gave a rise in mean sea level of about 20 centimetres by 2030 and 65 centimetres by the end of the 21st century.

The working group's 'judgement' was that an unequivocal detection of the enhanced greenhouse effect is not likely for a decade or more. The global mean temperature has increased by 0.3 to 0.6 degrees over the last 100 years, but this could be largely due to natural variability. 'Alternatively this variability and other human factors could have offset a still larger human-induced greenhouse warming.'

The scientists admitted that clouds, oceans, polar ice sheets, and the sources and sinks of greenhouse gases were 'only partially understood'. They could not rule out surprises – by which they meant startling new discoveries like the Ozone Hole, or unexpected processes, in the oceans for example. On ecological effects of the warming, the scientists offered the 'judgement' that some ecosystems might prosper, while others unable to adapt or migrate fast enough could become extinct.

Out of five study areas, the IPCC scientific working group predicted more frequent droughts in central North America and southern Europe, but could not achieve consistent predictions for India, Australia or the African Sahel, in a greenhouse world. Even if all the models agreed, the general misgivings about clouds would leave the regional forecasts less than reliable.

If the conclusions from the IPCC working group on scientific assessment of climate change are taken at their face value, the human species

Facing:
Changes in rainfall in computer models of climate. For a greenhouse world with doubled carbon dioxide, three leading models, British, Canadian and American, predict increases (blue) and decreases (red). These are for the mean precipitation in June, July and August, as compared with the present climate. Local disagreements speak for themselves, but all predict reduced rainfall in the middle latitudes and drastic changes in the Asian summer monsoon.

194

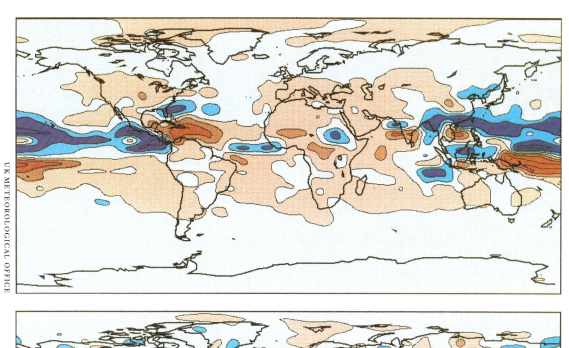

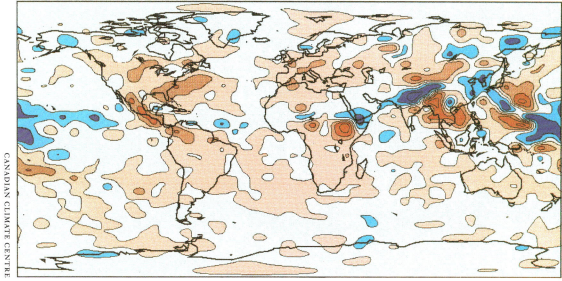

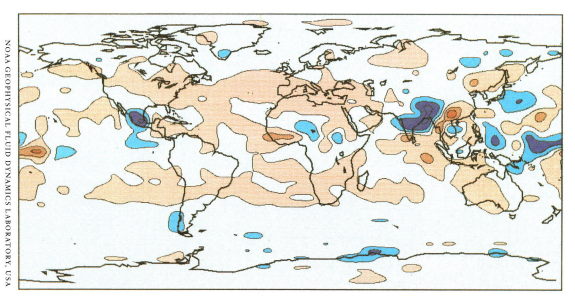

must expect major changes, and a fundamental choice between self-imposed economic disruption to cut the emissions, and piecemeal economic disruption resulting from the climatic shifts. The tortuous subject allows, though, a spectrum of possible expectations, from the most optimistic to the most pessimistic.

1. The greenhouse warming will be good for the whole human species, in creating a warm, moist, bountiful planet not known since the days of the dinosaurs.

2. It will be good for my region (or my country, or my business, or my military plans).

3. The warming is only a fashionable hypothesis, and no interference with normal economic activity is warranted until the evidence and predictions are clearer. (We may freeze, who knows?)

4. The warming may be a false alarm but it is only prudent to take precautionary measures to curb greenhouse-gas emissions.

5. The human species will immediately cut its greenhouse-gas emissions by the 60 cent needed to stabilize their concentrations at today's levels.

6. Enough of the world's nations will agree on (a) painless or (b) painful measures to control greenhouse-gas emissions, to avoid severe changes.

7. A greenhouse warming is already unavoidable, but the effects may not be as severe as predicted, because of self-correcting (negative) feedbacks in the Earth system.

8. Severe changes are unavoidable but the human world will adapt to them, successfully on the whole.

9. Severe changes of climate will bring famine, war and plague, and threaten the survival of civilization.

10. The greenhouse warming will run out of control because of reinforcing (positive) feedbacks in the Earth system, and threaten the human species with extinction.

Almost every opinion in the list is at least arguable. For example (item 3) the downward variation of a British model forecast, from 5.2 to 1.9 degrees C for doubled carbon dioxide, gave ammunition to sceptics like Allan Bromley, President Bush's science adviser, who wanted to defer action on the greenhouse warming until the science was surer. As for the extreme view (item 10), mechanisms on offer for a 'runaway greenhouse' include accelerated outgassing from bogs and changes in the ocean circulation. For the apocalypse one need only point to the extreme greenhouse of the planet Venus, with a surface far too hot for life.

The entirely incredible item in the list is 5. To close 60 per cent of the fossil-fuel power stations overnight, and take 60 per cent of vehicles off the roads, would require a nuclear war. Even a serious, urgent drive towards drastic curtailment of greenhouse emissions would mean an anti-industrial revolution in many parts of the world and probably the biggest economic slump ever. The Germans, when they set out to lead a crusade to save the world, spoke of cutting greenhouse-gas emissions by only 25 per cent over the next decade or two.

According to another working group of the IPCC, the one realistic way even to stabilize carbon-dioxide emissions at present levels, and then gradually reduce them, is by a huge investment in nuclear power stations. This would mean another volte-face for several countries that stopped investing in nuclear energy after the Chernobyl fire. Needless to say, the nuclear industry, anxious to point out that nuclear fuels produce no carbon dioxide, has taken a keen interest in predictions of global warming for longer than most people.

The strongest argument for action is not that the computer forecasts are reliable, but on the contrary that nobody really knows what the highest level of carbon dioxide in 160,000 years really implies. But the urge to prudence and the moderate action that seems likely to flow from this is unlikely to prevent the carbon dioxide in the air increasing further. Given time, energy conservation, alternative energy sources, and perhaps a major industrial shift to biotechnology may reduce the emissions greatly, but not quickly.

A hardheaded assessment must be that adaptation to change, rather than its avoidance, will be the norm in the 21st Century, if the modellers' predictions are correct. If so, a different kind of prudence requires that countries retain the economic vigour to build flood barriers or irrigate desiccating land. And as long as the rich minority of the world continue to put the lion's share of greenhouse gases into the atmosphere (as illustrated in proxy form by space images of street lights) the poorer countries will be in no mood to curtail their own development to moderate the emissions.

Greater trust in regional forecasts, when clouds and oceans are better handled in the climate models, will only tend to make differences in attitudes sharper. Some countries would benefit from a greenhouse warming, while others would suffer. Model runs with doubled carbon dioxide predict, in some cases, greatly enhanced rainfall in India, where unreliable monsoons have hampered development for many centuries. If this forecast persists, why should India turn down an opportunity to export grain to a drought-stricken USA?

The top climate modellers and the most vehement environmentalists happen to be concentrated in rich countries, along with the industrial style primarily responsible for the greenhouse emissions. On the basis of the computer models, some in the rich countries want to wish an anti-industrial revolution on the Third World. The issue of who is authoritative arises also in other areas of environmental concern, including the tropical rain forests. 'Authoritative' has quite different meanings in political and scientific contexts. It refers to power on the one hand and secure knowledge on the other, and there is no guarantee that the two go together, least of all when influence or pressure is being exerted on countries far away.

Rehabilitating the Altiplano

*I*N THE HIGH ANDES, just beyond the edge of the Amazon basin, a finding from prehistory should stir one's sense of wonder and humility, about people's interactions with the Earth system. When Spanish conquerors seized the lands of the Amerindians on the windswept Altiplano, they created large estates. These never achieved high yields but managed to produce some surpluses for sale beyond the local district. In Bolivia, 40 years ago, the estates were broken up and land was redistributed to the Amerindians, who adopted subsistence farming. By recent tradition they grow crops in rotation for three years and then let the plot go to pasture for twelve years, so that it can recover. Llamas, alpacas and sheep provide a little wool for warmth in a cold land almost bare of firewood.

To an expert eye, as well as to any casual glance, the Altiplano is a dead loss. Foreign agronomists note the impoverished soil, the erratic variations in rainfall, the hailstorms, and above all the almost nightly frosts that make the setting unsuitable for any but the hardiest of crops. The experts offer no way of boosting yields that Bolivians can afford. Yet all the colonial and modern experience of a barren Altiplano is contradicted by a large temple.

Not far from Titicaca, the great lake of the Altiplano, a godlike stone figure stands on the raised platform of the temple at Tiwanaku, facing the rising Sun. He clutches sceptres, and the same image has been found far and wide in the Altiplano. The temple was embellished with gold, when Tiwanaku was the capital of an agrarian empire. It flourished in the High Andes long before the Incas, when Europe was in its Dark Ages. For a thousand years this Andean civilization prospered on the very land where the descendants of the Tiwanakans now scratch a living from the reluctant soil.

In the 1960s archaeologists begin to read hints in the landscape about how the Tiwanakans managed it. Near Lake Titicaca, low humps on the ground separated by ditches turned out, in air photos, to make waffle-iron patterns across large areas. Raised fields, typically 5 to 10 metres wide and 200 metres long, were evidently the secret machinery of the Tiwanakan economy. In the 1980s, sustained work by Alan Kolata of Chicago and Oswald Rivera of La Paz unearthed the details.

Constructed as elaborately as a modern highway, with associated drainage and irrigation systems, the raised fields took care of the frosts of the Altiplano, as well as of the variable rainfall associated with floods and droughts. A layer of clay sealed the base of a field, and gravel and sandy soil made a sponge for the water. The chief 'secret' of the system

Raised fields on the Bolivian Altiplano. The rediscovery of prehistoric cultivation techniques that beat the frosty climate of the Andes are a timely reminder that modern high-tech cultures have no monopoly of knowledge.

199

is that radiant heat from adjoining ditchwater protected the crops from the nocturnal frosts.

The ditches also supported water plants, fish and ducks, and the rich organic sediments scooped from the ditches and spread on the fields provided the means of fertilizing the soil. The Tiwanakans re-engineered natural gullies to gather rainfall from the hills in a controlled fashion that prevented waterlogging and siltation. Aqueducts carried the water away across the plains to Lake Titicaca.

Climate research may shed light on why the Tiwanakan culture collapsed around 1100 A D, after a thousand years of sustained success. In this part of the world El Niño springs to mind, and 900-year-old atomic peculiarities in ice cores from an Andean glacier may be evidence for an exceptionally strong and long-lasting episode of anomalous warm water off the nearby coast. If that resulted in protracted drought in the High Andes, even the Tiwanakans may have been unable to cope.

The Bolivians are bringing the ingenious prehistoric system back into production on experimental raised fields, some that have survived from prehistory and others built afresh. Crop yields are some five times higher than those to which the farmers of the Altiplano are accustomed. These patches of greenery require no expensive chemical fertiizers, nor any miracle crop from the genetics lab – the local potatoes and quinoa will do.

On the other side of Lake Titicaca, on the Altiplano in Peru, another team of archaeologists has helped several communities to reactivate the raised-field system, with similar success. In other settings in Central and South America, including the old Maya heartlands and the coastal plains of Colombia and Ecuador, archaeologists are reviving prehistoric field systems that were adapted to lowland conditions. After half a millennium spent despising the Amerindians, Europeans are learning from their ancestors how to manage the land. In the care and maintenance of Spaceship Earth, expertise is where you find it – and not necessarily in the textbooks of high-tech countries.

Stop telling people what to do

R ETURNING FROM the Altiplano of Bolivia, I found on my desk a special issue of a famous science magazine. With the unthinking reflex of a driver stamping on the brakes, I flung it across the room. The words on the cover were 'Managing Planet Earth'. To close this book with a personal comment, let me explain why the phraseology on an otherwise excellent publication about the Earth system seemed to me deeply wrongheaded.

I had just deplaned from a circuit of the world, and from encounters in many settings with remote-sensing specialists and computer modellers, with geographers and scientists of diverse kinds, and with people going about their business as gardeners, miners or officials. At aircraft windows, a lot of time went in simply watching landscapes and clouds with remote-sensing eyeballs. After much previous, unreflective globe-trotting, I was for the first time awestruck by Spaceship Earth and its ingenious crew.

In Samoa, I met the villagers who bury food away, against cyclones and other mishaps. Joseph gave the Pharaoh much the same counsel when the climate of Egypt was dodgy, at the time when the Samoans' ancestors were riding the rare westerly winds of El Niño to discover their island group. In Java, I saw people defying a smoking volcano and official prohibitions to grow crops in the fertile ground created by their island's marriage to the sea. But I also saw African flocks running unattended through a degraded landscape, where the missing shepherds were being remoulded into schoolchildren in the name of progress. And I had looked down on the 20th Century's greatest monument to the would-be managers of Planet Earth: the grey, grim salt-flats of the Aral Sea.

Managing anything implies that it is manageable. The Earth system operated unmanaged for billions of years before humans existed, and may outlast them for billions more. For the time being, our species is a prominent piece of the system. Some sub-systems, including vegetation, rivers and minerals, are amenable to human manipulation, while the Earth's orbit is not, and neither are hurricanes, volcanoes or ocean currents.

A second requirement for management is knowledge of cause and effect in the Earth system: do this, and that will follow. Despite all the wonders of remote-sensing satellites and computer models, that is elusive. Basic pieces of knowledge are shockingly new, and they tend to raise as many questions as they answer. If any reader thinks that research of the kind described in this book amounts to a maintenance manual for the planet's life-support facilities, then something has gone wrong in the writing or reading.

Management also presumes at least a broad agreement about how the world should be. Environmentalists who read only one another's pamphlets delude themselves that a consensus is possible. Perhaps all reasonable persons could agree on a few environmental guidelines — in a monolithic, unchanging world with no cultural variations, class divisions, economic competition, scientific disagreements or technological change, and where there was total compensation for anyone out of pocket as a result of conservation policies. Most questionable of all is the idea that governments, at the focus of national and bureaucratic self-interest, are credible agents for a global consensus.

Finally, and most offensively, 'Managing Planet Earth' implies that there are managers – officers on the computer-filled bridge of the spaceship who tell the crew what to do. The scientists, environmentalists and politicians from the rich countries who aspire to this role are descended, mentally and often genetically, from those who bossed the world for 500 years as colonial officials, slave traders, missionaries, planters, whalers, miners, soldiers and development advisers.

In the new ecocolonial era the unbounded wisdom of Europe and North America is supposed to guide those unfortunate enough to be born in other places towards a better relationship with Nature. The abrupt switch in the Northerners' injunction from 'Develop!' to 'Conserve!' has of course left the 'developing' countries incredulous. But compulsive managers have short memories, and a quasi-racist inability to see other people's points of view. The harassment of Brazil about the Amazon rain forest is an example. How would Europeans or Americans feel about demos in Rio to save the Christmas Tree from automobile pollution?

Stop telling people what to do. For the more enlightened scientists and technical-assistance experts of a new school of thought, the primary task is to make sure that all countries have access to modern techniques, including remote-sensing images and computer models. Then they will be better able to make their own decisions about development and the environment.

To their undying credit, scientists in Europe and North America have played a leading part in alerting the world to environmental issues. They are still at the forefront of research on the Earth system, and the Global Change programme of international research has its headquarters in Stockholm. The best of the scientists know what a monumental task faces them. They will need all the remote-sensing satellites and supercomputers that their countries' taxpayers can afford for them, yet they must also maintain the child-like curiosity and open-mindedness needed for big discoveries. By slipping into prescriptive modes of thought they could bring Earth-system science to premature senility.

As for the money vortex that drives the global economy, this may be best regarded for time being as a quasi-natural phenomenon. Individual corporations and banks are increasingly alert to environmental issues. Enlightened self-interest nowadays includes averting the costs and opprobrium of avoidable pollution or land degradation, and anticipating the circumstances most propitious for business in a greenhouse or anti-greenhouse world. But markets have their own compulsions, revolving around money itself, and their effects on the distribution of wealth and economic activity may be inherently ungovernable, like hurricanes or volcanoes.

Hope lies with ordinary people minding their own business in their own localities, where their prosperity and even their survival depend on striking the shrewdest possible bargains with Nature. A key human number is population, and that is set mainly by the private decisions of billions of individual parents. For new scientific discoveries about the Earth system to have any practical payoff, they will have to be understood, interpreted and acted upon by those same ordinary people. They are the true watchkeepers of Spaceship Earth.

NOAA, GOES AND METEOSAT DATA, PROCESSED AT NASA GISS

Temperatures of the Atlantic region of Spaceship Earth seen from space on a July day. Different colour-coded scales for land, open water, snow and ice, and clouds, are in degrees K (273K = 0 degrees C). This image was synthesized from observations by two US and one European weather satellite.

Index